SOCIAL CLASS AND DELINQUENCY

SOCIETY TODAY AND TOMORROW

General Editor: A. H. Halsey

*Fellow of Nuffield College and Head of the Department
of Social and Administrative Studies, Oxford*

*

THE SECONDARY MODERN SCHOOL
by William Taylor *Principal Lecturer in Education, Bede College, Durham*

THE CUTTESLOWE WALLS: A Study in Social Class
by Peter Collison *Department of Social and Administrative Studies, Oxford*

CRIME AND THE SOCIAL STRUCTURE
by John Barron Mays *Eleanor Rathbone Professor of Social Science,
University of Liverpool*

SOCIETY IN THE MIND: Elements of Social Eidos
by Charles Madge *Professor of Sociology, University of Birmingham*

THE FAWLEY PRODUCTIVITY AGREEMENTS
by Allan Flanders *Senior Lecturer in Industrial Relations, University of
Oxford*

CONSTITUENCY POLITICS: A Study of Newcastle under Lyme
by Frank Bealey, J. Blondel, W. P. McCann

MODERN BRITISH POLITICS: A Study of Parties and Pressure Groups
by Samuel H. Beer

PROFESSIONAL EMPLOYEES: A Study of Scientists and Engineers
by Kenneth Prandy

THE ELITE IN THE WELFARE STATE
by Piet Thoenes

THE YOUNG WORKER AT COLLEGE: A Study of a Local Tech.
by Ethel Venables

WINCHESTER AND THE PUBLIC SCHOOL ELITE: A Statistical Analysis
by T. J. H. Bishop in collaboration with Rupert Wilkinson

POLITICAL MOBILIZATION: A Sociological Analysis of Methods and
Concepts
by J. P. Nettl

THE REVOLUTION OF THE DONS: Cambridge and Society in Victorian
England
by Sheldon Rothblatt

INTERNATIONAL SYSTEMS AND THE MODERNIZATION OF SOCIETIES:
The formation of National goals and attitudes
by J. P. Nettl and Roland Robertson

EXPERIMENT IN INDUSTRIAL DEMOCRACY: A Study of the John
Lewis Partnership
by Allan Flanders, Ruth Pomeranz, and Joan Woodward

METHODISM DIVIDED: A Study in the Sociology of Ecumenicalism
by Robert Currie

TECHNOCRACY
by Jean Meynaud

IS SCIENTIFIC MANAGEMENT POSSIBLE?
by Joe Kelly

TELEVISION IN POLITICS: Its Uses and Influence
by Jay G. Blumler and Denis McQuail

474 sociology

£3.25

Copy 1

WITHDRAWN

**Books are to be returned on or before
the last date below**

Social Class and Delinquency

Department of Sociology
McMaster University
Hamilton, Ontario

FABER AND FABER
24 Russell Square
London

First published in 1969
by Faber and Faber Limited
24 Russell Square London WC1
Printed in Great Britain by
Western Printing Services Limited, Bristol
All rights reserved

SBN 571 08474 5

PREFACE

The survey research for this book was originally done as a thesis at the London School of Economics. A London University Ph.D. was awarded for it in 1966 under the title 'A Study of Social Class and education in relation to Juvenile Delinquency'. This book is a revision and expansion of the thesis, based on the same data.

I would like to acknowledge the advice and encouragement of Mr. J. E. Hall Williams, Reader in Criminology at the L.S.E., who supervised the thesis, Dr. Alan Little, then on the staff of the L.S.E., and Dr. John Spencer, Professor of Social Administration, Edinburgh University, for their criticism at various stages, and Mr. Peter McNaughton-Smith, then at the Home Office Research Unit, for advice on the statistical handling of the data.

I would also like to acknowledge the generous help given by many people at all stages of the work. The education officers, headmasters and teachers of the schools whose children took part in the survey gave useful criticism, advice and information as well as making it possible to give the questionnaire in school time. The Children's Department and juvenile liaison police gave the necessary access to their documents. The children who took part in the main survey are especially appreciated. Their interest in the project and kindness in letting themselves become, in their terms, guinea pigs for science, made doing the field work a pleasure.

For my Grandparents
Harold Gray Eakins and Aileen Kennedy Eakins

CONTENTS

7

THE ISSUES

The person who sets out to study the causes of delinquency will soon find he has joined a most unusual company. His fellow-workers include philosophers, doctors, lawyers, police chiefs, psychiatrists, psychologists, sociologists, journalists, opinion pollsters, mothers, convicted criminals, social workers, politicians, religious leaders, truant officers and various anxious responsible citizens. He will encounter reports, theories, conclusions and opinions as variegated as would be expected from as diverse a group as the above. He will become acquainted with hypotheses on the causes of crime sufficiently wide ranging to include the following:

the shape of one's head
having a working mother
reading crime comics
the influence of capitalism
the spread of communism

He will have to delve his way through masses of material, a lot of which is irrelevant, unreliable, and badly thought out, if at all. He will discover researchers who have spent thousands of pounds of public money to find out that their view of delinquency was the right one after all. He will find no dearth of opinions but only scant hard evidence for any of them, even most of the better ones.

Perhaps worst of all he will find very little co-ordination of effort. Not many researchers have seriously taken into account the work of others. Consequently over time the list of facts and theories grows, but not in any systematic way. A researcher produces results consistent with his hypotheses. Yet he will not have controlled for other variables which may be equally up to the task of explaining his findings. So the theory which proposes these other variables as the crucial causal factors cannot be discarded. The two conflicting theories both remain on the books.

As well as the host of conflicting theories the literature abounds with conflicting 'facts'. Some very elementary and important points are in dispute. This book intends to deal with one such fundamental dispute and with several less important but related ones. And the other major task of the book is to test several of the better formulated but conflicting theories on delinquency etiology.

It will soon become clear that the questions on simple facts and the questions on the theories which attempt to explain these facts consist of the same variables. However for the moment some purpose is served by discussing these questions separately. Let us look at the factual problem first.

We do not yet know how delinquency is affected by social class. Specifically we do not know if working-class people are more delinquent than middle class, if they are less delinquent or if social class makes no difference at all. There is considerable opinion in favour of the idea that working-class people are more delinquent than middle class. But there are opinions, and, more to the point, research findings which would indicate that there are no differences between the social classes in amounts of delinquency committed. This issue is a most important one and the merits of both sides will be discussed in some detail later in the chapter.

The conflicting theories to be studied are all concerned with the source of working-class delinquency. They all assume that working-class people are more delinquent than middle class. (And admittedly this assumption has been unchallenged until quite recently.) The conflict between the theories then is confined to the specific causes of delinquency in the working class. Here there is an enormous variety of hypotheses from which to choose. The debate on this issue will, as well, be gone into fully later in the chapter.

It has been only in the last ten years that researchers have questioned the idea that working-class people are more crime-prone than others. However now that that question has been raised it is important that it be answered without delay. Obviously it would be futile to do research on theories which presuppose that delinquency is a working-class phenomenon if it should later be found that the presupposition were wrong. The idea that the

THE ISSUES

working class is more delinquent has been accepted too long without adequate empirical foundation.

The first protests to the idea consist of scattered references in
the American literature to the size and scope of middle-class and
upper-class delinquency.[1] It was thought that suburban high-
school boys were increasingly becoming involved in liquor
offences, car thefts, joy-riding, chicken-racing and property
damage. Some sociologists classified this behaviour as part of a
general youth culture not affected at all by social class.

At the same time there was a growing realization, and empirical
documentation of it, that upper- and middle-class people tend to
be more leniently treated by the police and courts. This made it
plausible that there were equal proportions of delinquents in the
classes, but that they emerged unequally in the official statistics
after very biased processing by the law enforcement agencies.

The first empirical work showing that there were not any
differences between the social classes in delinquency rates was
published in 1958.[2] Nye found no differences by class in admissions to delinquency made by 3,000 high-school boys and girls in
western and mid-western small towns in America. There were
enormous differences between the classes in the communities
studied in committals to approved schools.

Nye's questionnaire was sensitive enough to find some important associations between delinquency admission rates and rather
delicate aspects of family life. Questions on the children's estimated happiness of their parents' marriage, rejection of children
by parents and of parents by children, yielded results almost
entirely as expected by theory, although these were not always
significant. Only five per cent of the correlations were inconsistent
with Nye's theory that certain family relationships were the instigators of delinquency. For our purposes what he did not find is
more important than what he did. And he did not find any
significant association between the children's social-class background and the delinquencies to which they admitted.

[1] David Matza and Gresham M. Sykes. 'Juvenile Delinquency and
Subterranean Values.' *American Sociological Review*, v. 26, 1961, p. 715.

[2] Ivan Nye, James Short and Virgil J. Olson. 'Socioeconomic Status
and Delinquent Behavior.' *American Journal of Sociology*, v. 63, 1958,
p. 381.

F. Ivan Nye. *Family Relationships and Delinquent Behavior*. New
York: John Wiley, 1958.

The Nye-Short study is also important for the method it employed. It is the first large survey to use a measure of admitted delinquency rather than official. This merits some attention. Only a very small fraction, perhaps no more than one per cent, of all indictable offences committed actually result in the offender's conviction. There is every reason to suspect that the offenders who are charged or convicted are not representative of offenders who either escape detection or who are not charged anyways. The low-status, badly educated, poorer members of society are the ones least able to avoid detection and most likely to be charged and convicted.

Crime in a community has been described as an iceberg with only the small tip visible.

prison

conviction

charge

crime known to police

admissions to crime

actual crime

No one would claim that the crimes or delinquencies admitted to form the whole bulk of crimes actually committed by the same people. (Surveys on admitted delinquency are anonymous and confidential and so probably elicit a good proportion of the actual amount.) But clearly the level of admissions to crime is much closer to the true state of affairs than any other level. Thus the cross-section of delinquents found in a study of admitted delinquency will be much more accurate than the cross-section obtained in any other way.

For purposes of studying the distribution of delinquency through the social-class structure this matter of obtaining an accurate cross-section is crucial. The Nye-Short study will later be criticized for bias in this respect. But theirs was the first large survey to attempt to obtain an adequate sample.

The Nye-Short findings form an important stage in the development of etiological theory. Their conclusion that social class was not a factor in delinquency commission led to a much more refined handling of the class factor by researchers seeking to discredit their results. Though not the first to do so, Nye and Short gave empirical evidence of the distorted nature of official records on delinquency. Their findings have resulted in an improved standard of research generally in the field. They probably deserve much of the credit for the belated demise of research based on the comparison of an institutionalized delinquent group and a noninstitutionalized nondelinquent control group.

A few years after Nye and Short's publication of results, two other sociologists did a similar study which produced similar results. Dentler and Monroe[3] used a five-item theft scale based on Nye's theft questions. They took a sample of seventh- and eighth-grade boys and girls from suburban, rural and rural nonfarm homes. The authors found significant differences by a number of variables – all focused on relationships within the family.

However, they did not find any association between admissions to thefts and social-class background or mobility. The study can therefore be seen as a corroboration of the Nye-Short findings and an extension of them to a younger age group and to a slightly wider social group (to include children from rural areas and farms as well as small towns).

Work published by Erickson and Empey[4] in 1965 produced findings basically concurring with the above two studies. Erickson and Empey did find a statistically significant relationship between social class and admitted delinquency, but it was a very slight one. And this correlation was due mostly to differences between the highest social class and the other two; there were no significant differences between the middle- and lower-class groups. And it is the differences between these groups that have been the focus of the dispute on the social-class distribution of delinquency. Having delinquent associates and commitment to a peer group were far more predictive of admitted delinquency than social class.

The areas from which Erickson and Empey drew their sample were roughly similar to those used in the other two studies. Erickson and Empey's subjects came from a Utah community of population 40,000. The area is actually more urban than the population figures would suggest as it is contiguous to several other communities. The main point, however, is that the area sampled, like those in the two earlier studies, was not a large city. For reasons to be explained below, size of community is an

[3] Robert A. Dentler and Lawrence J. Monroe. 'Early Adolescent Theft.' *American Sociological Review*, v. 26, 1961, p. 733.

[4] Maynard L. Erickson and Lamar T. Empey. 'Class Position, Peers and Delinquency.' *Sociology and Social Research*, v. 49, 1965, p. 268.

important factor affecting the social-class distribution of delinquency.

In 1961 Reiss and Rhodes[5] reported some research which for the first time pointed out the importance of the size variable. These findings put the Nye-Short and Dentler-Monroe findings into a different perspective. In view of the similarities between the Erickson-Empey findings and the other two they may also be applied to the Erickson-Empey results. The Reiss and Rhodes study, it must be noted, was of official delinquency, so the explanation derived from it is not necessarily applicable to the admitted delinquency findings. However, work by Clark and Wenninger published in 1962,[6] which was based on admitted delinquency, offered a similar explanation and so substantiates Reiss and Rhodes.

With data on 9,000 boys and girls aged 12–16 Reiss and Rhodes calculated delinquency rates by social class, using two different concepts of social class. Criterion for the first, ascribed status, was the usual: father's occupation. For the second they used the concept of social-status area – the prevailing class of the neighbourhood. They found that though rates varied by ascribed status within each area, they varied even more for all classes of an area compared with all classes of a different area. The areas used were elementary school districts, which are small enough to be fairly homogeneous.

Thus working-class boys in a middle-class area were less delinquent than others of their class in a working-class area. Likewise middle-class boys in a working-class area were more delinquent than boys of similar middle-class standing who lived in a middle-class area. Unless this data is incorrect, it provides an explanation as to why Nye and Short found no differences by social class in their study.

The areas in the Nye survey were small and medium-sized towns in the west and mid-west. The Dentler and Monroe subjects came from roughly similar areas: suburban, rural and rural nonfarm. The subjects for the Erickson-Empey study were from a

[5] Albert J. Reiss, Jr. and A. Lewis Rhodes. 'Delinquency and Social Class Structure.' *American Sociological Review*, v. 26, 1961, p. 720.

[6] John P. Clark and Eugene P. Wenninger. 'Socio-Economic Class and Area as Correlates of Illegal Behavior Among Juveniles.' *American Sociological Review*, v. 27, 1962, p. 826.

small Utah town. No cities were included in any of the samples. All the communities studied were small and homogeneous.

Reiss and Rhodes maintain that their findings disprove certain aspects of Cohen's theory giving status frustration as the source of delinquency.[7] One specific prediction they extrapolate from Cohen's theory is that lower-class boys in middle-class areas would commit more delinquency than lower-class boys who live in lower-class areas. Lower-class boys in middle-class areas would, through the stiffer competition they faced, actually suffer more frequent and more severe status defeats than lower-class boys in a lower-class area. As well the lower-class boys in the mixed area would be more intensely aware of their failures as they would be surrounded by the evidence of middle-class success.

Reiss and Rhodes's findings support the view that there is some aspect of working-class culture that is productive of delinquency and is transmissible by ordinary day to day contact. It is passed on from person to person within the family and even more so from person to person in the neighbourhood.

This leaves us with some of the more dynamic but more subtle aspects of the social-class complex untouched. Perhaps middle-class people who live in a working-class area are not middle class in style of life, child-rearing techniques, political and religious affiliations, education and leisure activities. Possibly they are middle class only by occupation. Likewise, working-class families in middle-class areas may have largely middle-class reference groups.

The Reiss and Rhodes data do not begin to distinguish what it is within a working-class neighbourhood that children from middle-class homes acquire that makes them more delinquent, or what it is about the middle-class neighbourhood that prevents working-class children committing their quota of delinquency. Possible sources are the example of the peer group, time at risk for delinquency, desirable objects of theft and opportunities for concealment of offences, control exercised by parents, police and official organizations. Or it could be the case that families who choose to be a minority in a neighbourhood have more affinity with the behaviour pattern of the majority than would be expected from objective assessment of their status.

[7] Cohen's theory is discussed in more detail on pages 44 to 47 in this chapter.

Another American study, this one of admitted delinquency, found differences in delinquency rates by status area as Reiss and Rhodes did.[8] Clark and Wenninger took four distinct status areas: an industrial city, a lower-class urban area, an upper-class urban area, and a rural farm area. They found that rates of admitted delinquency decreased in that order.

Discussion of the hypotheses tested in the Clark and Wenninger study, and its other findings, will be included later in this chapter. This is necessary as half of the hypotheses were derived from theories which have not yet been discussed.

A replication, though not an exact one, of the Nye study is the last of the American empirical contributions to be reported.[9] Akers's survey was published in 1964, after both the Clark and Wenninger and the Reiss and Rhodes articles had been published. But unfortunately Akers had completed his data collection before their work had been published, and therefore had not taken into account the significant advances they had made both in research design and theoretical formulation.

Akers gave a written questionnaire to 1,000 children in junior high schools in an Ohio community of population 275,000. The delinquency questions were the same as in the Nye study except that the questions on liquor and sexual relations were omitted. No differences by socio-economic status in rates of admitted delinquency were found.

In addition to the tabulations and the chisquare tests, a correlational analysis was made with the data. Scores of delinquency were calculated from only five scale items. These were:

    driving without a licence

    skipping school

    taking things of under $2.00 value

    defying parents' authority directly

    damaging or destroying others' property

The correlation coefficient of occupational scores and delinquency scores was nearly zero.

[8] John P. Clark and Eugene P. Wenninger. 'Socio-Economic Class and Area as Correlates of Illegal Behavior Among Juveniles.' *American Sociological Review*, v. 27, 1962, p. 826.

[9] Ronald L. Akers. 'Socio-Economic Status and Delinquent Behavior: A Retest.' *Journal of Research in Criminology and Delinquency*, v. 1, no. 1, January 1964, p. 38.

It is suggested that this test for correlation is a most inappropriate one. Not all of the five 'delinquency items' are delinquencies.
Skipping school is so widely practised that it is meaningless to
consider one admission of it as delinquency. Defying parents'
authority is not necessarily a delinquency and in the vast majority
of instances would not be. Open defiance should not be confused
with incorrigibility; it would not be sufficient evidence for an
incorrigibility conviction even in a state with very strict delinquency legislation. Driving without a licence, though a delinquency, is not a serious one. It also happens to be an offence for
which middle-class children, having more access to cars, are at
higher risk.

Akers's scale contains a majority of items which are not serious
delinquencies. Of the two real delinquencies, theft and property
damage, one is confined to small amounts, that is, theft under
$2.00.

In the same article, Akers reports the rank order of delinquencies in frequency of conviction. In decreasing order, and
excluding traffic offences, they are:

> stealing
> auto theft
> run away
> destruction of property
> incorrigibility
> sex offences
> truancy
> intoxication

Of this list of eight offences only two were on the delinquency
scale, and one of these was the stealing item which was limited to
values less than $2.00. The three most numerous official delin-
quencies were not on the scale. This is not to assert that the
offences most frequently dealt with by the police are those most
widely committed. Rather, it is suggested that the delinquencies
which are officially dealt with provide a better basis for rating
delinquency commission than minor misconduct items and traffic
offences.

Akers also computed mean delinquency scores for each socio-
economic group. No significant differences between the groups
were found, although there was a slight trend, for boys only, in
the direction of higher delinquency as the social level decreased.

However, these mean scores were based on the scale items only. So the same criticism applies; namely, that it is misconduct that is being measured, not delinquency.[10]

Notwithstanding this criticism, a few of Akers's points cannot be dismissed. There were some serious offences on his questionnaire and for these, as with the trivial offences, he found no significant differences by socio-economic status. Two of the three serious offences referred to were not on the scale but were included on the delinquency list – theft over \$2.00 and car theft. The other item on the scale was property damage.

There is only one British study which has any direct bearing on the present subject of the social-class distribution of delinquency.[11] The major finding of this study was that social-class differences in delinquency rates had diminished radically throughout the decade of the 1950's. By the end of the decade, the authors concluded, what remaining differences there were were very slight.

Little and Ntsekhe compared proportions of lower-class delinquents from studies in the early part of the decade with proportions they found in 1959. The early studies were the Mannheim, Spencer and Lynch study of sentencing in London juvenile courts and the Morris study of Croydon probation cases.

Little and Ntsekhe state that as there had been no policy change in processing cases by police or courts throughout this period, or any change in the social-class distribution of the population, there must have been a change in the social-class distribution of those who commit crimes. In the early 1950's, and presumably in earlier years as well, offenders came predominantly from the lower social groups. By 1959 the social-class distribution of offenders resembled fairly closely the distribution of the whole population. However, even in 1959 the two highest social classes were slightly under-represented in the groups of official delinquents.

For the study of 1959 cases, the authors drew a random sample from three official sources: London juvenile courts, an approved school, and seven remand homes. The proportion of lower-class

---

[10] There will be further comment on Akers's statistical analysis in Chapter 4, when his results will be compared with those of this study.

[11] W. R. Little and V. R. Ntsekhe. 'Social Class Background of Young Offenders from London.' *British Journal of Delinquency*, v. 10, 1959, p. 130.

people in all three groups was smaller than in the Mannheim or Morris study. No tests for statistical significance were applied.

It should be noted that the authors used the Registrar-General's classification for their social-class groupings. In it, forty-two per cent of the population is grouped in the third class – which contains a substantial range of manual and nonmanual occupations. So there might be differences between the manual and non-manual persons in this third class which are obscured by the classification.

Table 1.1, taken from the article, shows the changes over the decade in the social-class distribution of delinquency.

TABLE I.I

Comparison of Findings on Social Class and Official Delinquency

	1 per cent Sample	Little and Ntsekhe	Mannheim (1952)	Morris (1952)
I	2·8	0·5	13·0	0·0
II	15·6	5·5		
III	42·2	50·5	34·1	20·2
IV	14·0	15·2		24·1
V	10·5	19·7	53·0	55·7
Uncl	14·9	8·9		
N		381	400	79

The Little and Ntsekhe article is a very important item in the review of the literature. So far, from the American studies reviewed, evidence has been brought both to support and to denigrate the theory that the working class is more delinquent than the middle class. Later it will be shown that almost all of the literature on delinquency in Britain is in favour of the view that the working class is more delinquent. There have been only a few specific empirical tests of the social-class delinquency rate theory in Britain. The first one (and, at the time this research was planned, the only one) was the Little-Ntsekhe study. As well, since that study was based on official sources of delinquency, its unexpected findings must be accorded some attention.

A study with a representative national cross-section of the

population, published several years after this study, showed opposite results to those of Little and Ntsekhe.[12] In Douglas's sample the rate of official delinquency (measured several ways) for children from manual homes was twice that of children from nonmanual homes. There were differences as well within both major social-class groups, with the lower group having the higher delinquency rate.

There are two large studies of admitted delinquency currently under way, both in the London area – that of the Survey Research Unit at the London School of Economics and the Family Development Study of the Cambridge Institute of Criminology. At the time of writing neither had published results so cannot be discussed here. Both will probably make important contributions to the literature.

As many of the studies producing data on the social-class distribution of delinquency that have been published have now been reported, it is now appropriate to turn to the theoretical question – to discuss the theories promulgated to explain the causes of working-class delinquency. As this is a study of British society, primary consideration will be given to the British theoretical and empirical works. American theories will be included for comparison at certain stages.

Theories of Working-class Delinquency

There are two theoretical schools providing explanations as to the source of working-class delinquency. One is essentially a cultural explanation. It suggests that delinquency is one outgrowth of a life characterized by different values, norms and daily living habits. The other explanation, heretofore applied primarily to American society, is based on anomie theory. It suggests that working-class persons have the same basic values as middle-class persons, especially as they share an orientation to high achievement and a belief that they have equal opportunities for this. However, working-class people, after failing to achieve the goals by abiding by the rules, feel they must abandon the rules. They continue to strive towards the socially inculcated goals, but now by using delinquent means.

[12] J. W. B. Douglas *et al.* 'Delinquency and Social Class.' *British Journal of Criminology*, v. 6, 1966, p. 294.

The cultural school bases its theory on observed differences between the middle and working classes in various crucial aspects of life. For the age group involved in this study (14), these can be broken down into the influences of the home, the neighbourhood and the school. If an older group were being considered occupational differences would also have to be included. The boundaries of these concepts will be discussed more fully later. For the moment, the concept of the neighbourhood should be considered as residual, that is, those influences that do not arise exclusively from within the family circle nor are a part of formal education. Thus peer group activities, recreation, and after-school employment would all be counted as influences of the neighbourhood.

Early Socialization in the Working Class

It has long been observed that interaction within the family is itself as different from class to class as it is between different ethnic groups. A large number of studies, using a wide range of methods, have found differences in child-rearing techniques, attitudes, educational and vocational aspiration, use of language and leisure activities. A few of the studies that show how the working class is different, in ways that could make it more criminogenic, have been selected for review.

One of the best known studies that makes a case for high working-class delinquency is Betty Spinley's *The Deprived and the Privileged*.[13]

Spinley's work was based on participant observation and some Rohrschach testing. The purpose of her research was empirically to demonstrate the existence of a basic personality type and its subtypes, that is, the English personality and its subtypes by social class.

Spinley compared child-rearing practices between a traditional working-class part of Paddington and an upper middle-class group. She summarized by sketching the modal life cycle of the (lower) working-class child from his unplanned and frequently unwanted entry into life to his own haphazard marriage. Upon marriage, he transmitted the pattern to his progeny. Altogether, Spinley found this culture highly conducive to delinquent be-

[13] B. M. Spinley. *The Deprived and the Privileged*. London: Routledge & Kegan Paul, 1964.

21

haviour. The effort to develop an abstract conscience in the child was noticeably absent. The child learned that he could usually get what he wanted by being devious. He might not be punished even if he were caught; if his mother was so disposed she would punish him, if it were too much bother she would not. He was not taught to defer gratification and tended to think only of the present in making decisions.

The child did not learn to feel guilt or anxiety at the thought of doing wrong. He lacked a consistent association between misbehaviour and punishment for it. Punishment was not geared to how right or wrong he was, but to what sort of mood his closest parent was at the time. Punishment was something that intruded from an unpredictable external world; it was not something over which his actions had any control.

Terence Morris[14] also adheres to the school of thought that working-class persons have values and norms different from those of the middle class. Morris supports his position with social psychological material, especially the findings of Davis and Havighurst on class differences in child rearing. He also draws on Mays's Liverpool material, Spinley's Paddington study and Jephcott and Carter's Radby study. Like Spinley, Morris sees differences between the classes at all stages of life. From permissive socialization in earliest childhood to his unprovided-for old age, the working-class member is described as pleasure seeking for the present, heedless of the future.

Morris is describing the less skilled section of the working class, but in some respects the differences between these and middle-class practices would hold for the whole of the working class. For example, there would be less cohesiveness in the working-class nuclear family – at least in so far as mothers and fathers maintain separate leisure activities. Disagreement between parents, when it arises, could be expected to be more visible, loud and violent in the working class. And there is much evidence of there being less emphasis on abstract moral training in the working class.

Moreover, the child in a small flat, overcrowded with other children, an overtired mother and a paucity of activities such as clubs or hobbies, would be forced to spend time with his peer

14 T. P. Morris. *The Criminal Area*. London: Routledge & Kegan Paul, 1957.

group on the streets. If he receives little attention at home, he will become emotionally dependent on the street group. This would lead him to absorb the group's norms. The alternative for him would be to do without group support of any kind.

In his discussion, Morris referred chiefly to the 'mass of unskilled workers'. The defining characteristic of this group, according to him, is its lack of opportunity for upward mobility. Skilled manual workers who have incomes comparable to middle-class persons should not be included in this lower group but should be counted as middle class. Their style of life is gradually approaching that of the middle class.

There is one other qualification to be applied to the concept of working class as used in the studies here reviewed. The economic conditions described as a part of working-class life, and said to facilitate the onset of delinquency, are ceasing to be an inevitable corollary of manual work. The continual fear of unemployment, the intermittent crisis of unemployment, bad housing conditions, large families, overcrowding in the home itself, the housing area, and the schools are all becoming less of a problem.

These changing conditions apply especially to the skilled working class. They have led to a tentative reformulation of the cultural explanation (Morris's is an example) by applying it now exclusively to the unskilled sector of the working class. Whether or not skilled workers are now closer to nonmanual workers than to unskilled workers in certain respects of course is an empirical question. It is one for which an answer will be sought in this study, for at least the one aspect of delinquency admissions.

There are parallels to the explanations given above in the American literature on the subject. The most well known of these is Walter Miller's and it takes perhaps as extreme a stand on the criminogenic nature of the working class as the British contributions.[15] Miller, a social anthropologist, accounts for gang delinquency as the natural outgrowth of a more general parent culture, the culture of the lower class. He isolated six concepts: trouble, toughness, smartness, excitement, fate and autonomy, around which goals and attitudes differ between the working- and middle-class cultures.

[15] Walter B. Miller. 'Lower Class Culture as a Generating Milieu of Gang Delinquency.' *Journal of Social Issues*, v. 14, 1958, p. 5.

Miller saw toughness, a highly regarded value in the lower-class culture, as psychic reaction formation against the female-dominated household which is more prevalent in the lower class. Miller's model is the home in which a woman may live with her children, her own mother, possibly also a sister and, for various lengths of time, a man, who will likely be the father of various of her children. The lower-class boy who is socialized in such circumstance would develop very different norms, values and attachments from those of a boy socialized in a typical middle-class nuclear family. By merely conforming to his ideas of acceptable behaviour, the lower-class boy would automatically violate some middle-class norms, which, unfortunately for him, also happen to be the legally enforced rules of society. These delinquent boys should not be seen so much as rebelling against middle-class norms as adhering to those in which they and their ancestors have been brought up.

Miller considers that his theory accounts for the delinquency of a large segment of the population. His original work was done in a heavily Negro area, but with data from a broader range of sources he estimated that the parent lower-class culture influences from forty to sixty per cent of the American population. While he terms this criminogenic subculture a lower-class culture, he is clearly referring to a much larger group than is conventionally thought of as lower class. Forty to sixty per cent of the American population would include the families of stable skilled workers and probably some middle-class families as well as rural and farm families. His theory is not of a slum culture, as it appears on first sight, but really of a simple working-class culture.

When this is borne in mind, the theory appears a most extreme one, with a few very unlikely implications. Miller states that delinquency ensues automatically as people of the lower-class culture (about half the population) merely go through life abiding by the norms in which they have been brought up. This implies an enormous dissensus in American society. Half the society subjects the other half to an alien normative structure and punishes it when it fails to conform.

In the last ten years some work has been done on language usage which may prove to be very important in explaining delinquency etiology, as well as other social phenomena. Basil Bernstein, though he does not explicitly apply his ideas to delinquency, offers in his theory some insights that are directly applicable to the problem of explaining working-class delinquency.[16]

He describes two kinds of language usage, one an elaborated code, the other a restricted code.[17] Working-class people, especially semiskilled and unskilled persons, are generally confined to the use of the restricted code. Middle-class persons characteristically have acquired the use of both.

Which type of language code a person develops depends on the nature of his social relationships, particularly the earliest ones in the family. The number, variety and range of social experiences differ greatly from class to class. In its simplest form, the difference is that in the middle class there is more emphasis on individual achievement. The type of language developed within these essentially different types of social relationship in turn regulates the perception, effect and organization of future experiences.

One tries to avoid the functionalist circuit in discussing the institutions of a society or group, but in the case of the language code development of a social class the significant point is its circularity. Working-class children are taught a certain language code which they use. (One can refrain from explaining why, only to point out that it is functional for maintaining and protecting this way of life.) This code is the only one they are exposed to for the first five years of their lives and it is the one used by their families and friends throughout their lives. When these children come into contact with people who use the elaborated code they experience both humiliation and rejection. This increases their dependence on their own group again and reduces any motivation to acquire the other as well. This isolates them further from users of the elaborated code making it less possible for them to learn the new code.

Bernstein describes at length points on which the two forms of language usage can be contrasted. These points of contrast affect

[16] Basil Bernstein. 'A Public Language; some Sociological Implications of a Linguistic Form.' *British Journal of Sociology*, v. 10, 1959, p. 311. 'Language and Social Class.' *British Journal of Sociology*, v. 11, 1960, p. 271.

A. H. Halsey *et al. Education, Economy, and Society.* New York: Free Press of Glencoe, 1963.

[17] In his earlier writing Bernstein used the term 'formal language' for what he now calls an elaborated code, and 'public language' for the restricted code.

all aspects of life. The implications of this for a restricted code speaker, who must live in a society governed by elaborate rules, are devastating. The points of contrast are summarized below. Those most salient to delinquency etiology are marked with an asterisk and will be discussed further later.

Method of making moral decisions*
Method of legitimizing authority*
Sense of cause and effect*
Experience of guilt and shame*
Ability to generalize, analyse
Curiosity
Ways of facing new experiences
Problem solving
Dependence on group for emotional support
Facility for relationships on one to one basis
Capacity for expressing tender feelings
Range of aesthetic experiences

For the person with only a restricted code, Bernstein explains, certain experiences simply never become part of his life. Guilt and shame are not experienced in the same circumstances as they would be for a speaker of the elaborated code. Feelings of guilt are not associated with an understanding that an act is wrong.

'It is suggested that speakers limited to a *public* language have more terms which serve to minimize guilt and that these terms are generalized to include a greater range of activities than have speakers of a formal language.'[18]

Middle-class magistrates see this phenomenon every court day. A working-class accused will state, with courtesy, that he knows he did something morally wrong. Yet he will not exhibit the remorse and horror at his action that the middle-class person brought before a criminal court typically shows. The magistrate, if he can picture himself in the dock at all, knows what overwhelming a sense of shame he would experience and expects others to share these feelings. Awareness of wrongdoing and the imminence of punishment for it mean very different things to the middle-class and working-class person.

With a lower level of conceptualization persons with a restricted

[18] Basil Bernstein. 'A Public Language; Some Sociological Implications of a Linguistic Form.' *British Journal of Sociology*, v. 10, 1959, p. 311.

code are confined to a lower order of causality. Consequently they see themselves as less responsible for certain acts. The same social factors, through language, affect the facility for handling both moral and intellectual content. The child growing in intellectual discernment is at the same time acquiring the capacity to make complicated moral decisions. And the child lacking in abstract analytical capacity is lacking also in the fundamental structure of the middle-class conscience.

Speakers of only a restricted code are more resistant to change and have less intrinsic interest in novelty. They see innovation as threatening because it could result in their being rejected from their group. And social isolation is a more terrifying prospect for a person who habitually does things in groups, with his mates, than to a person who is accustomed to doing more things by himself.

For the restricted code speaker there is yet another pressure towards reliance on the group. The child who is dealt with arbitrarily by his parents will have learned to respond in stereotyped ways. As he has not learned to think through his problems logically he will be less likely to attempt to work them through himself. Instead he will turn to the group for direction. If this is the case then it is easy to see how, given the presence of delinquent models in an area, younger working-class boys growing up in it would quickly become involved in delinquencies.

In the case of delinquent activity the range of prospective victims that a restricted code speaker could identify with and not want to hurt is limited. A person speaking an elaborated code would be aware of a number of reasons why stealing is wrong. A restricted code speaker probably would not be thinking of theft as such, or its rightness or wrongness. He would feel it wrong to steal from Mrs. N's grocery store because Mrs. N is a kind person who never hurt him and who needs all the groceries she has in the shop. He might not have the same feelings about stealing from a chain store. He could not appreciate the rights of shareholders in the same way that he could visualize Mrs. N's needs. Nor would he consider the proscription of theft in the Ten Commandments and from that deduce that all theft, even shoplifting from chain stores, is wrong.

According to Bernstein there is a profound difference between restricted and elaborated code speakers in the way they legitimize

27

authority. The restricted language speaker ascribes legitimacy to persons in terms of the relationship he has with them. The elaborated code speaker refers to principles rather than the relationship itself. He is thereby able to see a wider network of figures, to even the more remote of which he can respond consistently.

This arises as the restricted language speaker as a child has been exposed to rules of behaviour without explanation. A direction given and the reason for it are confused within the same statement. This has both social and logical implications. The child learns that the justification for the direction lies in the relationship he has with the speaker, not with the logic for doing it.

Bernstein gives as an example:
'Father to Son: "You're not going out."'
'Son: "Why?"'
'Father: "You're always going out."'
'Son: "Why can't I go?"'
'Father: "I told you you're not going out. Now shut up." '[19]

Bernstein's theory holds great promise for criminology. It gives an explanation that is at the same time comprehensive and deep. By showing how social-class differences become rooted in language usage the tenacity of these influences on working-class people's lives can be appreciated.

However it must be emphasized that there is as yet very little empirical data in support of the theory. A large-scale test of the theory is being undertaken but it will be some time before results will be available from which the theory can be properly evaluated.

Education in the Working Class

The literature reviewed up to now has treated certain aspects of working-class family life as the chief source of delinquency in this society. The family's internal relationships, values and methods of transmitting these to its offspring have all been considered. There is another possible, though less direct, source of delinquency which is now to be discussed. That is the sector of the education system through which most working-class children go, the secondary modern school.

[19] A. H. Halsey *et al. Education, Economy, and Society*. New York: Free Press of Glencoe, 1963, p. 312.

THE ISSUES

Curiously, it is never openly stated that the secondary modern school generates or in any way assists or acts as a catalyst for the production of delinquency. Yet it is commonly asserted by the academics and professionals concerned that the grammar school almost never has a delinquent in it or from it. This clearly implicates the secondary modern. Discussion about delinquency and the secondary moderns is usually carried on with a tone very sympathetic to the schools. The schools have to cope with numerous delinquents who come bringing their delinquent behaviour with them, which they acquired from some extraneous source.

If there is something about life in a grammar school that inhibits delinquency, and it is not contained in the secondary modern, then it follows that there is something about secondary modern life that engenders delinquency. It is one of the purposes of this study to see if there are differences in delinquency patterns, irrespective of social-class origins, between the children of these two school types. So it is a task of this chapter to review the theories and research that deal with educational factors in explanation of delinquency.

In spite of the mass of writing on the school and related aspects – delinquency treatment, social structure, mobility, self-concept, aspiration and so on – there is almost nothing that is clearly relevant to and definitely helpful for this study.

The surveys that have been done on social class and selection, achievement, early leaving and vocation have been thorough and in sufficient number for their broad conclusions to be undisputed. The review of the literature on this section of the background thus becomes unusual in two respects. A good part of the literature is so well known and so characterized by unanimity on its essential points that it needs no exposition, defence or even compilation. At the present time no empirical or theoretical work can be added that contradicts it. The other part of the question, on the schools' role in delinquency etiology, has been almost completely neglected. Thus there is almost nothing to review.

It seemed best to summarize the points of contrast between the grammar and secondary modern schools that could explain higher delinquency rates on the part of secondary modern children. The table is well footnoted so that the reader can easily refer to the sources. But only a few of the more important points on this table will be discussed here.

THE ISSUES

The comprehensive, public, private and technical schools are not dealt with in this review. It was not possible to include a third type of school, which would have been the comprehensive, in the field work. So it would have been pointless to raise questions which would then only have been left unanswered. However some of the literature on the comprehensives is included as it contains detailed descriptions of the differences between grammar and modern schools which are germane to this issue.

TABLE I.2

Comparison of Grammar and Modern Schools

	Grammar	Modern
middle-class values and norms (achievement, deferred gratification, punctuality, orderliness, manners, quiet behaviour)	attempt to inculcate these values and norms, fairly successful 2, 7, 33	attempt is made, but is not very successful 6, 27
teacher's view of the pupil	bright, able and willing to learn, appreciative 24, 29, 31, 33	dim, not able or willing to learn 26, 31, 32, 40, 46
social relationships (1) peer	concentrated on middle class 7, 22, 29	concentrated on working class 18
(2) teacher-pupil	greater similarity of background, social and educational 8, 22	less similarity of background both social and educational; if teacher has working-class background may over-conform to middle class 1, 14, 16
formal education	great emphasis, use of evaluation, exams, motivation to achieve 7, 17, 33, 39, 43	less emphasis, little use of exams, little incentive to achieve 7, 10, 30, 32, 40, 41, 42, 44, 45

	Grammar	Modern
(1) process	more analytic, reasoning, organizing ideas 4, 9, 34	more concrete (copying paragraphs, etc.), practical 4, 9, 32
(2) teaching	teachers with degrees, higher prestige, higher salaries 31, 33, 34, 35	teachers from training colleges, less prestige, lower salaries 31, 33
(3) teacher's role	convey knowledge and develop academic ability 7, 33, 43	supervise discipline, teach what you can under poor conditions 22, 26, 30, 32, 36, 41, 42, 44
(4) child's attitude to school	pride, source of satisfaction 3, 4, 9, 33, 36, 43	failure, source of humiliation 2, 4, 27, 32
official purpose	give academic education to those who can profit from it; train for the professions, keep talent flowing upwards into the middle class 32, 40, 41, 42, 45, 46	give secondary education to the ordinary child 4, 41, 45, 46
parents' attitude	support school norms, give motivation, keep informed 11, 12, 25	do not support; apathetic, fear the school 11, 12, 40

[1] Roger Armfelt. *Our Changing Schools*, 1950.
[2] Olive Banks. *Parity and Prestige in English Secondary Education*, 1955.
[3] G. Z. F. Bereday. 'The Problem of Social Equality in English Education', 1953.
[4] Basil Bernstein. 'Social Class and Linguistic Development', in Halsey, ed. *Education, Economy and Society*, 1963.
[5] N. S. Burke and A. E. Simons. 'Factors which Precipitate Dropouts and Delinquency', 1965.

THE ISSUES

[6] W. H. Burton. 'Education and Social Class in the United States', 1953.

[7] Flann Campbell. *Eleven-plus and All That*, 1956.

[8] R. R. Dale and S. Griffith. *Down Stream*, 1965.

[9] H. C. Dent. *The Education Act, 1944*, 1944.

[10] H. C. Dent. *Secondary Modern Schools*, 1958.

[11] W. B. Dockrell. 'Secondary Education, Social Class and the Development of Abilities.' *British Journal of Educational Psychology*, 1966.

[12] R. A. Ellis and W. C. Lane. 'Structural Supports for Upward Mobility', 1963.

[13] J. Floud, ed. *Social Class and Educational Opportunity*, 1957.

[14] A. H. Halsey *et al.*, eds. *Education, Economy, and Society*, 1963.

[15] H. David and H. Hargreaves. *Social Relations in a Secondary School*. London: Routledge & Kegan Paul, 1967.

[16] R. J. Havighurst and B. L. Neugarten. *Society and Education*, 1957.

[17] R. E. Herriot. 'Some Social Determinants of Educational Aspiration', 1963.

[18] H. T. Himmelweit. 'Social Status and Secondary Education since the 1944 Act: Some Data for London', in Glass, ed. *Social Mobility in Britain*, 1954.

[19] David Holbrook. *English for the Rejected*, 1964.

[20] D. N. Holly. 'Profit from a Comprehensive School, Class, Sex and Ability', 1965.

[21] Brian Holmes. *Problems in Education*, 1965.

[22] Brian Jackson and Dennis Marsden. *Education and the Working Class*, 1962.

[23] K. Andreas M. Kazamias. *Politics, Society and Secondary Education in England*. Philadelphia: University of Pennsylvania Press, 1966.

[24] D. McIntyre *et al.* 'Social and Educational Variables relating to teachers' assessments of primary school pupils.' *British Journal of Educational Psychology*, 1966.

[25] Fortune V. Mannino. 'Family Factors Related to School Persistence', 1962.

[26] Martin Mayer. *The Schools*, 1961.

[27] J. B. Mays. *Education and the Urban Child*, 1962.

[28] National Society for the Study of Education. *Juvenile Delinquency and the Schools*, 1948.

[29] A. N. Oppenheim. 'Social Status and Clique Formation among Grammar School Boys', 1955.

[30] A. T. Ravenette and J. H. Kahn. 'Intellectual Ability of Disturbed Children in a Working-class Area', 1962.

[31] Frank Riessman. *The Culturally Deprived Child*, 1962.

[32] Brian Simon. *Intelligence Testing and the Comprehensive School*, 1953.

[33] Frances Stevens. *The Living Tradition*, 1960.

[34] Asher Tropp. *The School Teachers*, 1959.

[35] John Vaizey. *Education for Tomorrow*. Harmondsworth: Penguin, 1967.

[36] Thelma Veness. *School Leavers*, 1962.

THE ISSUES

[37] John Webb. *The Sociology of a School*, 1962.
[38] Peter Wilmott and Michael Young. *Family and Class in a London Suburb*, 1960.
[39] W. Percy Wilson. *Views and Prospects from Curzon Street*. Oxford: Basil Blackwell, 1961.
United Kingdom
[40] The Hadow Report, 1926.
[41] The Spens Report, 1938.
[42] The Norwood Report, 1941.
[43] The Crowther Report, 1959.
[44] The Newsom Report, 1964.
[45] Ministry of Education. Pamphlet No. 1, *The Nation's Schools: Their Plan and Purpose*, 1945.
[46] Ministry of Education. Pamphlet No. 9, *The New Secondary Education*, 1947.
[47] Ministry of Education. *The Certificate of Secondary Education*, 1961.

Before going on to discuss a few of these points some comment about the dichotomies should be made. Grammar schools that are composed chiefly of working-class children will depart considerably from the ideal depicted. And modern schools with a large middle-class population will resemble the grammar school at some points. A comparison of this sort tends to exaggerate the points of contrast. Later, in the discussion of the results, more account will be taken of the range of possibilities within each type of school, as well as the differences between the types.

The table, in its entirety, should convey the impression that in the grammar school middle-class influences are conscientiously taught, encouraged, rewarded and required. In the secondary modern school, middle-class attitudes are taught with less fervour and fewer rewards. The child who goes to a grammar school is drawn increasingly into a network of middle-class influences and relationships. The infrastructure of the secondary modern is middle class, as are so many institutions of the state. But between the formal purpose and outcome there is a loss of middle-class intentions and an operational acceptance of working-class practices.

The idea that grammar school selection keeps delinquents and potential delinquents out, thereby sending them to secondary modern schools, is an objection that could be raised, and which should therefore be answered. Selection for the grammar school occurs by age 11, before most children who will become official delinquents are defined as such, and before they actually commit much delinquency, either officially known or not. Selection does not require a clear police record. Nor is any prediction made that the child will remain nondelinquent. There may be the occasional case of a child being rejected on the grounds of bad behaviour, which could include delinquency. However, this number of cases would be too few to account for the reputed infrequency of delinquency in the grammar schools. Moreover, it is far-fetched to believe that enormous numbers of teachers have independently discovered accurate criteria for predicting at age 11 which of their pupils will become delinquent.

Selection is based on some combination of intelligence and academic achievement. If high intelligence precluded delinquency eleven-plus selection would keep delinquents out of the grammar schools. And there is considerable expression of public opinion to this effect. However, it is contradicted by sufficient studies of the intelligence of criminals to be thoroughly unacceptable. There are no significant differences between criminals and the rest of the population in measured intelligence, and as this holds for institutionalized criminals, who are on the average deficient in some respects, it should surely hold for the wider group of unofficial delinquents and criminals.[20]

There may be differences between delinquents and nondelinquents in academic achievement, and there is some evidence to support this. If this were true it would mean that potential delinquents were kept out of the grammar schools. To the writer's knowledge there has been no specific test of the association of academic achievement and the commission of delinquencies. Most studies on schooling and delinquency have used institutionalized populations for delinquents. But since committal to an institution is often as much a result of a bad school record as a bad police record, the association of low academic achievement and delinquency is a foregone conclusion.

It is known that there are proportionately more middle-class children in the grammar schools, and of course proportionately more working-class children in the secondary moderns. Any differences between children from the two types of school could

[20] Herbert A. Bloch and Frank E. Flynn. *Delinquency: the Juvenile Offender in America Today.* New York: Random House, 1965.

Daniel Glaser. *The Effectiveness of a Prison and Parole System.* New York: Basic Books, 1964.

be entirely due to their differences in social background. This effect can of course be controlled in the research design; however it is more difficult to control for this conceptually in studying the literature. Often in studies of this sort there is no attempt to distinguish between the social background of the home and the social environment of the school.

The only good piece of research with direct bearing on this problem is that by Toby and Toby.[21] The Tobys hypothesized that delinquent behaviour and participation in delinquent gangs was preceded by low academic achievement. They traced the development of delinquency as follows:

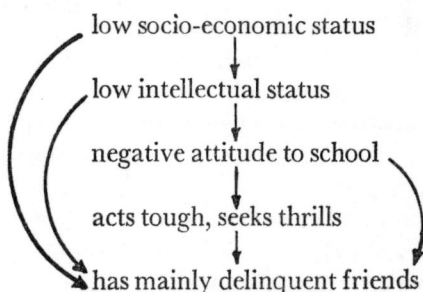

low socio-economic status
↓
low intellectual status
↓
negative attitude to school
↓
acts tough, seeks thrills
↓
has mainly delinquent friends

The authors concluded that low intellectual status did occur before delinquent activity. This is an important finding as the opposite explanation, that low performance follows from participation in a delinquent subculture, is a most plausible one. Of course the child's level of achievement could drop still lower after he has begun his delinquent career.

Low intellectual status was itself preceded by low socio-economic status. The chronology is that low social standing leads to low achievement, which turns the child against the school and forces him to seek satisfaction outside of it. In this case, the substitute satisfaction comes from behaviour antithetical to that taught by the school.

British writers have paid considerable attention to the question of low achievement, but have not dealt with its implications for delinquent behaviour. At least one of them, Bernstein, does not

[21] E. Jackson Toby and Marcia L. Toby. *Low School Status as a Predisposing Factor in Subcultural Delinquency.* United States Office of Education and Rutgers University, 1957.

underestimate the possible detrimental effects of the schools' régime. He describes the reaction of restricted code speakers to the formal educational process as one of 'critical psychological distress'. This he says occurs especially at the secondary level. The process he outlines is worth repeating in some detail.

'This analysis has indicated the critical importance of the early stages of education; for that which is not efficiently learned and applied correctly will prejudice the pupil's success at the secondary level. The character of the educational process changes at the secondary level. It becomes increasingly analytic and relies on the progressive exploitation of what Piaget calls "formal operations", whereas the lower working-class child's linguistic history tends to restrict him to the *concrete* operational stage. . . . The discrepancy between what he can do and what he is called upon to do widens considerably at the secondary level. Society reinforces his perception of this discrepancy by often allocating him to what many people consider an inferior educational institution. . . . Failure, despite persistence, often ensues. Insulation from this failure is accomplished by denying the relevance of education and by the mechanical assertion of his own values. By fourteen years of age many lower working-class children have become "unteachable".'[22]

Jackson and Marsden point out that when the working-class child does gain a grammar school place, and especially if he goes on to the sixth form, he identifies whole-heartedly with the régime. He drops his friends of pre-eleven-plus days. He works long hours at his studies and in his spare time participates in school societies and sports.

From this part of the review of the literature, it appears that there are many ways in which grammar and modern schools are different, some of which could explain their pupils' different proclivities for delinquency. The schools' effect is made as high as the level of value formation to as low as the level of daily routine.

At the level of social relationships, the school can enormously extend or restrict the scope of the child's friendship network. In a grammar school it will increase the child's middle-class contacts.

Spatial environment as well as mental is different between the two school types. The grammar school takes in children from a large catchment area while the modern school catchment area is

[22] A. H. Halsey *et al. Education, Economy, and Society.* New York: Free Press of Glencoe, 1963, p. 307.

so small that it keeps the child close to home and an already familiar neighbourhood.

For the grammar school pupil, a larger portion of the day falls into the sphere of the school's influence. In doing homework and participating in supervised school activities, even his out-of-school hours are affected by the school. For the secondary modern pupil his out-of-school hours are his own. They will be spent less on constructive pursuits and less in solitary activity.

In setting its standards for success the school affects the child's concept of himself. The school helps to determine whether he sees himself as successful or unsuccessful, whether he feels he can try to achieve or whether he feels his efforts would be ineffectual, whether he sees himself liked and accepted or not.

A parallel can be drawn between the effect of area, as dealt with in a few of the American studies, and the effect of school type as the system exists in Britain. Many of the features that make one area different from another in America, and in Britain as well, are those which make one type of school different from another here. The mediating concept is that of the prevailing class.[23] Each child is affected by the social class of the home he comes from; this can be seen in both societies. But the host of other influences – peer groups, recreational facilities, attitudes to school, achievement and authority – are affected by the prevailing attitudes and customs of the social environment in which the child lives. These are usually set by the majority in the area or the group concerned.

There is a sense in which attendance at a grammar school is like living in one neighbourhood, while attendance at a secondary modern is like living in a different kind of neighbourhood. It has been shown that there are differences in delinquency rates by type of area as well as by social class.[24]

These findings suggest that a similar situation of differences in delinquency rates by type of school may exist in this society.

[23] In the American studies 'prevailing class' is used in reference to neighbourhoods only, but there is no reason why it could not be applied to the school situation as well.

[24] Albert J. Reiss, Jr. and A. Lewis Rhodes. 'Delinquency and Social Class Structure.' *American Sociological Review*, v. 26, 1961, p. 720.

John Clark and Eugene Wenninger. 'Socio-Economic Class and Area as Correlates of Illegal Behavior Among Juveniles.' *American Sociological Review*, v. 24, 1959, p. 164.

For the most part in this discussion emphasis has been laid on the broad cultural and structural differences between the types of school. Doubtless some kind souls will raise the objection that as there are well-educated, conscientious and humane teachers in the secondary moderns some children's experience must be very different from that outlined. The answer to this criticism must be an abrupt 'no, not likely'. There is yet to be a valid demonstration, or any demonstration, that a good teacher has any measurable effect on such a formative system.

One American writer, from an analysis of what scattered research there has been on this subject, concluded that the teacher's contribution to his students' achievement, at least in the short run, is minimal.[25]

The sociologist must deal with what happens, and while he should not ignore good intentions he must remain sceptical and judge on results. This researcher came into contact with numerous competent and highly motivated teachers and heads in secondary modern schools. But even so she accepts the pessimistic interpretation given above.

What will become increasingly more clear throughout this book is that there are enormous differences between middle-class and working-class children, between grammar school and modern school children. Some of the evidence for this is based on empirical studies of the differences in socialization, language use, leisure patterns, attitudes to authority and so forth. The other aspect of this argument is not just that these differences are observed and held to exist. It is that the whole system of education (based on awareness of this difference) divides the children and, in separate groups, further socializes the children to become more like the average of the group to which they have been assigned.

The persons at the highest policy-making and administrative levels either judged that there were different types of children with different types of mind or else relied on the unanimous advice of the professionals concerned that this was so. The descriptions repeatedly made of children in reports to the ministers or boards of education over the last fifty years make them out to be very similar to Bernstein's restricted code speakers, and extreme

[25] Rossi in A. H. Halsey *et al. Education, Economy, and Society.* New York: Free Press of Glencoe, 1963, p. 270.

cases at that.[26] This observation then became the fundamental point of reference for policy decisions regarding the structure of the school system.

As late as 1947 the Ministry of Education could say:

'Everyone knows that no two children are alike. Schools must be different, too, or the Education Act of 1944 will not achieve success. They must differ in what they teach and how they teach it.'[27]

People tend to become what is expected of them. This occurs at least as much when they are expected to be inferior, dull, uncreative and lazy. It can be seen clearly in the studies of the effect of streaming.[28] Children of lower streams are less intelligent than children of higher streams. But by being stamped 'dim' some of the children in the lower streams failed to progress in reading at even a pace commensurate with their ability. Similarly children who are labelled 'secondary modern' probably become less able as they conform with what the system expects of them.

Secondary modern education, in this writer's opinion, provides a perfect example of the self-fulfilling prophecy. A study made by psychologists in the same East London borough as this study comes to similar conclusions.[29]

They found that the verbal ability of older boys, referred to the local child guidance clinic, was much lower than their performance scores. Amongst younger boys there was no significant difference. Presumably in the intervening years the boys' verbal ability diminished. What is important is that it was clearly something social rather than constitutional that was affecting these verbal intelligence scores.

The school system, by separating children by ability, makes

[26] This includes Hadow, Spens, Norwood, and even Newsom although he is less dogmatic about it.

[27] Ministry of Education. *The New Secondary Education.* H.M.S.O., 1947, p. 22.

[28] Alfred Yates, ed. *Grouping in Education.* New York: John Wiley, 1966.

J. C. Daniels. 'The Effects of Streaming in the Primary School. 1: What Teachers Believe.' *British Journal of Educational Psychology,* v. 31, 1961, p. 69.

[29] A. T. Ravenette and J. H. Kahn. 'Intellectual Ability of Disturbed Children in a Working-Class Area.' *British Journal of Social & Clinical Psychology,* v. 1, pt. 3, 1962, p. 208.

these abilities diverge even more. The children who are not academically educable are sent, it is always said in their best interests, to schools that do not attempt to 'force book learning at them', but which have 'realistic standards', and a practical and 'concrete' curriculum related to their immediate interests and environment.[30]

The head of a hypothetical secondary modern was made to say:

'One thing's clear. If the children had been in need of the grammar school they'd have been sent to one. They haven't. That means that it's not grammar school education they want.'[31]

Note the identity between what children need, what they want, and what is provided for them. Of course it is well known that many more children want to go to grammar schools than ever obtain places in them. And the determination of the number of grammar school places in any area has little to do with how many want them or have the ability to make use of them.

At some point it is decided that certain children are not academically educable. Accordingly they are assigned to non-academic secondary schools. Now another curious progression of thought and policy helps to keep the unimaginative, concretely oriented children unimaginative and oriented to the concrete. The secondary modern school was designed to serve the ordinary non-academic child. If it gives its children academic work, or prepares them for external examinations (a sure sign of giving them academic work) it is criticized for neglecting the needs of the ordinary non-academic child.

The curriculum of the grammar school is oriented to university entrance requirements, though only the top minority will go on to a university. The junior school is geared to preparation for grammar school selection, though only its top minority will go on to grammar school. The interests of the elites of these two schools are served at the expense of the average child. But the secondary modern is deemed unfair and unegalitarian if it gives special attention to its superior children.

Needless to say many secondary moderns have attempted to

[30] Norwood Report. Board of Education. *Curriculum and Examinations in Secondary Schools.* H.M.S.O., 1941, p. 21.

[31] Roger Armfelt. *Our Changing Schools.* London: H.M.S.O., 1950, p. 51.

give some of their pupils an academic education, prepare some of them for external examinations and for later entry into a grammar school. Indeed, as the ingrained and life-long orientation of teachers has been to this end it should be expected that they would strive towards such recognized goals for their charges.

Proponents of the grouping by ability system can claim some success for it. The children in the lower streams do badly, proving that they were of lower ability. The children in high streams do well, proving that they deserved to be there. The children in the lower streams are far behind the children in the higher in subject matter, proving that it would have been impossible for a teacher to teach both groups within the same classroom.

However these claims do not stand up even to good criticism, certainly not to research which has been set up with adequate controls. A survey of streaming practices in Western Europe and the United States points out how confused are the causes and effects in this matter.

'It is largely because grouping tends to sustain the differences on which it is based that it has been possible to claim success for some of the selective procedures that have been practised. To isolate an able minority of pupils at an early age and to accord them preferential educational treatment – better facilities and equipment, more highly qualified teachers, and a longer period of schooling than are provided for their fellows – not unnaturally results in their producing superior levels of attainment. We are inclined to agree with those who have argued that to predict that they will do so in such circumstances is a self-fulfilling prophecy rather than a vindication of the practice.'[32]

Delinquency and the Working-class Neighbourhood

The explanations of delinquency covered so far have been that certain influences, in the family itself, and then in the secondary modern school, have caused the relatively high rates of delinquency in the working class. There is one further source of working-class influence to be discussed, that of the neighbourhood.

Use of the concept of neighbourhood or area leaves the subject

[32] Alfred Yates, ed. *Grouping in Education*. New York: John Wiley, 1966.

open to a multiplicity of misunderstandings. As was explained at
the beginning of this chapter, the concept is to some extent a
residual category. It is suggested that there are experiences that
affect children – to what degree is an empirical question – that
should be conceptually distinguished from the experiences of both
the family and the formal educational system. There are some
intrafamilial experiences over which parents have virtually complete control, that cannot be affected by neighbours or the type of
neighbourhood lived in. Early socialization of the child, discipline,
the atmosphere of family meals, family outings and holidays,
some formal recreation, hobbies, reading and sports are examples
of the experiences over which parents have considerable control.

There are other facets over which parents can exercise some
control, but which are to some extent subject to the elements of
the neighbourhood, physical and social. Informal leisure, street
play groups, the use of local sports facilities, cinemas, bowling
alleys, cafés, street corners, time spent walking to school and back
again, are examples of experiences over which the parents'
influence is mitigated by that of the other residents of the area.

A middle-class family in a working-class area can do a lot to
isolate the child from working-class influences. The family may
manage to stimulate and supervise the child into a grammar
school. It may enrol the child in constructive leisure pursuits. It
may attend a predominantly middle-class church, and participate
in organized activities there that implicitly strengthen middle-
class attitudes and abilities. The child may be kept home to study
in the evening. He may be sent to camp in the summer. Yet, however much the family works at it the middle-class child in a working-class area will likely be faced with more working-class
experiences than a child from a similar family that lives in a
homogeneous middle-class area.

In the same way, a working-class family that lives in a middle-
class area will inevitably be affected, actively and passively, by the
middle-class institutions surrounding it. If there are no fish shops,
cafés, billiard halls or other hangouts near by, and if there is no-
body else who wants to and is allowed to hang around, the working-class boy will not spend his time hanging around.

To summarize the argument it is suggested that there is such a
thing as the prevailing class of the area, and that it has an influence independent of that of the individual homes of the area

concerned. The nature of this influence is determined by the numerically predominant class, which has an effect by virtue of its collective demand for certain types of facilities.

Josephine Klein in her very useful compilation of cultural data describes some of the indirect effects of the neighbourhood influence.[33] She contrasts the situation in which the parents approve of the prevailing mores of the neighbourhood to one in which the parents are a disapproving minority. The neighbourhoods have themselves different effects on the children. As well, it is suggested that they affect the climate of socialization within the home itself, although not at the earliest stages of development. Where parents approve of neighbourhood standards, and allow their children to participate in its activities, they can rely upon the local tradition to inculcate personality traits they value. They are more relaxed in their handling of their children.

Where the parents cannot trust the neighbourhood to socialize their children properly they may take an extreme stand on some matters. For example, in a situation where roughs and respectables live side by side in the same districts or the same streets, the respectables may have a conscious problem of maintaining their standards.

'Certain forms of childish behaviour are given particular attention because the child will be misclassified as a rough if he engages in them: shouting, swearing and fighting are obvious examples at this level. Table manners and more refined speech forms would be pre-occupations a little higher on the social scale.'[34]

However, there are instances in which the influences of the home and the area cannot be separated. This would occur when a family chooses to live in a certain area because the area's standards (the neighbourhood influence) coincide exactly with their own. Morris found that this happened in some parts of his Croydon sample. The families with the most delinquency tended to live on the same streets and crescents of the council estates. The nondelinquent families moved away from these corners as soon as they could. Delinquent families from more respectable parts of the estate would then move in, to get away from neighbours with

[33] Josephine Klein. *Samples from English Cultures*. London: Routledge & Kegan Paul, 1965.
[34] Josephine Klein. *Samples from English Cultures*. London: Routledge & Kegan Paul, 1965, p. 632.

higher standards whom they considered stand-offish. This movement, clearly the preference of both rough and respectable tenants, was supported by the housing department.[35]

The vast majority of people of course do not live in areas in which the influence of home and neighbourhood are so intertwined. Thus the influence of the area would be a separate factor in most cases.

From the American literature one of the most relevant studies of the influence of the neighbourhood on the behaviour of adolescents is Turner's *The Social Context of Ambition*.[36] Turner found that the type of area lived in (the prevailing class of the area) significantly influenced social-class values and aspirations. This was not a delinquency study, but can be used merely to show the impact of the neighbourhood on related behaviour in the same age group.

Theories of the influence of the area on crime commission go back to the early part of this century. However these theories, which were based solely on the area influence, have disappeared. New theories have incorporated the explanations of both the area and the family and, to some extent, the school. Discussion of the older, narrowly ecological accounts will be included only as an introduction to the later and fuller discussion of theories which incorporated their observations.

The early theories ignored psychological and other social factors. Sutherland, for example, at the earliest stage of the development of his theory of differential association even denied that psychological factors had any independent effect. 'Personal traits have a causal relation to criminal behaviour only as they affect the person's associations' – a position from which he later departed. These traits themselves he asserted to be a function of earlier associations.

Differential association theory explained how a boy living in a delinquent area became a delinquent. It did not explain how the area became delinquent in the first place.

[35] T. P. Morris. *The Criminal Area*. London: Routledge & Kegan Paul, 1957.

Roger Wilson. *Difficult Housing Estates*. London: Tavistock, 1963.

J. H. Nicholson. *New Communities in Britain*. London: National Council of Social Services, 1961.

[36] Ralph Turner. *The Social Context of Ambition*. San Francisco: Chandler, 1964.

From this beginning several accounts were eventually developed that attempt to explain the origin of the delinquent areas themselves. The first of these to be discussed is that of Albert Cohen.[37] Cohen's theory made an enormous advance by incorporating into it both psychological and sociological factors. Doing that, it found common ground in theories and observations previously considered unrelated and even mutually exclusive. The theory was published in 1955 and has had a considerable impact on subsequent theoretical formulation and empirical research. *Delinquent Boys: The Culture of the Gang* reports no empirical testing of the theory itself. It is only a statement of theory supported by reasoned application of the observations of other writers. The book, however, comes late enough to have had the benefit of lengthy attention to the phenomenon of the delinquent gang. (Thrasher's *The Gang* was published in 1927; Clifford Shaw was publishing in 1929; and Robert Park's more general ecological investigations go back to 1914.)

Cohen's theory, very briefly, is that gangs of delinquent boys exist in response to a commonly perceived need for alternative satisfaction of thwarted status aspirations. Boys, having been socialized to expect a certain status, and having accepted the belief that they have a just chance of obtaining this on their own, find during adolescence that they cannot. They band together to give each other emotional support, creating status within their own group and developing and reinforcing norms of behaviour which give them the sense of achievement they do not get in the larger community.

The delinquent group is exclusively male. For an explanation of this Cohen refers to work by Talcott Parsons. Boys in an industrial urban society are socialized primarily by their mothers. Fathers' occupational roles are not shared, and are not shareable, with their sons. In any event, bringing up children is considered a largely feminine task. Thus boys, at adolescence, to establish their masculine identity, must repudiate feminine attachments and characteristics. To maintain the ideal behaviour taught by their mothers would indicate that they were effeminate, cowardly and childish. Moral behaviour, because of its association with the female authority on morality, is confused with feminine behaviour. Girls, however, do not have to reverse the total

[37] Albert K. Cohen. *Delinquent Boys*. New York: Free Press, 1955.

behavioural standard of their mothers to establish their individual and independent femininity.

Boys are also more critically affected by status striving in that the goal of occupational success is far more their concern than it is girls'. When they fail – and this becomes evident at adolescence – they react far more strongly than girls.

Cohen treats the malicious nature of delinquent gang activities as reaction formation against middle-class norms of hard work, saving for the future, and respect for property. According to him, working-class boys, when they sense their failure to achieve middle-class goals, repudiate the norms that are associated with those goals and regulate the race towards them. This point of view is probably the one most disputed by other criminologists. Their alternative accounts will be considered later.

Cohen's explanation of the process of gang formation is fundamentally different from that of writers in the cultural schools. Yet the description Cohen gives of the delinquent gangs is much the same. Miller, writing after Cohen, isolated six characteristics (trouble, toughness, smartness, excitement, fate and autonomy) that are not dissimilar to Cohen's description of gang activity: non-utilitarian, negativistic and malicious. The emphasis is different but the descriptions are not inconsistent one with another.

Altogether Cohen's theory is a good attempt to fill a gap in theory. Differential association theory explained how a subculture incorporates new members, but not why it exists in the first place. Psychogenic theories explained why certain children individually would turn to delinquency, but not why great numbers of non-disturbed youngsters did the same thing.

Of course these conflicting psychological and sociological explanations of delinquency etiology are yet another version of a very old theoretical dispute, that of heredity versus environment. It has taken a long time in the field of criminology for the two sides to begin to incorporate the findings of the other into their own body of knowledge.

The criticism of Cohen's theory that touches its most salient features is that of David Matza (1964).[38] Matza accuses Cohen, amongst other theorists, of analysing too many things in terms of opposites, of neatly discovering dichotomies everywhere. This he says comes out pointedly in Cohen's description of the values of

[38] David Matza. *Delinquency and Drift*. New York: Wiley, 1964.

46

delinquents, as being in direct opposition to those of conventional society.

Cohen has an explanation for this in reaction formation, the process to which he attributes the rise of new, delinquent values in gangs. At this Matza in effect accuses Cohen of choosing the process to fit the result. He points out that just because reaction formation conveniently would result in the development of opposite values, and allows for a good description of the nature of delinquent behaviour, it is not necessarily the process that is operating. Moreover, Matza in describing reaction formation as the most radical of defence mechanisms infers that it is the least likely one to be operating. And in fact Cohen has given no support for his contention that it is.

Other, more useful, criticisms of Cohen's theory appear sporadically throughout the literature. Those that are based on empirical testing of the theory will be discussed along with the work of the particular researcher concerned.[39]

Anomie in the Working Class

There is at present one major dichotomy in the explanation of lower-class juvenile delinquency. Some writers attribute it to criminogenic cultural influences, variously traced to the home, the school, the area or some combination of these. Other writers, of whom Cohen has been the first example, maintain that the lower-class culture is not that different from the middle class. It is not *per se* any more criminogenic. These writers hypothesize that delinquency in the lower class is one of the results of status frustration.

They hold that middle-class values of success and achievement are the values of the whole (American) society, held just as firmly by the working class as the middle class. They then observe that at adolescence the working-class boy becomes very aware that he has failed in terms of these middle-class standards. He is not getting on at school, will not go on to college, and has only a routine

---

[39] Albert J. Reiss, Jr. and A. Lewis Rhodes. 'Delinquency and Social Class Structure.' *American Sociological Review*, v. 26, 1961, p. 720.

John Clark and Eugene Wenninger. 'Socio-Economic Class and Area as Correlates of Illegal Behavior Among Juveniles.' *American Sociological Review*, v. 27, 1962, p. 826.

job to look forward to. He cannot expect to earn the income needed to acquire the possessions and symbols of success others have. The working-class boy is believed to share the same criteria for success, but it is he that becomes aware that he does not have the same opportunities for gaining it.

This account of working-class delinquency is derived from anomie theory, particularly as developed from Durkheim by Merton. Merton's analysis is that in America the value of high achievement, judged in monetary terms, is held by people in all social strata. It is coupled with a belief that there is equality of opportunity for high achievement. Yet the places at the top are few.

There is equality of opportunity only to the extent that there are no legal barriers or absolute social obstacles for a person of low status rising. In fact, the majority of the places most desired are occupied by the children of people who themselves held high positions in society.

Merton describes contemporary American society as an extreme example of anomic society. There is a vast discrepancy between culturally prescribed goals and the realistic means of the lower-class person's achieving them. In the culture the goal of high achievement is stressed more than the norms which regulate the ethical route to success. Desire for the goal is great and there is little reward, monetary or emotional, for adhering to the norms of society. The process goes on:

'A mounting frequency of deviant but "successful" behaviour tends to lessen and, as an extreme potentiality, to eliminate the legitimacy of the institutional norms for others in the system. The process thus enlarges the extent of anomie within the system so that others, who did not respond in the form of deviant behaviour to the relatively slight anomie which first obtained, come to do so as anomie spreads and is intensified. This in turn, creates a more acutely anomic situation for other and initially less vulnerable individuals in the social system.'[40]

Merton's theory does not require that all, or even larger proportions of the working class than the middle class, adhere to unrealistically high goals. It only requires that a substantial minority of them hold them. From this minority sufficient will be

[40] Robert K. Merton. *Social Theory and Social Structure*. Glencoe, Illinois: Free Press, 1957, p. 180.

unable to attain the goals. Of these, many will turn to deviant behaviour.

Merton suggests that deviant behaviour, that is the continued adherence to the goals but detachment from the norms, is only one of five possible responses to failure. Which type of response people turn to depends in part on the inhibitions and attitudes of the social strata in which they have been brought up. Middle-class people for example may turn to ritualistic behaviour, performance in accord with the norms, but without striving towards the goals. Lower-class people would be particularly prone to turn to deviant behaviour.

Merton's formulation should hold even if there are differences between the classes in adherence to high-achievement goals. Thus, if the theories that emphasize cultural differences between the classes are empirically verified, this would not preclude the possibility of Merton's anomie theory being concomitantly operative. Only if virtually no lower-class persons were found to have high goals, or if working-class persons were found to attain high goals at an equal rate with middle class, should Merton's theory be dismissed.

Merton's theory is an attempt to account for the responses to failure made by people differentially placed in the social hierarchy. In particular, it is an explanation as to why people in the lower class commit proportionately more crime than people classes above them. The theory is at a high level of abstraction. The variables that it takes into account are few: strata, values, norms, legitimation of norms, and withdrawal of legitimation. It does not account for any possible variables of personality structure within the lower class, socializing groups within the lower class or opportunities for acquiring specialized delinquent roles.

A few sociologists have tried to extend Merton's rather general theory to fit their more detailed picture of delinquent behaviour and lower-class structure. In doing this they have actually refuted nothing of Merton's but have drawn conclusions from his general points and applied these to more particular theoretical problems.

Cohen's theory is an extension of Merton's to explain one particular manifestation of lower-class deviance, juvenile gang delinquency. Cloward and Ohlin's is another, attempting to explain the same thing, but extending Merton's theory further still. As far as the explanation of Merton's theory has been given above, Cohen and Cloward and Ohlin would agree. It is from this point that Cloward and Ohlin depart from Cohen.

Cloward and Ohlin fault Cohen's theory with the observation that not all working-class boys who experience status frustration join delinquent gangs. For this they postulate that there is differential access to certain illegitimate success goals in the same way as there is to legitimate goals. The illegitimate world has its own criteria for entry, own rules of behaviour, and own channels of upward mobility.

Differential association theory explains the process of acquisition of delinquent skills, contacts, aspirations and satisfactions, while anomie theory explains why working-class boys would want to turn to delinquent behaviour at all. By applying the opportunity concept to both legitimate and illegitimate avenues it can be seen how certain boys who should be highly motivated to delinquency (by virtue of status frustration) do not participate in delinquent gangs – because they do not make contact with a gang or are not accepted by one.

The Cloward-Ohlin theory describes three types of gang: conflict, criminal and retreatist. They are related to stratification within the illegitimate opportunity structure and the nature of legitimate society surrounding it. Thus, a boy who could not make the grade in a certain criminal gang (and places in these groups are strictly limited) might then turn to a retreatist gang which has easier entrance requirements. Outside New York City, and perhaps a few other cities, the Cloward-Ohlin theory is far too sophisticated for the gangs that actually exist. One sociologist who looked for these types of gangs in certain working-class boroughs in London did not find any that met the description.[41]

These has been to date only one specific test of the theory in America, a survey of admitted delinquency by Clark and Wenninger.[42]

Clark and Wenninger set out to test the two conflicting accounts of working-class delinquency – the Cloward and Ohlin

[41] David Downes. *The Delinquent Solution: a study in subcultural theory.* London: Routledge & Kegan Paul, 1966.

[42] John Clark and Eugene P. Wenninger. 'Socio-Economic Class and Area as Correlates of Illegal Behavior Among Juveniles.' *American Sociological Review*, v. 27, 1962, p. 826. 'Goal Orientations and Illegal Behavior Among Juveniles.' *Social Forces*, v. 42, 1963, p. 49.

theory and the cultural theory described by Miller. They deduced two hypotheses from each theoretical school for testing. From the cultural school they hypothesized that there are differences in goals held by members of the two classes and that lower-class goal orientation is directly related to illegal activity. From the anomie school they hypothesized that socio-economic status is directly related to illegal behaviour rates.

The authors took four distinct status areas: an industrial city, a lower-class urban area, an upper-class urban area and a rural farm area, a sample of 1,200 subjects altogether. Their questionnaire consisted of a list of misconduct items and three sets of questions on values and focal concerns. One was derived from Robin Williams's pervading values of American society, one from Miller's lower-class focal concerns and one from Cohen's middle-class focal concerns.

They found differences in admitted misconduct rates by status area. The industrial city area had the highest, followed by the lower-class urban, the upper-class urban, and the rural farm area. The same order was found to hold for adherence to Miller's lower-class concerns.

Within each status area there were no differences between the social classes in goal orientation. In connection with this it should be noted that Reiss and Rhodes found differences by class within each area in delinquency rates, though the differences were not as great as between whole areas.

Goal orientation was not found to vary for the middle- and upper-class groups between status areas. There were differences, however, between the lower-class groups from area to area. Clark and Wenninger suggest in explanation that middle- and upper-class groups are less influenced by their area of residence in formulating values than lower-class groups are.

Perceived chances for obtaining goals without illegal behaviour did not vary by social class within each status area. To put it in other words, in each area the children had an opinion as to how good their chances were to obtain goals without illegal behaviour. And all the children of the area, despite their class differences, basically concurred in this opinion. Yet the opinions differed from one area to another.

Delinquent and nondelinquent groups were characterized by differences in their adherence to middle-class American values,

51

the delinquent group being less committed to middle-class values. The delinquent group also differed from the nondelinquent by perceiving its chances of obtaining goals without illegal behaviour as less than that of the nondelinquent group. Thus all the initial hypotheses received some support. The authors concluded:

'Miller's theory has received support in that significant differences can be found between the focal concerns of the lower and middle classes. However, these differences are not great, which also tends to support the position of Merton and others, that values are essentially similar throughout the social strata.'[43]

The authors, in adding support to both sides of the conflict, have not made its resolution any easier. Had they been determined to evade the issue they could not have come up with more suitable results or interpretation. However, their work was thorough and such were their findings.

Adherence to working-class values and perception of opportunity as limited are both associated with high delinquency admission. Now the problem must be approached more delicately. How large must a city be in order that class differences in adherence to values occur? Are the values on which the classes do agree held with equal tenacity and affect?

Anomie in the British Working Class

The question as to how applicable the anomie theory is to British society is in my opinion a very difficult and complicated one. Yet amongst sociologists there is remarkable consensus that British society is not remotely anomic. It is insisted that there is no great discrepancy between goals and means in any part of the social structure. Working-class persons are observed to adhere to lower goals and to internalize different norms in the first place. Thus, when they achieve at a lower level, there is no frustration and, more importantly, no weakening of commitment to the normative structure.

The British working-class boy has not been educated to believe he has an equal chance to rise to the top of the social scale. Unlike the well-publicized path from the log cabin to the White House,

---

[43] John P. Clark and Eugene P. Wenninger. 'Goal Orientations and Illegal Behavior Among Juveniles.' *Social Forces*, v. 42, 1963, p. 56.

everyone in Britain knows that the only path to the throne is from the palace nursery. The British working-class boy can accept his low status without the guilt that it is his own fault, that he failed to make use of his God-given opportunities. Indeed, he can even indulge in inverted snobbery.

Actually there is some evidence already that lower-class persons in Britain adhere to unrealistically high goals. A survey done by Himmelweit et al. in 1952[44] was the first to suggest such a state. Results from this survey indicate that 40 per cent of middle- and working-class children in secondary modern schools thought their chances of upward mobility greater than their fathers'. While in the grammar schools investigated, 78 per cent of the working-class and 65 per cent of the middle-class children thought they had better chances than their fathers for upward mobility.

There were great differences between the classes in perception of opportunity, but note that this was complicated by stratification in the school system. The modern school boys had appreciably lower expectations, but these were unrealistically high in view of the current mobility pattern. The working-class boys in grammar schools had very high expectations, which were fairly realistic as they were comparing themselves with their fathers, not with middle-class boys.

When asked, 'Do you think that you have as good a chance as other boys of moving up in the world?', 85 per cent of all respondents said they thought so. There were no significant differences by social class. As the question elicited such uniformity of response not too much attention should be paid it. However, a fair comment would be that these boys to a great extent accept the belief of equality of opportunity. Though they were undoubtedly referring to quite different groups when they compared themselves with 'other boys', still they were seeing opportunity as being equally available.

By comparing the boys' expected jobs with their fathers' jobs the effect of the type of school is made more clear. Working-class boys at grammar schools expected to obtain jobs on the average two prestige levels (in a range of five) above those of their fathers. Middle-class boys at modern schools expected to be one prestige level lower than their fathers. Even then, 14 per cent expected to

[44] H. T. Himmelweit et al. 'The Views of Adolescents on Some Aspects of Social Class Structure.' British Journal of Sociology, v. 32, 1952, p. 148.

be one level higher. And 40 per cent gave a 'wish job' a level higher than their fathers' actual jobs.

When these attitudes are seen in the light of the vertical mobility presently taking place, the problem becomes obvious. The children's goals are too high. Most of them will not achieve the status for which they hope.

Throughout the last hundred years in Britain there has been more downward mobility than upward. Havighurst, in an article based on the data reported in *Social Mobility in Britain*, stated that the mobility pattern for the last century in Britain has been:

  40 per cent of the population stable

  27 per cent upward mobile

  33 per cent downward mobile[45]

There has been no change in this pattern throughout the last 100 years. And in other industrialized countries mobility rates have been constant for the same period of time. So there is no reason to expect that mobility will now change in direction or pace in this country. Note that in the United States the mobility rate remained the same for the same period of time despite a great expansion in secondary and higher education. This was, however, one of net upward mobility. The commonly held view that there is greater opportunity now for the individual to get ahead is not founded in reality. There is no promise for this if past experience is referred to and no promise for it when projections of the future are made.

The present, though limited, data on trends in the distribution of income do not give any cause for optimism. Titmuss thoroughly discredits the evidence for the popular view that in recent decades the lower-income groups have gradually increased their share of the national income. He carefully words his conclusions:

'There is more than a hint from a number of studies that income inequality has been increasing since 1949 whilst the ownership of wealth, which is far more concentrated in the United Kingdom than in the United States, has probably become still more unequal and, in terms of family ownership, possibly strikingly more unequal, in recent years.'[46]

[45] A. H. Halsey, Jean Floud and C. Arnold Anderson. *Education, Economy, and Society.* New York: Free Press of Glencoe, 1963, p. 106.
[46] Richard M. Titmuss. *Income Distribution and Social Change.* London: Allen & Unwin, 1962, p. 198.

THE ISSUES

Should Titmuss's assessment be correct, and continue to be, British society will increasingly fill the requirements of an anomic society.

A survey by F. M. Martin[47] done at the same time as the Himmelweit study also revealed unrealistic aspirations for social advancement. This was seen in an inquiry into the preferences of parents for their children's secondary education. There were important differences by social class (in the expected direction) as to the nature of secondary education desired. The point is, though, that the aspirations of all the classes exceeded existing opportunities. Fifty-four per cent of all classes expressed a preference for grammar school education at a time when there were places for less than 20 per cent. And of those parents who wished their children to go to grammar schools, 30 per cent also wanted them to go to university. Thus, the parents of 18 per cent of the age group wanted their children to go to university when there was the opportunity for only four per cent.

In another part of the same study information was collected on the reaction of parents to their children's not obtaining grammar school places.[48] The proportion of working-class parents who wanted grammar school places for their children was lower than that of middle-class parents. Yet the proportion of working-class children who actually obtained them was so low that the majority was disappointed. Proportionately far more working-class parents saw their ambitions frustrated than middle-class parents.

Table 1.3 shows the proportions in each social group, in two areas, who expressed the desire that their children go to grammar schools. The third and fourth columns show the percentages of those who wanted their children to go to grammar schools, but who did not obtain places. Almost all the parents in all the groups who wanted their children to go to grammar schools said they experienced frustration when their children did not obtain places.

From these studies it would appear that the case for the working class lacking aspiration is not as well supported as believed. Interestingly, the evidence gathered from these surveys corroborates one of the main findings of the participant observation studies,

[47] David Glass, ed. *Social Mobility in Britain*. London: Routledge & Kegan Paul, 1954, p. 160.
[48] J. Floud, ed. *Social Class and Educational Opportunity*. London: Heinemann, 1957, p. 82.

that is, that aspiration is lower in the working class than in the middle class. The point is, however, that even with lower aspiration there is more frustration.

TABLE I.3

Parents' Preferences for Grammar School Education

	Prefers Grammar		Prefers Grammar, Sent Elsewhere	
	Herts.	Middlesbrough.	Herts.	Middlesbrough.
Professional and business	82%	87%	49%	27%
Clerical	77	67	59	55
Foremen, etc.	61	68	70	68
Skilled workers	48	53	72	80
Unskilled workers	43	48	79	84

It appears that the same situation obtains in America. Turner found in his study of San Francisco high-school students that the high-status students were aiming at higher goals than the lower-status students. But in relative terms the lower-status students were more ambitious. That is, their goals were not as high as the high-status students', but considering the place from which they were starting they involved a greater step upwards.[49]

The results of another survey add further evidence for this interpretation.[50] Veness asked a broader question than the previous researchers – 'Are the British ambitious?' She concluded that they are, both in having high motives for social advancement and for wanting material possessions. Veness found differences between grammar school and modern school children in their status orientations. Both groups of children were, however, very highly oriented to status achievement in terms of the actual mobility taking place at the present time.

Veness did not ask father's occupation in her study, and so the proportions of each social class in the grammar and modern school groups cannot be determined. It could be that the differ-

[49] Ralph Turner. *The Social Context of Ambition.* San Francisco: Chandler, 1964.
[50] Thelma Veness. *School Leavers.* London: Methuen, 1962.

ences she found are differences of class more than type of school. In either case they indicate unrealistic ambitions on the part of modern school boys, most of whom will actually be taking low-status jobs when they leave school.

TABLE I.4

Success Orientation at Different Educational Levels

	Modern School				Grammar School			
	A Stream		B Stream		A Stream		B Stream	
	No.	Per cent	No.	Per cent	No.	Per cent	No.	Per cent
status through effort	35	34·6	26	25·7	47	92·0	15	55·5
status without effort	14	13·9	9	8·9	4	7·8	10	37·1
fantasy status	29	28·8	48	47·5	0	0	0	0
status disregarded	23	22·7	18	17·9	0	0	2	7·4
Total	101		101		51		27	

(Veness, 1962, p. 164 – data for boys only)

The conditions that Merton posits for anomie may be much closer to being fulfilled in this society than most sociologists think. Note that Merton's theory does not require that the majority of working-class persons adhere to goals beyond their means of achieving (which they do not), or even that proportionately more working-class than middle-class persons do so. This does not happen either. It only requires that there be a substantial minority of persons in the lowest-placed group of society experiencing this discrepancy between goals and means.

Most British sociologists, however, do not think that anomie theory is applicable to British society. Mays, for example, finds fault with anomie theory *vis-à-vis* British delinquency and also endorses a pure subcultural explanation.[51] In his earlier writing he had given detailed documentation to the theory that lower-class culture directly and naturally produced crime.[52] From his Liverpool dockland research he concluded that there is a juvenile subculture conducive to delinquency, but unrelated to status frustration amongst the young persons concerned. He gave as reasons

[51] J. B. Mays. *Crime and the Social Structure*. London: Faber & Faber, 1963.

[52] J. B. Mays. *On the Threshold of Delinquency*. Liverpool University Press, 1959.

57

for the prevalence of crime in that subculture: excess of leisure time, absence of adequate parental models and discipline, young people's natural desire for daring and dangerous pursuits, and the presence of adults who encouraged or condoned minor offences and larceny.

Mays rejected as inapplicable to modern English society the thesis that subcultural crime is the result of discrepancies between culturally prescribed goals and the means of achieving them. He stated:

'Subcultural juvenile delinquency in Britain is more historical in origin and due to class differences which have thrown up traditionally variant ways of living. In the U.S.A., the criminal subculture is more explosive in nature and arises much more from the fact that aspirations have been blocked, not only by class divisions, but because some individuals and groups have been able to get ahead at a more rapid pace than others and so oblige their less fortunately placed fellow citizens to climb the ladder of success by illegitimate means.'[53]

Mays makes a strong case against the applicability of the anomie theory to delinquency in Britain. But his argument seems inadequate in a number of respects. As it is representative of considerable British opinion, it will be criticized in detail.

Delinquent areas in the United States have long histories as crime-producing areas, as have delinquent areas in this country. Shaw and McKay's ecological studies demonstrate this. And the manner of living differs markedly between the classes in America, if not so much as it does in Britain. Surely Mays's statement that some groups in the United States are placed so as to get ahead more rapidly than others is just another way of saying that people are divided into different social strata, and consequently have different opportunities.

Mays also stated that his study, the Morris Croydon study and the Jephcott and Carter Radby study all agreed that delinquent subcultures in Britain were a less serious problem than in the United States. Admittedly, violence and narcotics addiction are more prevalent in America, and make delinquent subcultures more visible and dramatic. However, it is another matter to say that the problems generated are less serious. The British lower-

[53] J. B. Mays. *Crime and the Social Structure*. London: Faber & Faber, 1963, p. 97.

class subculture influences low educational achievement, unemployment, mental and physical illness and broken homes.

Summary

This study cannot hope to solve the dispute as to whether or not anomie theory is applicable to British society. The data will add some information of use and some comments on the theory will be made. But there is a more fundamental question to be solved first, and this is the prime task of this piece of research. The question of course is as to whether or not working-class children admit to more delinquency than middle-class children. From the data used initially to answer this question much further analysis will be possible.

If there are differences by social class in admission rates, then the matter can be pursued. The subject then is what specific aspects of working-class life are associated with these higher rates – class of the area or the influence of the secondary modern school. This data can then be used to reflect on the theories discussed. If delinquency rates were found to vary greatly by area this would support the cultural transmission explanation. Should this be the case, and should there be no differences by the social class of the home itself, this would make an even stronger case for the cultural theory. On the other hand, should there be differences by social class but not by the area the cultural theory would be discredited and anomie theory would receive indirect support.

The data can also be applied to the question as to what period in the child's life is the most formative for delinquency. This is a matter that has not been explicitly discussed so far. If the association of delinquency admissions with the social class of the home were important, but those with area or school were not, it would seem that the critical delinquency-producing factors were active in the early years. Conversely, it would seem that the later influences of peer group and leisure activity were more powerful if the area and school type associations were important and the social class of the home not.

Clearly the data to be collected in this survey cannot speak, except in a very indirect and inferential way, to the controversy between the cultural and anomie theories. The data will be very relevant to the first question discussed, as to the actual social-class distribution of delinquency admissions. And it is essential to solve the first query before the theoretical controversy is approached. Any solution to the second without adequate data on the basic one would be meaningless. Predictions from both types of theory are of course the same – that working-class rates of delinquency will be higher than middle-class rates.

Even though little ground may be covered in solving the theoretical dispute the discussion of it, and the bringing together of diverse research findings on it, are worthwhile. It has been suggested that the conditions of anomie are more in evidence in British society than is usually supposed, and that they can be expected to increase. The far-reaching changes presently taking place in British social structure will, as well as produce more of the prerequisites of anomie, act to break down differences between the classes.

With the spread of comprehensive education, the expansion of universities and technical colleges, people will increasingly come to believe that the system is fair. 'Education is provided for those who are able.' More and more children will be encouraged to compete in the system. With greater flexibility in the comprehensives children who do not do well initially will still be encouraged to keep their sights high; there is always the chance they will improve and may even eventually go to university. Heretofore such children would have given up and accepted their place in secondary modern life.

One of the necessary conditions for anomie is a substantial group of people with unrealistically high goals. Should ambitions rise faster and higher than suitable positions for fulfilment of them status frustration will be an obvious result.

The same improvements in the education system – especially the spread of comprehensive schools – will result in a lessening of class differences. Of course this is looking well into the future. But it is a basic, and irreversible, trend. And it is supported by long-range changes in the economy. Increasing prosperity may not lessen the gap very much because with every gain of the lower-income groups there will be proportionate gains by the middle and upper groups. But the sheer increase of material possessions, leisure and transportation to broaden experience will make enormous changes for working-class people. They will have the same possessions, leisure and security of middle-class people today.

Yet one should not talk of increasing prosperity with unqualified optimism. The wages and prices freeze of 1966 should have taught one thing: even a Labour government will create unemployment to deal with an economic crisis. While working-class people today have far more security than they ever did before they are still much more vulnerable than middle class. When some sacrifices must be made they will be the first to be obliged to make them.

With this qualification in mind then let us assume gradually increasing prosperity for all, and consider some of the other implications. The major prediction here to be made is that increased prosperity will probably act to increase anomie. American society forms the obvious example. In America the belief in the availability of upward mobility was made possible by the fact that the lower classes were becoming better off. They were not gaining at the expense of the higher strata, but they did see improvements in their standard of living over time. The fact that they did see substantial gains made them raise their goals even higher, to compete at a level at which many could not succeed.

Also in America there has been an expansion of professional, semiprofessional and skilled jobs, with a corresponding decrease of jobs in the unskilled sector of the occupational structure. So there has been more upward mobility than downward in the last 100 years. This has not been the case in Britain and there is no reason to expect this to change in the future. With net downward mobility and with rising aspirations an increasing number of people are bound to be disappointed. As well, in America the influx of immigrants (more recently of Negro migrants from the rural south) to take the least desirable unskilled jobs has provided a thrust from the bottom, pushing second-generation and older Americans up the scale. There is no equivalent force in British society.

These broad trends suggest that the social-class factor will continue to be an important factor in influencing delinquency. Though the differences between the classes will diminish, making social class apparently less important, with increasing anomie social class will likely assume greater importance in other ways.

2

THE DATA-COLLECTION PROCESS

The path through the literature was beset with many obstacles. However by the end of it the importance of a few interconnected variables should be obvious. For our purposes what emerges from a study of the literature is a small set of hypotheses on the relationship of these variables. These hypotheses are now to be set out explicitly. As the discussion will soon turn to a testing of them they will be stated in the usual form for testing – the null form.

1. That there are no differences between the social classes in rates of admitted delinquency.

2. That there are no differences between grammar and secondary modern school children in rates of admitted delinquency, controlling for social class.

3. That there are no differences in rates of admitted delinquency between children of different levels of academic ability, controlling both for social class and type of school.

4. That there are no differences, controlling for social class, between children who live in four specific socially distinctive areas.

It should be clear from the previous chapter that a considerable number of studies on admitted delinquency have been conducted so that a substantial fund of experience on the techniques involved in this sort of research is available. So the task of compiling and administering a questionnaire on admitted delinquency becomes a relatively simple one. There are two distinct problems to solve. The more straightforward one is to construct and give a questionnaire taking as much advantage as possible of the previous American work. And the other is to cope with the problems that are exclusively British. There are a number of problems here but the most difficult one, and the one that must be solved first, is that of gaining approval for the study from officials who control access to the needed subjects.

The whole question of obtaining permission for research is probably the most difficult, time-consuming and frustrating problem faced by social researchers in this country. It is a problem almost never discussed in the literature. Curiously, the few writers who have mentioned it have glossed over the real issues, lamely excusing the officials who have hindered their research on the grounds that they were over-worked.

This sort of exposition must be criticized for two reasons. Firstly it is simple dishonesty to omit mention of the most pertinent facts and to promote secondary considerations into primary ones – so that the primary ones can be hidden. Even worse, this deception does nothing to assist other researchers who must solve the problem in some way themselves. A scientist is obliged to report his work in sufficient detail for others to be able to replicate it. In this particular field of research the most difficult problem of method to overcome for anyone wishing to replicate a study is obviously that of obtaining permission for the study. And on this subject researchers are characteristically either silent, facile or patently dishonest.

Of course many social scientists in writing up their research are at the same time concerned about obtaining subjects for their next piece of work. One appreciates their fear of offending officialdom. So perhaps the outsider must take on the responsibility of being particularly open, honest and explicit. It is hoped that the following remarks are as well helpful.

The research planned was threatening to certain officials both for its delinquency content and its queries on social class. The social-class questions were far and away the more threatening. Every official who was at all worried about the questionnaire found fault with the questions on parents' occupations. Only one headmaster found the delinquency questions more worrisome. Many heads who were not at all concerned about the delinquency questions were adamant that the social-class questions not be asked.

The education officers and heads were moved by a variety of fears, some reasonable and some thoroughly irrational. Most were afraid that parents would complain – to the headmaster or education officer, or worse yet to the education committee, local council, their MP or the press. The fear of complaint was all-powerful. There was no thought that a satisfactory answer might be given to a complaint, or that a complaint might be harmless anyway.

The fact that questions on social class and delinquency had been asked many times without unfortunate repercussions did not help. The questions had not been asked before in their particular areas. 'You could get away with this in Liverpool, but never have such questions been allowed in the south', explained an education officer in the home counties. This is not true. Some of the best social surveys that have been done anywhere have been done in England, on a national level and certainly in the home counties. And a fair number of them have asked much more impertinent questions.

Some education officers explained more reasonably that the committees to which they were responsible did not permit the schools to obtain information on social background themselves. So they could hardly be expected to allow an outside researcher to make such inquiries. These officials did not seem to object to this policy and of course there was no attempt to persuade the committees otherwise.

Some headmasters were convinced that the children would rebel against such a prying questionnaire and refuse to answer the questions. Perhaps they feared the revolt would spread and that the teachers would have difficulty re-establishing control. Or perhaps the mere vision of classes of boys flouting authority was itself too much to take.

Some felt that the boys would go through the questionnaire denying having committed any delinquencies. (Subsequent results showed that only four per cent denied having committed any form of petty theft. Twelve per cent denied all the misconduct items. A question each on lying and disobedience to parents was asked, but were not analysed as delinquencies. Again the proportion of denials was only four per cent for each.)

Several officials maintained that if the schools allowed questions about delinquency to be asked they would be open to the charge that they were encouraging delinquent behaviour. The argument continues that if the schools showed they approved of delinquency the children would themselves suddenly be persuaded that delinquency was a good thing. The schools' pro-delinquency example would automatically free them from all previous inhibitions.

Thus the school would become responsible for a crime wave. The psychological assumptions involved in this sort of reasoning are too ludicrous for discussion and so the matter will not be pursued.

None of the education officers and heads who disapproved of the research seemed to be at all interested in any kind of educational research. They could not conceive that research findings might ever be put to any good use, either for educational advancement or for the general welfare of the pupils.

Finding education officers and headmasters who were in favour of the research took considerable time. In fact it took over three months of trial and error work. As this stage of the research was of such vital importance the process is described in some detail.

The first step was to attempt to gain approval from county education officers. This attempt was totally unsuccessful. After two months of negotiations the last county for which entry for the survey was sought gave a total 'no' – applying even to schools which had approved the project.

In fact no county ever did give permission for the questionnaire. Eventually advice was received – and the advice proved good – that access be sought at the level of the borough. Only certain boroughs, termed 'excepted boroughs', have autonomy in education matters, and only these could be used. A sufficient number of them fortunately were of a suitable social-class composition.

The use of these boroughs meant that the county level could be skipped. Only two tiers of officials had then to be faced: borough education officers and headmasters. As the survey required schools located close to each other the borough was a sufficiently large area.

The next step was that the researcher's supervisor contacted the education officer of the borough, explaining the project to him in the most amorphous terms, omitting all mention of content if possible. After letting this impression of a respectable and innocuous inquiry take hold the researcher would contact the education officer and arrange to see him. The tone of being uninvolved with the research was the one that seemed to induce the most favourable reaction. The emphasis was on how common the questionnaire was, how questions on it were routine in both British and American surveys.

The questionnaire was described as being only a rough draft. If the person then objected to anything it could be said that that was one of the things that could easily be changed anyway. He was left with no good objection on which to base a total refusal.

After the questionnaire had been given at the pilot stage this could be used as proof of its being respectable and harmless. This fact, quite reasonably, was most reassuring to officials and heads. In fact a good piece of advice for anyone doing social research in this country would be to complete some kind of pilot test, no matter how trivial or inappropriate, before seeing any official.

With the education officers it was emphasized that in the other areas the procedure was for the researcher to see them, then see the heads concerned, who of course could approve or veto the project. The purpose of this obviously was to make the official not feel any pressure to say 'no', as the way would still be open for the head to refuse later. With the heads it was emphasized that the education officer was in full approval, although of course they had the right to refuse!

In fact the education officials of the areas eventually in the survey were fully behind it and offered to find other schools if the ones originally chosen did refuse. It may well have been the case that the areas that refused would have no matter how well devised the method of presenting the idea to them was. And in the same way the areas that participated might have even if the project had been presented in the bluntest, most inept manner. So the approach should not necessarily be credited with the successful eliciting of help from education officials.

There was an enormous difference between the areas that refused and those that helped – in attitude, method of discussion and the whole approach to research in schools. There was no intermediate stand. The areas that refused appeared not to have considered the proposal on its merits. The officials that helped carried out their part of the operation efficiently and professionally, and were both reasonable and kind throughout.

There was one other problem to solve that would not have been a problem had the research been done in America, or in certain other countries. It is a problem that harasses a large number of researchers in the social sciences. This is the lack of computing facilities. The data for this survey were supposed to have been largely processed by the end of November, 1964. Yet the first correct results did not appear until May, 1965. Most of the results had been produced by August, 1965. However the operation had to be finished mechanically as the computer staff erased most of the tapes and lost some of the cards on which data were punched.

This case is an extreme one admittedly, but there are very many other tales of woe nearly as bad and in a large variety of fields.

The problems discussed above, of obtaining subjects and computing facilities, are the sort of problems that seriously hinder research. Failure to solve either of these problems satisfactorily means either that the research must be abandoned or that much lower standards for the work must be adopted. The finest theory and the most well-developed research techniques are of no avail if the researcher cannot obtain the needed sample and adequate computing facilities.

The Questionnaire

It will be seen below that what are normally the main tasks of a survey, constructing the questionnaire and analysing and interpreting the data, were relatively simple tasks compared with that of obtaining the subjects. The questions were taken for the most part from previous surveys. The analysis as well was similar to that of previous studies.

Perhaps the chief characteristic of the delinquency questions was that they consisted of delinquent activities that were described, rather than criminal categories that were defined. The child was not asked if he had or had not committed certain offences. He was not asked if he had been convicted of any delinquencies, nor if he had ever been dealt with by the police. He was rather presented with a list of situations, some delinquent and some not, and asked how many times in the last year he had engaged in them.

The earliest admitted delinquency studies[54] used legal definitions of crimes but the trend since then has been to present situations as a child might normally encounter them. The delinquency items can of course later be regrouped as specific criminal offences. So nothing is lost in the analysis by using delinquent situations and the situations are more meaningful to the respondents.

The items were grouped into five distinct offence types: serious theft, petty theft, property damage, violence and misconduct. Analysis was carried out on the items separately and on the whole groups of offences.

As the delinquency items set out situations rather than specific criminal categories it could be suggested that they measure only misbehaviour rather than delinquency proper. Indeed some of the questions clearly are of misbehaviour that almost always would not make the person liable to criminal prosecution. For example most children who admit to lying have not committed perjury. Most children who admit to disobedience have not been 'beyond control'.

It is, however, very easy to eliminate confusion on this point although many of the studies in this field have not. The items of misbehaviour normally not involving delinquency were analysed separately from the delinquency items. These non-delinquent items are referred to throughout the book as the misconduct items. The rest of the items, though they are not labelled as delinquencies or crimes on the questionnaire, are in fact just that.

The definition of delinquency in this work is a legal one. Delinquencies are actions that could result in prosecution, and which would probably so result if sufficient evidence for them were available. The definition is different from that of court appearances or convictions in that it includes the great mass of undetected delinquencies.

The delinquency items, as with many other questions, came from previous American questionnaires.[55] Two questions were

[54] Austin L. Porterfield. *Youth in Trouble.* Fort Worth, Texas: Leo Potishman Foundation, 1946.

[55] F. Ivan Nye. *Family Relationships and Delinquent Behavior.* New York: John Wiley, 1958.

John P. Clark and Eugene Wenninger. 'Socio-Economic Class and Area as Correlates of Illegal Behavior Among Juveniles.' *American Sociological Review,* v. 27, 1962, p. 826.

taken from a British study.[56] Those questions which were not taken from other surveys were modelled as closely as possible on those which were.

The method used to deal with the social-class questions proved to be particularly effective. The strategy was a very simple one: to ask the questions on parents' background in several ways, with the expectation that the child would answer one or more of them, if not all, giving enough information for him to be classified.

The first question on this, no. 30 in the questionnaire, was 'Father's occupation'. Immediately after it came a further one: 'Describe his job', with a couple of lines left for this. Earlier in the questionnaire there had been questions on father's and mother's school-leaving age (whether 14 or later) and whether or not they had been to a college or university. In cases where the occupation was ambiguous this information was referred to.

What little hostility was aroused by the questionnaire seems to have been engendered by the social-class questions. Very few of the delinquency items were left unanswered but many boys failed to answer one or more of the social-class questions. A few wrote 'None of your business' in reply to 'father's occupation'. One claimed his mother was a prostitute. But generally the response was satisfactory. The distribution of the social classes in the schools sampled was quite close to the distribution of the classes in the boroughs concerned. So it appears that the subjects' answers were by and large truthful. Certainly the claim by many education officials that the children of unskilled workers would upgrade their parents' occupation was without foundation. There were many labourers, dustmen, street-sweepers and charwomen in the group.

Several ratings on social class were used in the analysis. Both parents were rated according to the Registrar-General's five social classes and to job type – whether manual or nonmanual. However the Registrar-General's classification was used in its original form only for a small part of the analysis, usually where comparison with census material was necessary. For most of the analysis the social-class rating was based on only the father's occupation. If this information was missing then the mother's occupation was used. There were 65 cases, out of 920, which could not be classified when only father's occupation was used.

[56] Robert G. Andrey. *Delinquency and Parental Pathology*. London: Methuen, 1960.

Only 16 remained unclassified when the information on the mother was turned to.

The Registrar-General's classification can be used in two forms, both of which are unsatisfactory for most survey data, this study included. When just the five social classes are used the sample is divided into very unequal groups. The class I group contains less than five per cent of the population while the class III group contains almost half. What is even more unsatisfactory for the purposes of this study is that class III includes both manual and nonmanual workers. Thus for half the sample the fundamental point of contrast is obscured.

It is possible to use the Registrar-General's classification with the three central classes further divided into manual and non-manual groups. However this yields an eight-fold classification which would require a very large sample to fill.

A workable compromise was reached by breaking down the social classes into their manual and nonmanual sectors, the eight-fold classification, but recombining the groups. The revised classification has two groups of nonmanual workers, called the upper middle and lower middle classes, and two groups of manual workers, the upper working and lower working classes.

The upper middle class contains all professionals, managers and proprietors; the lower middle class has the clerical workers, shop assistants, salesmen and all other nonmanual workers. The upper working class has all skilled workers and foremen. The lower working class has all semiskilled and unskilled workers. The four groups are of fairly equal size although the upper working class is slightly larger than the others.

The revised classification groups the Registrar-General's classes as follows:

upper middle: R-G's I and II nonmanual
lower middle: R-G's III nonmanual and IV nonmanual
upper working: R-G's II manual and III manual
lower working: R-G's IV manual and V

A more refined rating on class, termed, from the Registrar-General, 'socio-economic group', was also made. There were sixteen categories in all in this, although a few, agricultural and military occupations, were not represented in this sample. The two managerial and two professional groups were combined, as shown below, so that ten categories were actually used.

1. higher managerial ⎱ combined
2. lower managerial ⎰
3. self-employed professional ⎱ combined
4. professional ⎰
5. intermediate (lower professional)
6. junior (clerical)
7. personal service
8. supervisory
9. skilled
10. semiskilled
11. unskilled
12. own account

As the study's main task was to determine and analyse class differences in delinquency admission rates it was useful to have both simple and more stratified classificatory systems. If no differences by social class were found using the simpler classification it would still be possible to carry the study one step further. Since the four-fold classification combines some sociologically different groups it could be that significant differences had been blurred by the classificatory tool. A more refined scheme would make them visible.

For example, in this study foremen are counted as skilled workers and are placed in the upper working class. In other classifications they are considered lower middle class. Own-account workers, usually with very small shops in working-class neighbourhoods, are ranked as class II nonmanual by the Registrar-General and so go into the upper middle class. Yet by their low level of education and routine nature of their work they might better be thought of as working class.

The classification of these marginal groups in opposite directions could obscure significant differences in delinquency rates by making the middle-class groups more working class and the working-class groups more middle class. With the socio-economic status rating the marginal occupations can be temporarily extracted and additional tabulations and chisquare tests made.

The Pilot Stage

In view of the number of times the essential questions on the questionnaire had been put before the information needed from pilot testing was not too extensive. It was necessary to make sure that the questions, revised for English consumption, were actually comprehensible to the boys. The few questions that were not were then further revised.

More important it was necessary to see if the boys interpreted the delinquent situations as they were intended. Did their concepts of what was right and wrong coincide with the legal ones? There was no hesitation or ambiguity on this point. The boys had a precise and accurate knowledge of what was legal with regard to theft, property damage, attempted theft, attempted damage and violence.

Though people may use the most extraordinary excuses in a courtroom – 'I was only borrowing it, my lord' – they are under no illusion as to what belongs to them and what does not, what they can touch and tamper with, and what they cannot. Numerous borderline examples of delinquent acts were suggested to the boys in the pilot sample. The response in this discussion was that of near unanimous and correct appraisal. The boys could not define the crimes, but they certainly knew what applied. When asked what precisely made something an offence they could not explain. Yet when given two close examples, one legal and the other illegal, they knew which was right and which was wrong.

The boys did not have much idea as to the value of the goods involved in theft. In the pilot questionnaire the questions on theft were broken down into £1, between £1 and £10, and over £10. The boys could not name items that would fall into the categories and did not know how to categorize such commonly stolen articles as transistor radios and automobile parts. Consequently the theft questions on the final questionnaire had to be rearranged. One was kept for general theft over £1, one for shoplifting over £1, one for shoplifting under £1. For theft under £1 other than shoplifting the questions were divided according to place of offence or object taken.

The pilot stage was carried out in a college of further education. The subjects were 40 apprentices taking sandwich courses there. Two classes of boys had been asked if they would take part in the project and all agreed to. The boys were extremely cooperative and their frank comments were most useful.

The boys were almost all from secondary modern schools, the one exception being a boy from a technical school. However they were highly unrepresentative of secondary modern boys. Most were from the top streams. Some, according to the college, could have done grammar school work but did not manage to obtain places. The fact that they were doing apprenticeships indicates that they were without exception headed for skilled manual jobs.

The pilot testing probably had to take place at a college of further education. At least it had to be outside the secondary school system for tactical reasons (yet it had to take place in some kind of school setting). Any complaint from parents, especially if it did go to a council meeting or to the press, could have jeopardized the whole operation. It would obviously have been more desirable to test the questionnaire on secondary modern boys rather than apprentices who had left school a year previous. But the risk did not seem worth the probable gain.

The boys actually in the pilot project were more knowledgeable about their social origins than boys still in school. They had already made vocational plans and so were simply more aware of job requirements, benefits and distinctions. Also probably they were more open in this respect. These boys had been asked to take part in the survey but had been explicitly told they did not have to.

The Sample

In the early planning of this project it was hoped that a neatly balanced sample of four areas could be obtained:

one entirely middle class,
one entirely working class,
and two mixed –
   one predominantly middle class,
   the other predominantly working class.

The areas eventually found for the survey did not of course fall conveniently into the categories desired. But they did present a good range in terms of social-class composition.[57] The four areas, with fictitious names to preserve confidentiality, were:

Suburb   65·8 per cent middle class, in the
               Greater London area, formerly
               Middlesex;

[57] The middle class is over-represented because there are a disproportionately large number of grammar school boys in the sample.

West Country	39·2 per cent middle class, a small city;
North London	32·6 per cent middle class, in the Greater London area, formerly Middlesex;
East London	15·3 per cent middle class, in the Greater London area, formerly Essex.

There was no way of knowing the class composition of the schools or areas before actually giving the questionnaire. The education officers had only a vague impression of the social composition of the catchment areas of their schools. Some schools had the information in their files, or at least some information on some of their pupils; others had almost no information.

The education officers and heads typically gave the impression that they were above being interested in the subject of social class. They appeared to believe that interest on their part would suggest that there was discrimination in the system. In the context of being knowledgeable of the background of their areas they would give some description of them in social-class terms. However even this was given a little reluctantly. In no area was there evidence of any effort to relate the children's social background to their academic progress in any constructive way.

The areas for the study were the catchment areas of the three schools in each borough. The schools chosen within each borough were as close to each other as possible; in most cases contiguous catchment areas were used. This was important as both type of school and area were variables to be studied independently. It was essential to separate the variable of the school influence from the more general social influence of the neighbourhood. Obviously if the grammar school had been taken from one end of the borough and the secondary moderns from the other it would have been impossible to say whether any differences found between them were due to the differences between the type of neighbourhood each was in or to differences in the kind of education offered.

The simplest way to separate the variables is to find areas small enough to be homogeneous and yet large enough to contain both grammar and modern schools. Proximity of schools to each other would mean at the very least that the physical amenities within each area would be substantially the same. The areas are themselves further described in Chapter 5, when the data on the area influence are discussed.

THE DATA-COLLECTION PROCESS

Administration of the Questionnaire

The questionnaire was given during a three-week period in late September and early October, 1964. It was thought very important to get through the stage of giving the questionnaire fast. Any complaints that might arise hopefully would not be processed through the educational bureaucracy in time to prevent the questionnaire from being given in the rest of the schools. In retrospect all this caution seems paranoid as in fact no complaints ever did arise at any stage. However in view of all the difficulty faced in merely obtaining permission for the study this preoccupation with security measures is perhaps forgivable.

The questionnaire was given by the writer in school time and in the ordinary classrooms. A teacher stayed in the room, but did not take part at all. The children were told that the questionnaire was anonymous and confidential. They were not to sign their names and no one at the school would see the forms.

No warning or advance information about the questionnaire was given. Rather, just before giving the questionnaire the researcher would give some brief information about the research project and her background as a graduate student. Emphasis was on the fact that the questionnaire had been given many times before in America. One of the purposes therefore was to compare the answers of British boys with the Americans.

No attempt was made to hide the fact that there were delinquency questions on the questionnaire. This part of the explanation was treated very lightly. The researcher would say that the boys were going to be asked some very personal questions, for example such things as, 'Have you taken sweets from shops?' This invariably drew laughter in response, and sometimes the challenging remark, 'Oh not us, miss!' The researcher would continue with the comment that it was quite obvious from their response that such things of course happened. They certainly should not mind answering questions of that sort since only the researcher would see them – not their teachers, head or parents. Usually by this time there would be some snickering and giggling and certainly curiosity about what was coming. Occasionally there were seriously put questions, such as:

'Are you sure the head won't see this, miss?'

'Of course he won't. I shall be taking the questionnaires away with me after you've answered them. No one else will see them.'

Very solemnly, 'It'll be the truth then, miss.'

In most schools the children were seen in sets, which made the giving of the questionnaire easier for all concerned. The more able children would finish the questionnaire in from twenty minutes to half an hour. The less able needed forty minutes or even up to an hour.

In the schools in which it was expected that there would be nearly illiterate children it was usually possible to keep the least able together, to give them more time and more help. In quite a few classes these children were taken to a corner or kept after the others had left so that the questions could be read out loud to them, while they followed and answered. This worked out very well in dealing with the children who had been absent the first time the questionnaire was given, and who tended to be the least literate.

Only two children had to be excluded because they could not read the questionnaire. These were Indian boys who did not know enough English to understand the questions even when they were read out loud to them.

Extra attention is essential if the nearly illiterate children are to complete questionnaires. In most surveys using written questionnaires the questions are simply not answered properly and these cases are discarded at the coding stage. Since there is good reason to suspect that children of low ability are more delinquent than other children the exclusion of these subjects from the analysis must be expected to distort the results. (And results from this study did show that the less able children were more delinquent.)

In many surveys the questionnaires are actually given in the classroom by the teacher. It is suggested that such a practice is a poor one if only for this purpose of keeping the nearly illiterate children in the sample at all cost.[58]

This problem can also be solved by interviewing the children instead of giving them a written questionnaire. However interviewing would have been unacceptable for this study on grounds

[58] The need for this help can perhaps best be shown by example:

'I know my father's occupation, miss, but I can't spell it.'

'If you will tell me what it is I'll tell you how to spell it.'

'Cook.'

of cost and, more important, on grounds of being unacceptable to schools. It seems that use of a written questionnaire, with special attention to those children who have difficulty with it, turns out to be a satisfactory compromise.

Absenteeism in the Sample

The problem of dealing with absenteeism in the sample is similar to the problem of dealing with the nearly illiterate children. In both cases failure to include a substantial proportion of these groups must be expected to result in serious bias in the sample.

Absentees are disproportionately lower class, delinquent, secondary modern and illiterate. So a large percentage of absenteeism could interfere with all aspects of the study. Despite the known importance of this group previous surveys have not made any attempt to include them in the sample. It should not be too difficult to figure out what to do with this group: keep coming back to the school to give the questionnaire to the absentees when they eventually put in an appearance at school.

The plan was to administer the questionnaire a second time and, if necessary, a third time in the schools that had a high proportion of absentees. This proved to be permissible in all but one school. The exception was a suburban secondary modern.

Table 2.1 indicates the extent of absenteeism in the various schools and areas.

By going back to the schools to give the questionnaire to absentees when they returned the original non-response was cut by more than half. And as the absentees proved to be more delinquent than average the worthwhileness of this extra effort was demonstrated. This became apparent even at the time when two charming boys at an East London secondary modern gave to the researcher an excited and detailed description of their breaking and entering adventures of the previous day, which took place while they were truanting.

Conclusions

The basic features of the research design have been described. It is obvious that the ideal research plan could not have been put into practice and compromises were made at various stages.

These changes or compromises can be attributed to two causes. The less important factor was that there was only one researcher to do all the work. The more important limiting factor was that the research was being done in a system that discourages the asking and answering of fundamental questions. 'Things work best when not understood' is a popular saying in Britain. And while the reference intended is more often the monarchy it could also be said of the education system. It sounds incongruous to say that the education system is fraught with anti-intellectual strains, but so it appeared frequently to this researcher.

TABLE 2.1

Non-response Due to Absenteeism

	no. of boys in 4th form	present at 1st question	present later	total non-response	per cent non-response
East End grammar	57	49	0	8	14·0
East End modern 1	59	41	13	5	8·4
East End modern 2	99	58	32	9	9·1
North London grammar	41	39	0	2	4·9
North London modern 1	85	78	7	0	0
North London modern 2	55	52	0	3	5·8
West Country grammar	119	113	0	6	5·1
West Country modern 1	113	108	0	5	4·4
West Country modern 2	73	68	0	5	6·8
Suburb grammar	128	123	0	5	3·9
Suburb modern 1	64	55	0	9	14·1
Suburb modern 2	82	67	13	2	2·4
Total	915	851	65	59	6·1

Yet despite certain barriers the research method is an improvement on earlier work. For example the pitfall of confusing misbehaviour with delinquency has been avoided, through changes in both question wording and analysis.

This study is the first, of studies employing a written questionnaire, to keep non-response to a low level. A large group of absentees was included in the sample. As well all but two of the children who were illiterate or nearly illiterate were kept in the sample.

Another feature of this study is that it makes the most thorough analysis of the social-class distribution of delinquency to date. The results do not stand or fall on the use of only one – perhaps an inappropriate – social-class measure. Both highly stratified and very crude classificatory systems are used.

Previous studies, with one exception,[59] have not dealt with both official and unofficial concepts of delinquency. In this study the hypotheses on the association of social class and type of school were tested for both versions of delinquency. The earlier studies have either confined their sample to convicted delinquents and not made any reference to delinquency in the community, or have taken a sample of schoolboys but have not related their findings to the social-class distribution of official delinquency.

This study goes beyond the earlier ones also in that the type of school attended is a variable along with social class and area. Probably any study of admitted delinquency in Britain would look at the school variable. So the fact that this one does is little more than a reiteration of the fact that this is the first study of admitted delinquency in Britain.

The theories tested in these studies are a part of the British literature on the subject as well as the American. It seemed desirable to put the hypotheses on the social-class distribution of delinquency to a test in a society where the social-class differences are more pronounced. As well it seemed time to collect some basic data on social class and delinquency in Britain from the point of view of admitted delinquency as well as official.

[59] Maynard L. Erickson and Lamar T. Empey. 'Court Records, Undetected Delinquency and Decision-Making.' *Journal of Criminology, Criminal Law and Police Science*, v. 54, 1963, p. 456.

3

SOCIAL CLASS AND DELINQUENCY

Now that the questions to be studied have been discussed and the method by which they are to be answered outlined the findings can be reported and commented on. This is the first chapter in which survey data are reported and it is the data directed to the most fundamental question that are discussed here. Stated as the null hypothesis it is that there are no differences by social class in rates of admitted delinquency. Stated as it is throughout the literature the question is: Are working-class children more delinquent than middle-class children?

There are a number of ways of analysing the data collected in the survey. The most basic one used, and the most frequently used in the American surveys, was a comparison of the proportions in the four social classes who admitted to the offences in question. Accordingly tables were constructed and the chisquare test for significance of difference was made. As this is the first data to be reported the tables have been kept in the text for easy reference.

For these tables the four-fold classification of social class was used: upper middle, lower middle, upper working and lower working. There is also an unclassified group so there are four degrees of freedom in most tables.

However it could happen that there are differences by social class which are not statistically significant when a table with so many degrees of freedom is used. The differences might be significant when the two middle-class groups are combined and compared with the two combined working-class groups. This would reduce the degrees of freedom from four to two. In cases where differences appeared but were not significant this additional test was made. The actual tables resulting from this test are not set out in this book.[60]

One further method of analysing the data was used. This was to look at the extent of involvement in delinquency rather than just the distribution of admissions and denials. When answering the questionnaire the boys were given a choice of four frequencies:

very often
several times
once or twice
not at all

It could be that there are differences in the frequency that the offences are admitted to by members of the different classes. That is working-class boys may admit to having committed actions very often or several times more frequently than middle-class boys. Yet when total admissions and denials are considered the proportions in the classes may be the same. Since so many of the offences are admitted by the majority of boys it could be that there is something very different about those who admit to having committed offences very often and those admitting only minimal involvement.

It could also be surmised that when middle-class children become involved in delinquency they do it in a more serious way. As the barriers to committing crime are greater for them the important step might be the first one. Once they have gone through the barrier they may become more seriously involved. While this hypothesis has little to recommend it in this researcher's opinion it is a possibility discussed in the literature. So the data should be explored for it.

Accordingly tables were constructed to compare the proportions admitting to the different frequencies of the offences by social class. The social-class groups were dichotomized as otherwise there would have been insufficient numbers in the cells for most of the items to be analysed. These data are set out in detail in Appendix B.

For each group of offences analysis has taken place in three

[60] Any reader wishing to see tables not contained in the book can refer to the extensive appendices of the thesis for which this work was originally done, or the writer. The thesis is at the University of London, entitled *A Study of Social Class and Education in Relation to Juvenile Delinquency*, by Mary Lynn McDonald, 1966.

parts. Tables of admissions to the delinquencies by the four social classes have been constructed and the differences tested for significance. Where there were no significant differences but a trend was apparent a further test was made with the social-class classification collapsed into two groups. Then, in all cases, tables by social class and the frequency of admission of delinquent acts were constructed.

Serious Theft

The serious theft group of offences comprises the bulk of crime that is considered serious enough to be dealt with by the police. And the theft items on the questionnaire embrace the bulk of situations for which juveniles are most often prosecuted. So this section, though looking at delinquency at the admitted level, is dealing with the behaviour that most closely approximates official delinquency.

Seven instances of theft behaviour were described on the questionnaire:

shoplifting
larceny
breaking and entering
taking a car
car possession
taking a motorcycle
taking a motorscooter

As well as the analysis done on each item separately the bottom four offences were grouped together as 'vehicle theft'. Admission to any of those four offences was counted as an admission to the category. Thus there are two more items in the analysis:

vehicle theft
serious theft

Of the possible theft situations only for larceny and the overall vehicle theft item were there statistically significant differences between the four social classes in rates of admission. However for four others there was a slight trend in the direction of higher-working-class admission. This occurred for shoplifting, car possession, theft of a motorcycle and scooter. This trend appeared also in the overall theft category.

These differences can be seen in table 3.1.

TABLE 3.1

Theft Admissions by Social Class

offence	UM*	LM	UW	LW	X²	df	P
serious theft							
(per cent admitting)	33	34	35	37	0·70	3	> 0·80
shoplifting	8	9	10	12	6·95	4	> 0·10
larceny	6	9	13	17	13·50	3	< 0·005
b and e	22	22	23	22	2·23	3	> 0·50
taking car	4	6	7	5	1·41	3	> 0·70
car possession	6	8	10	11	4·43	3	> 0·20
taking cycle	3	7	8	9	6·41	3	> 0·05
taking scooter	4	7	6	11	6·49	3	> 0·05
vehicle theft	12	15	16	22	8·35	3	< 0·05

* Upper middle, lower middle, upper working, lower working.

When the tables were dichotomized into just the middle-class and working-class groups the social-class differences for one further offence, taking a motorcycle, become statistically significant.

The test for differences by class in frequency of admission is not a good one for this category of offences as the absolute numbers admitting to them were not large. The serious theft group is the group with the lowest proportions of admissions. For some of the offences there were not sufficient numbers for a test of significance to be applied when the admissions were broken down into the four levels.

Amongst the items for which there were sufficient numbers for this analysis there were none for which frequency of admission was different by social class. Even for those for which there were differences when overall admissions and denials were considered there was none when the degree of involvement was.

This means that in so far as middle-class children admit to these thefts they admit to having committed them with similar frequencies as working-class children. When middle-class children break the delinquency barrier (with respect to serious theft) they become just as involved as working-class children – not any more and not any less.

In the group of serious theft offences the differences by social class were not too great. For the majority of offences they were not statistically significant. When the social-class classification was collapsed into two only one further offence showed statistically significant differences. When further analysis of the data was made, utilizing the less refined class categorization but measuring the frequency or involvement in delinquency, this did not uncover any additional class differences. While this is only one category of offences being studied it must be noted that it is the most important one so far as official crime is concerned.

However while the social-class differences for the theft offences were not great there was a clear trend in the direction of higher working-class admission. As well as the two for which there were statistically significant differences there were four for which there was a consistent step by step trend. And in the overall serious theft category this non-significant trend could be discerned as well.

The findings on the serious theft admissions are unusual in that it was expected that the differences between the classes would be more pronounced and significant for more items. From nearly all the diverse components of the literature the prediction of higher working-class delinquency rates would have been warranted. The participant observation studies conclude that working-class children routinely commit vast amounts of delinquency, including serious theft. Psychologically oriented writings state that middle-class children would not admit to delinquencies if they did commit them. Both agree that middle-class children are less exposed to delinquent opportunities.

As well as all this indirect evidence there is the very relevant material gathered in the American surveys. In America it has been found that in cities where people live in areas composed mostly of one class children admit to different amounts of delinquency, according to the class of their area. From this one would have predicted even greater differences in admission rates in the United Kingdom as class differences are more pronounced here.

There is only one piece of research reported in the British literature which would give rise to any expectation that the differences between the classes would be slight. This is the work by Little and Ntsekhe.[61] These writers found only slight underrepresentation of the highest social groups and over-representation

[61] W. R. Little and V. R. Ntsekhe. 'Social Class Background of Young Offenders from London.' *British Journal of Delinquency*, v. 10, 1959, p. 130.

of the lowest in the records of official delinquency they studied. However the material is not too well suited for comparison as Little and Ntsekhe used the Registrar-General's five-fold classification, which does not always distinguish between manual and nonmanual groups. Also as Little and Ntsekhe did not apply any statistical tests it is their inspection of the data that must be relied on.

The Little-Ntsekhe material was based upon offences of all kinds. Yet, as it included only offences that were serious enough to bring the offender into court, it is comprised for the most part of the serious theft offences. When this fact is borne in mind it can be seen that the findings of the present study are not entirely inconsistent with the Little-Ntsekhe findings. It will be shown that the differences by social class for the damage and violence offences are much greater, and even those of the petty theft and misconduct groups are somewhat greater than the serious theft. Certainly the serious theft offences show the least strong of all the differences by social class herein studied. So the findings of weak social-class differences in the Little-Ntsekhe study, predominantly of serious theft offences, is not out of line.

Damage

When the results of the analysis of the rest of the offences are reported it will be seen that the serious theft group was an exception to the pattern. The first of these other groups, the damage offences, is a good example. It shows strong and significant differences by social class in rates of admission. In this it is similar to the violence group. The other two groups, petty theft and misconduct, fall between the serious theft and the damage and violence groups in strength of social-class differences.

There were seven damage situations on which data were collected:

railway damage
throwing stones
car damage
lavatory damage
fence damage
general damage (to any public or private property)
building site damage

Of these seven items there were statistically significant differences by social class in rates of admission for five. As well, the differences for the whole damage category were significant. For one of the exceptions, railway damage, there was a slight trend in the direction of higher working-class admission. For the other, general damage, the trend was irregular. However the combined working-class groups did admit to more delinquency than the combined middle-class groups. This difference was significant.

The complete tables have been relegated to the appendix. But for a quick glance at the range of admissions for groups of offences abbreviated tables will be provided in the text.

TABLE 3.2

Damage Admissions by Social Class

offence	UM	LM	UW	LW	P
damage	67	67	78	81	< 0·005
throwing stones damage					
(per cent admitting)	51	47	64	73	< 0·001
railway damage	21	23	24	27	> 0·05
car damage	27	31	40	44	< 0·005
lavatory damage	17	16	24	30	< 0·01
fence damage	21	23	32	37	< 0·001
general damage	28	38	35	42	> 0·05
site damage	14	21	23	27	< 0·02

When frequency of admission is considered even more evidence of the strong class differences in admission rates is discovered. For the general damage and the throwing stones items there were significant differences by social class in depth of involvement. That is, of those who did admit to the offences, proportionately more of the working-class boys than the middle-class boys admitted to having committed the damage very often or several times.

For a substantial proportion of the damage situations there was a significant and consistent progression of higher rates of admission as the social levels were descended. And, though not all the trends were perfectly regular, for no offence was there a trend at variance with the dominant one.

The absolute amounts of admission for this group of offences ranged from 21 per cent (building site damage by upper middle-class boys) to 73 per cent (throwing stones by lower working-class boys). The rates of admission were high. But it was still the case that the majority of boys denied having committed the majority of offences in the last year. The one offence that drew a simple majority of admissions from all classes was that of throwing stones at street lights, windows and so forth. It is the offence that requires the least amount of forethought and probably the least degree of malicious intent.

For the whole group of damage offences the absolute amounts of admission were much higher than for the serious theft offences. Undoubtedly the behaviour admitted to was for the vast majority of cases not too serious. It is behaviour which is usually not even reported to police by the victim. And in British courts as the value of damage involved would usually be less than £50 it is behaviour which would usually be dealt with by summary conviction.

Clearly there is no cause for hesitation in suggesting conclusions for this part of the study. The rates of admission increase significantly as the social scale is descended. This holds true step by step for five of the seven offences. The differences exist although the trend is less perfect for the other two.

Violence

The pattern of admission to the violence offences was very similar to that of the damage offences. There were significant differences by class, of some kind, for all the items. And for four of the five offences there was a perfect step by step increase in the rates of admission as the social levels were descended.

There were five items of behaviour in the violence category:

    fist fight (being in a fist fight)
    fight start (starting a fist fight)
    assault (beating up someone without provocation)
    possession of a weapon
    gang fights

For the first four offences there were significant differences by social class. For the last offence, gang fights, there was a significant difference only when the sample is dichotomized into a middle-class and a working-class group and two degrees of freedom are lost.

SOCIAL CLASS AND DELINQUENCY

The range of admissions can be seen easily in table 3.3.

TABLE 3.3
Violence Admissions by Social Class

offence	UM	LM	UW	LW	P
violence	60	64	71	78	< 0·005
fist fight	72	75	81	83	< 0·05
fight start	44	42	50	57	< 0·05
assault	24	22	32	33	< 0·05
gang fights	33	39	49	51	< 0·001
weapons	16	30	22	24	< 0·02

When the measure of frequency of admission was turned to only one further difference appeared. This occurred for the assault offence. Not only did more working-class boys admit to assault than middle-class boys, but as well those who did admitted to more of it than middle-class boys.

It was shown that there was a similarity in the pattern of admissions by social class between the damage and violence offences. It also happens that the absolute amounts of admissions in the two groups are similar. In the violence group, as in the damage group, there was only one offence for which there was a clear majority of boys from all social classes admitting. This was for being in a fist fight. It is the least serious item in the group and probably should not be counted as an offence. It still is the case that the majority of boys deny having committed the majority of offences. Yet those who do admit the offences are a substantial minority.

The conclusions for the violence section are as straightforward and obvious as they were for the damage offences. The evidence, without exception, was in one direction – that of higher working-class delinquency. Statistically significant differences by social class (for one offence only with the combined classes) were found in all cases.

Rather different patterns of admissions appeared when the last two categories of delinquency, petty theft and misconduct, were examined. Certain questions drew responses indicating that there were no differences in the proportions of each social class admitting to them. Other answers indicated that there were differences, although in one case the middle-class rates were higher. Altogether for neither petty theft nor misconduct was the pattern as clear as in the previous three categories.

Petty Theft

The petty theft group contained a variety of offences which have only two characteristics in common. They were all offences which are widely committed and yet they involve only items of little monetary value. The twelve items were:

petty shoplifting (under £1)
neurotic theft (of small things not wanted)
family theft (from friends or family)
school theft (from desks or lockers)
bad loans
cinema (not paying)
bus fares (not paying on bus or train)
automatic machine (not using money in machine)
holiday theft (on holiday or outing)
receiving
site theft (from building site)
fruit theft (from fruit stand or stall)

At times probably these items would involve values of more than £1, which is the cut-off point between serious and petty theft. Theft from a building site, from family members, theft while at school or on a holiday could easily involve large amounts. However at the time the questions were compiled it was decided that these items should be included in the less serious category as in most cases the values involved would be small. One of the points learned through the pilot study was that the boys were not able to estimate values of goods commonly stolen. So it would have been inappropriate to add similar questions, but with higher values stipulated, to the serious theft category.

The serious theft offences drew an exceptionally low rate of admission. One of the reasons for this may have been that too many items were subsumed into the petty theft category that represent behaviour at the serious theft level.

The findings in the petty theft groups were very mixed. There was one offence, theft from family members, for which middle-class boys had a significantly higher admission rate. Otherwise the findings could be broken broadly into two groups – those for which there were higher working-class rates of admission of some kind, and those for which there were no significant differences by class. For half the items there were significant social-class differences. This group included the following:

TABLE 3.4

Petty Theft Admissions by Social Class – I

offence	UM	LM	UW	LW	P
neurotic theft	23	29	34	30	< 0·05
bad loans	27	25	34	38	< 0·005
cinema	43	47	56	54	< 0·02
receiving	34	45	44	48	< 0·05
fruit theft	27	33	40	46	< 0·005

Of the offences for which the working-class rates were higher six occurred *vis-à-vis* overall admissions and denials. There were two items, not paying at the cinema and not using money in an automatic machine, for which there were significant differences both in overall admissions and in depth of involvement.

The group of petty thefts for which no significant differences were found is shown in table 3.5.

TABLE 3.5

Petty Theft Admissions by Social Class – II

offence	UM	LM	UW	LW	P
petty shoplifting	52	61	58	63	> 0·10
school theft	26	25	25	24	> 0·90
bus rides	84	88	86	80	> 0·30
holiday theft	29	31	29	38	> 0·25
site theft	20	29	30	29	> 0·05

In the response to these offences no clear trend appeared. For one of them the lower working-class children had higher admission rates and for one other there was a slight, though not consistent, trend in the direction of higher working-class admissions.

However the statement is better left without any qualification; the differences were not significant and no clear trend appeared.

There was no apparent pattern in the division, between the groups of significant and nonsignificant differences, which might be used to explain the response. It could only be said that for a bare majority of items in this category there was some significant degree of higher working-class admission.

There was one offence, theft from family members or friends, for which there was a significantly higher rate of admission on the part of middle-class children. This was the only item, and there were 43 in all, in which a finding of higher middle-class delinquency was made.

However there is a very obvious and plausible explanation for this otherwise unusual finding. It could simply be that working-class children, with less precise concepts of property ownership, did not regard as theft the taking of things from family and friends that middle-class children did. Working-class children could be more prone to see their action as borrowing.

It is in this sort of situation that definitions of crime can differ by class. But as soon as the crime involves the world beyond the kin and friendship group the situation becomes very clear. The boys in the pilot study, who were mostly working class, had concepts of crime accurately in line with those of the written law.

One other comment about the finding on theft from the family should be made. This offence is usually treated as evidence of disturbance but it would seem quite wrong to treat it as such in this case. Between a quarter and a third of the sample admitted to the offence. As it is unlikely that this proportion of the sample suffers some emotional disturbance it is more reasonable to conclude that very inconsequential actions are included. Probably very small values are involved in the thefts and probably the thefts are not too uncommon amongst normal children.

No pattern emerged with respect to the kinds of offences for which there were class differences and those for which there were not. It was thought that there might be higher, or at least equal, middle-class admissions to neurotic theft. Yet this turned out to be one of the offences for which there was a clearly higher working-class rate. It was thought that there might be higher middle-class admissions to theft on holidays and outings as middle-class children more frequently go on holidays and outings.

Also if they were going to steal at all they might feel more free to do so when away from home. For this offence, however, there were no differences between the classes.

There were no differences between the classes in admissions to theft at school. Yet this is one offence for which all the preceding writing on the subject would suggest higher working-class admission. Of course the same explanation that was suggested for theft from the family may hold here – that working-class children demarcate theft from borrowing at a different point from middle-class children. However as the classes admitted to the *same* amounts this brings up another difficulty. It could be the case that working-class children steal more at school but happen to admit to exactly the same amounts as middle-class children. However this coincidence is most unlikely.

There is another possible explanation for this unexpected shortage of working-class theft. The head of one East London school said that theft is so common in his school that the children do not leave anything unguarded. They keep their jackets on and never leave things in the cloakroom or in their desks. Also it is noticeable in these schools that the children have very few possessions that could be stolen. Many did not have a pen or pencil with them at school, and very many had no books or paper.

One comment should be made about the petty shoplifting admissions. This item evoked a substantial rate of admission – over half the sample. Yet the serious shoplifting item drew an unusually low rate of response, only about 10 per cent of the sample. It is probable that some of the children who should have admitted to the shoplifting item for £1 or more admitted only to the petty shoplifting one.

The findings in the petty theft section show at least one thing conclusively, that children of all classes admit to large amounts of minor delinquency. Average admission rates were as high as 85 per cent – for failure to pay bus fares. Even for petty shoplifting admission included over half the sample. And shoplifting is an offence that requires overt taking and concealing. Moreover the shoplifting crimes that bring children into court not infrequently involve amounts of less than £1.

The interpretation of findings in the petty theft section has been given in the form of very tentative suggestions. Unlike the other types of delinquency conclusions did not follow automatically from the data. In some situations working-class children admitted to more delinquency, but not always in the sort of situations they would be expected to. A few questions had been included to tap the likely delinquencies of middle-class children. These did not succeed. The working-class children admitted to higher or equal amounts. The one offence for which middle-class children admitted to higher amounts was one which the literature describes as a typical working-class offence.

There are enough inconsistencies in both the theoretical and empirical literature for there to be support for any kind of finding in this bracket of offences. So there would seem to be little point in referring to the literature to defend either the predicted or the unusual findings.

One conclusion should be obvious from this discussion. It is that the finding of greater or equal working-class admission depends on the situation. One cannot fruitfully speak of 'theft' or 'petty theft' as homogeneous categories in discussing class differentials in admissions to these offences. It seems that exposure to the theft situation has something to do with the number of times it is admitted. Yet by itself this is not a sufficient explanation.

It does not appear that either class has any fixed propensity to commit petty theft that is applied consistently to all instances of temptation or opportunity. Nor does it appear safe to extrapolate from the participant observation studies for predictions as to what children actually will admit.

Misconduct

There were twelve items grouped together under the label 'misconduct'. They were all matters which are not the subject of criminal legislation. In fact some of them are not even matters for summary conviction when practised by adults. (For example: buying and consuming liquor, running away from home, truancy, keeping late nights and bad company.)

Neither are some of these items the subject of specific legislation for juveniles. But they are taken into consideration by juvenile courts in making dispositions. This sort of misbehaviour could result in a child's being dealt with as 'beyond control'. He would not technically be defined as delinquent but would be liable to be treated as one.

The misconduct items were:
    driving a car (without a licence)
    driving a motorcycle
    driving a motorscooter
    truancy
    run away
    liquor (buying or consuming without parents' permission)
    swearing (nuisance in public)
    pornography
    late nights
    bad company
    betting
    school misconduct

As with the petty theft section the results on class differences in admission rates were very mixed. The category split nearly into halves. For seven items no significant class differences were found. For five items there was some amount of higher working-class admission.

For three offences the working-class children admitted to significantly higher rates, as follows:

	UM	LM	UW	LW	
school misconduct	59	62	67	76	< 0·01
truancy	32	29	38	49	< 0·005
bad company	29	37	47	52	< 0·001

For two further offences there were significant differences by class in the number of times the items were admitted. The school misconduct item qualified on both grounds, frequency of admission and overall admissions and denials.

    pornography: 17 per cent WC, only 11 per cent MC admitted very often
    late nights: 21 per cent WC, only 12 per cent MC admitted very often
    school misconduct: 19 per cent WC, only 8 per cent MC admitted very often

Within the groups of offences with no significant differences by class no trend in the response could be discerned. For two of the items (pornography and swearing) admission rates by the upper middle-class boys were higher than all others.

The absolute amounts of admissions were very high in this section. A majority of children in the sample actually admitted to half the offences. Several offences were admitted to by three-quarters of the sample. This section of the questionnaire was supposed to be the least threatening and it proved to be that.

These findings should cast doubt on the popular conception that working-class children have the monopoly on misconduct as well as actual crime. The working-class children had markedly higher admission rates for the damage and violence items – which in terms of volume in the criminal statistics are relatively un-serious offences. So to that extent the view that working-class children commit large amounts of nuisance offences is not a far-fetched one.

As the offences involved in those sections are often trivial and unpremeditated the concept of petty crime as a part of the normal course of working-class life is tenable. But it must be qualified by the findings in the misconduct bracket. For along with the finding, in some cases, of higher working-class admissions are findings of equal admission rates by the classes. And whether or not the rates are similar by class the rates are high. So if this diffuse mis-behaviour is to be thought of as a normal part of working-class life then to quite an extent it must also be thought of as normal to the middle class.

However, if this suggestion is pursued to its logical end it arrives at a theory which this writer, amongst many others, would not wish to advocate. That is a youth culture theory. According to such theory delinquency and adventurous misconduct are part of the process of adolescence. As children of all classes go through adolescence they all go through a delinquent stage.

But the carrying of the observation of normal delinquency to these lengths is unwarranted if the evidence gathered from other parts of this survey is to be relied upon. Throughout the discussion of the data reference has been made to the proportions of children admitting to the offences. While these proportions were substan-tial for the less serious offences they were small for the more serious offences. Even when the total category of serious theft was considered only about a third of the children could be counted as delinquent. And the children who did admit to the serious offences for the most part admitted to having committed them only once or twice.

The picture that emerged was that most children admitted to having committed the very trivial delinquencies and misconduct. And of these an even larger proportion of working-class children admitted to them than middle-class children. Of the serious theft offences most children denied having committed any. And when any individual offence was considered the vast majority in both classes denied involvement. However, for a few items in that group there were significantly greater admission rates on the part of the working-class children.

When the damage and violence offences were considered the admissions were substantial for both classes, but in almost all cases the rates were significantly higher for the working-class boys.

The Depth of Involvement Concept

The delinquency involvement concept was included as an essential dimension in the measure of admitted delinquency. It was used here as in the Nye study and subsequent ones, although with opposite results. The evidence gathered in this study through use of the measure was not as conclusive as that acquired by the simple admissions and denials measure. But the involvement data did add perspective to the question. With this two further assertions about the survey findings can now be made.

More working-class boys than middle-class boys admitted to the various delinquencies.

Working-class boys admitted to more delinquencies than middle-class boys.

Of the 43 chisquare tests for differences by social class, in overall admissions, 19 were significant. Of the tests for differences by delinquency involvement only eight were significant. And, of these, four had already appeared in the admissions and denials bracket. So the involvement measure uncovered only four additional significant differences. The relevant tables are contained in Appendix B.

In the serious theft group, where differences by social class were the weakest, no new differences appeared through the involvement measure: For the most part the offences that showed significant differences in depth of involvement were the more trivial items. Even so the evidence was useful as it corroborated that obtained by the basic admissions and denials measure.

A Further Check on the Social-class Distribution of Delinquency

At the time the study was planned it was thought that an additional and more refined classification of the occupational levels would be necessary. In the event that no or very few social-class differences in admission rates appeared when the four-fold and two-fold classifications were used it would then still be possible to look further for some.

The four-fold classification is open to the criticism that it obscures sociologically meaningful boundaries. For example foremen are placed in the upper working class. It would be argued that they should be separated from the skilled workers and instead grouped with the lower middle class, as they are in some classificatory schemes.

Own account workers, many of whom operate small shops in working-class areas and have small incomes are classified in the upper middle class, along with professionals, managers of larger concerns and higher civil servants. Perhaps they should be in a lower group.

Shop assistants in this study are part of the lower middle class. Yet certainly in income they would often rank below skilled workers. Similarly many of the clerks or blackcoated workers would have lower incomes than skilled workers but are ranked in the middle class. Probably there is less controversy about their status than of the other groups as there is still much to distinguish clerks from skilled workers. But there is foundation for objection to the social class placement of all these groups.

These marginal groups could have acted to obscure differences in delinquency admission rates when the four-fold classification was used. However a very large number of significant differences by class did appear. So analysis by a more refined classification did not prove to be essential. It was useful though for the further analysis of the serious theft offences as this group showed very few social class differences. As well the additional analysis served to ascertain whether or not a purer classification would yield clearer and strong results.

The new social-class groups formed with this classification were composed as follows:

Refined middle class: employers, professionals and higher civil servants

– own account workers, clerical workers and sales workers were excluded

Refined working class: skilled, semiskilled and unskilled workers

– foremen were excluded

There were 18 items for which no significant differences in admission rates were found when the four-fold and two-fold classifications were used, or when the depth of involvement measure was used. On these 18 offences the further test using the refined classification was made. Only one further item, theft from building sites, showed statistical significance on this test. In view of the strong trends in the direction of higher working-class delinquency this finding was definitely not anticipated.

This unexpected finding can be used to comment on one aspect of the method of this survey. As the refined classification did not yield any additional significant results it appears that the ordinary four-fold classification, used throughout the study, was a most adequate tool. The four-fold classification did not obscure any significant differences despite its questionable placing of some marginal groups.

Conclusions

The conclusions based on the initial analysis reported in this chapter do not need any further qualification. They cannot be added to and as they are they reflect the full scope of the findings on this part of the survey. There are differences between the social classes in rates of admitted delinquency, measured several ways, consistently showing higher rates on the part of the working-class boys. This is particularly the case for the damage and violence categories of offences, less so for petty theft and misconduct. The same pattern appeared for the serious theft offences, but was less strong than the others.

4

DELINQUENCY AND THE SCHOOL SYSTEM

The task of interpreting the data on delinquency admissions and the school system turned out to be much more complicated than that of interpreting the data on social class in the previous chapter. This was well forewarned by the review of the literature. The sources drawn on for the review came from a variety of academic disciplines. Impressionistic as their evidence was, it did all lead to a simple conclusion. Stated summarily it was that there are a considerable number of important differences between the grammar and the secondary modern schools – at least some of which could be expected to have an effect on proclivities and opportunities for committing delinquency.

There can be little quarrel with this on theoretical grounds as such a wide range of theories lead to the same conclusion. Differential association theory, delinquency opportunity theory, reference group theory, early and late socialization theories all would predict higher delinquency on the part of secondary modern children.

The difficulty is encountered when one attempts to separate the influences of the school system proper from those emanating from the background of the home. The mingling of the two influences can be illustrated with the tabulations of the distribution of the social classes through the two school types in the sample.

In the grammar schools well over half the children (64 per cent) were from middle-class homes while in the secondary moderns an even higher proportion (71 per cent) were from working-class homes. On the basis of composition alone the grammar school must be thought of as a middle-class institution. And the secondary modern is even more clearly a working-class institution.

TABLE 4.1

Distribution of the Social Classes by Type of School

	UM	LM	UW	LW	Unclassified	Total
grammar number	131	74	95	20	4	324
per cent	41	23	29	6	1	100
modern number	72	89	274	147	12	594
per cent	12	15	46	25	2	100
Total	203	163	369	167	16	918

The distinction between the concepts of school influence and mere social-class influence should be elementary. But it has been ignored even in recent studies. And since the influence of the social class of the home has been unequivocably demonstrated the separation of the two concepts is crucial.

For the purposes of reporting data the concepts could easily be dealt with separately. The matter of interpreting the data was more difficult and will be left until the preliminary discussion of the results is completed. For the analysis two sets of tables were constructed, one for middle-class boys, the other for working-class boys. This provided the simplest way of eliminating the class factor in the school-type tables. Otherwise the data analysis is similar to that in the previous chapter. Proportions admitting to the offences, values of chisquare and probabilities of occurring by chance are all specified in Appendix C. Only very brief tables will be included in the text, and then only when strong differences are to be demonstrated.

Serious Theft

Of the seven serious theft offences there were only two for which the differences in admission rates by type of school were significant. This occurred for working-class boys only. However these differences obtained for two of the commonest offences, shoplifting and larceny. In fact of the theft offences that are prosecuted larceny, which includes shoplifting, forms the largest single group. And shoplifting would be an important component of the larceny group. Therefore the fact that significant differences by school have been found for these two offences is worth noting.

Also, although the differences between the two school types on the specific vehicle theft items were not significant, the differences for the whole vehicle theft category were, although only for working-class boys.

TABLE 4.2

Theft Admissions by School Type
working class boys only

	grammar	modern	P
shoplifting (per cent admitting)	5	13	< 0·05
larceny	4	17	< 0·001
vehicle theft	10	28	< 0·001

Significant differences were found for only three items out of the 18 comparisons made. However the trend was in the expected direction for the other theft offences. There were no instances of higher grammar-school admission rates.

The effect of type of school as a significant factor *vis-à-vis* the theft offences was slightly less strong than social class. However the trend was more consistent in the type of school analysis. In comparing the two factors it could be said that both social class and school type had some influence on theft admissions, but the effect of neither was very strong.

Damage

The effect of type of school with regard to the damage offences was no greater or less than it was with the theft offences. Amongst middle-class children there were significant differences for one offence, throwing stones, and amongst working-class children there were significant differences for that offence and one further, fence damage. While the trend was generally in the expected direction it was not nearly so consistent a trend as in the theft group.

The admission rates for throwing stones clearly show the differences that occur both by social class and type of school.

Middle-class grammar	43 per cent
Working-class grammar	50 per cent
Middle-class modern	59 per cent
Working-class modern	71 per cent

Although it is clear that type of school had some association with damage admissions, independent of social class, the association was not nearly so strong as that of social class itself. Social-class admission rates were significantly related for five out of seven offences in this category. But the effect of type of school was seen in only one offence, and, for working-class children only, one further. As will become obvious when more and more data are reported it is the basic factor of social class that distinguishes most effectively delinquents from nondelinquents.

If the social-class factor had not been eliminated from the tables of admission rates by type of school quite different and misleading results would have been obtained in a number of cases. This can be demonstrated by comparing tables of admission rates in which social class is not controlled with those for which it is. Comparison of the tables also illustrates the pervasiveness of the social-class influence.

TABLE 4.3

Rates of Damage Admission by Type of School, Not Controlling for Social Class

	grammar	modern	X^2	P
car damage (per cent)	31	39	6·21	< 0·02
lavatory damage	17	25	7·51	< 0·01
site damage	17	24	6·96	< 0·01
throwing stones	45	68	45·74	< 0·001
fence damage	22	33	11·61	< 0·001
N	324	588	df=1	

The five items for which significant differences by class have already been shown also showed statistically significant differences by school type, when the class factor is not eliminated. However, in table 4.4, where rates by school type were computed

TABLE 4.4
Rates of Damage Admission by Type of School and Class

	middle class				middle class			
	grammar	modern	X^2	P	grammar	modern	X^2	P
car damage (per cent)	26	34	2·76 > 0·10		41	42	0·03 > 0·80	
lavatory damage	15	17	0·36 > 0·50		21	26	1·02 > 0·30	
site damage	15	18	0·58 > 0·40		20	25	1·38 > 0·20	
throwing stones	43	59	9·27 < 0·005		50	71	16·91 < 0·001	
fence damage	21	23	0·24 > 0·50		25	35	4·24 < 0·05	
N	194	150			117	389		

separately for middle-class and working-class children, these differences were greatly reduced. Only one item, throwing stones, remained significant for both classes, and one other, fence damage, remained significant for working-class children only.

Within the two broad social classes the differences by type of school were not great. Rather, within each type of school the differences by social class were more important.

Violence

The degree of association between violence admissions and school type proved to be similar to that between damage admissions and school type. In neither case was the association strong. And in both types of offences the association of admission rates with social class was.

Of the five violence offences only for one, gang fights, was the association with type of school significant. This occurred for both middle-class and working-class children. However, for all but one of the other items the trend was in the expected direction of higher modern-school admissions. And, for the overall violence category the differences by school type – for middle-class children only – were significant.

It seems that for the traditional subcultural forms of delinquency, damage and violence, the most influential factor is the social class of the home itself. The case for this point will be made in some detail in the next chapter. There, when the data on damage and violence admissions by area has been presented, a better estimate of the comparative importance of the social class of the home will be possible.

Petty Theft

The strongest association between type of school and rate of admission was found in the category of petty theft offences. In fact type of school was associated with admission rates for the same number of offences that social class was. This was the only offence group for which type of school was as strong a factor as social class. And for no type of offence was the association with type of school stronger.

There were five offences for which there were significant

differences by type of school for both middle-class and working-class children. These are set out in table 4.5.

TABLE 4.5

Petty Theft Admissions by School Type and Social Class

	grammar		modern	
	MC	WC	MC	WC
petty shoplifting (per cent)	46	44	68	64
holiday theft	25	23	35	34
site theft	20	21	30	32
fruit theft	23	24	37	47
machine	35	42	51	48

For three other offences (neurotic theft, not paying at the cinema and receiving) there were significant differences by type of school but for middle-class children only.

Misconduct

In the group of misconduct items type of school and rates of admission were significantly associated for seven of the 24 comparisons made. Amongst middle-class boys there was an association in five cases: late nights, liquor, betting, driving a motorcycle without a licence, and school misconduct. Amongst working-class boys only two associations were significant: running away and school misconduct.

No suggestion of pattern could be discerned in this part of the data analysis. It can safely be said that type of school was not an important factor in influencing misconduct admissions. It was certainly not as important a factor as social class. Social class and the rates of admission were significantly associated for five offences out of 12. But of the 24 possible associations for type of school only seven were significant.

Discussion

So far type of school has been seen to be independently associated with admission rates for at least some of the offences in each category. Of the various categories it has had its greatest effect on the petty theft admissions. It has had considerably less effect on all the other categories. Its effect was clearly minimal on the damage and violence items. And its effect on serious theft admissions was not much greater. However social class itself was not greatly associated with serious theft admissions. So the low degree of association between school type and admission rates is not low in comparison.

The association of type of school with misconduct admission rates was not very strong. Again, however, this finding must be related to the association found between social class and misconduct rates. This association was somewhat greater, though still was not strong. Altogether the data on misconduct has been very mixed. No clear picture emerged with respect to either the social-class or the school-type associations.

The effect of the type of school attended need not fall evenly on both the social classes. It could be that only one or other of the social-class groups is affected. And in fact the literature clearly indicates that working-class children would be the more strongly influenced by the type of school they attend than middle-class children. Both British and American contributions would suggest this; the evidence is piecemeal, but there is a considerable amount of it.

When working-class children go to a grammar school they adopt its social habits and are accepted into its informal groups.[62]

They absorb its attitudes, or at least some measure of them. They cease to adhere to some working-class social practices.[63] They develop middle-class vocabulary, grammar and construction. It is not too much of an extension of this line of argument to suggest that working-class children might adopt the middle-class tendency to lower delinquency admission rates.

It could similarly be argued that when middle-class children attend a secondary modern school they would adopt its social customs, and in particular its delinquency rates. However there is an element in the situation of the middle-class child at a modern school that does not exist in the situation of the working-class

[62] A. N. Oppenheim. 'Social Class and Clique Formation Among Grammar School Boys.' *British Journal of Sociology*, v. 6, 1955, p. 228.

[63] Brian Jackson and Dennis Marsden. *Education and the Working Class.* London: Routledge & Kegan Paul, 1962.

child at a grammar school. The additional and, it is suggested, highly influential factor is the influence of the middle-class parent.

The fact that many secondary modern schools do not remotely resemble the image originally projected of them is in some measure to the credit of middle-class parents. The changes that have been made in the secondary moderns range from teaching methods and course materials to the total role of the secondary moderns in the educational system. The pressure of middle-class parents in introducing a more academic curriculum, external examinations and generally in simulating the life of the grammar school should not be underestimated.

However, active and effective middle-class parents are not uniformly distributed throughout the school system. And the changes in secondary modern schooling have not taken place in any systematic way. There is at present much variation in the kind of education offered and the nature of the social environment developed in secondary modern schools.

Still the overall result is that middle-class parents make the secondary modern schools their children attend more like middle-class institutions. Working-class parents do not have an equivalent effect on the grammar schools. The working-class child who attends a grammar school finds himself in a thoroughly middle-class environment. The middle-class child who goes to a modern school does not find himself in so profoundly alien an environment, and should therefore be expected to change less in his out-of-school behaviour.

We should expect working-class children in grammar schools to be affected by the delinquency inhibiting atmosphere there, but not expect middle-class children to be so strongly influenced by the greater proclivities and opportunities for committing delinquency in their schools.

This prediction was not borne out by the data. There was no tendency for either class to be the more affected by type of school. What associations were found between type of school and admission rates held to the same extent for each of the major social classes.

Attendance at a modern school has as much effect on the behaviour of middle-class children as attendance at a grammar school has on working class. If this finding is correct there are a lot of important implications.

We are looking at two processes of resocialization. One of them, socialization into grammar-school life, has received considerable attention in the literature.[64]

From its earliest times the grammar school has prided itself on its ability to recruit the ablest children from the working class and socialize them for a middle-class life.

The corollary of this process is usually neglected. It is that the secondary modern school recruits the academically least able children from the middle class and socializes them for a working-class future. This entry into a working-class milieu, at adolescence, involves amongst other things greater amounts of certain delinquencies.

The data from this survey show that middle-class children at secondary modern schools admit to more delinquency than their counterparts at grammar schools. Whatever the advantages of a middle-class upbringing may be they are not effective in protecting the child from the peripheral influences of the modern school. There is no evidence that these differences between children of the two schools could be due to differences in intelligence.[65] What does seem a reasonable conclusion from the evidence at hand is that the secondary modern influences the middle-class children who come to it in a wide sphere of behaviour and attitudes, including behaviour that is delinquent.

In the discussion of theory and in the analysis of data great care was taken not to confound the effects of social class and type of school. At the same time it has been made clear that the intermingling of these influences in reality is a matter for empirical determination. It has been well documented in the review of the literature that grammar-school education is intrinsically middle class in its goals, methods and social atmosphere. And it has likewise been shown that, despite some elements of middle-class ideology and régime, the secondary modern does much to perpetuate a working-class style of life.

Still the attempt has been made to isolate the effects of formal education – curricula, daily routine, the schools' goals and

[64] Brian Jackson and Dennis Marsden. *Education and the Working Class.* London: Routledge & Kegan Paul, 1962.

Richard Hoggart. *The Uses of Literacy.* London: Chatto & Windus, 1957.

[65] See page 34.

methods, even with their immutable class associations, from the influences of social class that emanate from the home itself. The finding that the type of school attended is significantly associated with admitted delinquency is to be discussed in that context.

It is suggested that the effect of type of school, of course controlling for social class, is for the most part just an extension of the effect of social class. It is not a new dimension. Because it is not a new dimension it is probably more a function of the general social environment of the school than its formal educational life.

Support for this interpretation lies in the fact that there was an overlap in the offences for which there were significant differences by school type and those for which there were by social class. The differences are of course independent of each other, but they happen to occur for the most part on the same specific items. There were 22 offences for which there were significant differences by type of school. Of these there were only eight for which there was not a difference by social class as well. If the social environment of the home produced these effects then the social environment of the school could easily produce the same ones as well.

Type of school has an effect on delinquency admissions in so far as it intensifies either middle-class or working-class experiences. Because there is an association between being middle class and being less delinquent there is an association between being a grammar-school pupil and being less delinquent. Grammar schools succeed in their function of making children more middle class than they would otherwise be, at least in so far as admissions to delinquency are of concern.

Which type of school a boy attends affects the structure of his daily existence as well as in a profound way the course of his life. If the superficial aspects of opportunity to commit delinquencies, such as unsupervised time, are important in delinquency etiology one would predict that the type of school attended would affect a greater range of offences, and affect more than the ones already affected by social background. In fact if it should be that only the superficial aspects are important the effect should be spread evenly throughout all offences.

Great care must be taken in suggesting to what extent the secondary modern school initiates delinquent behaviour. It appears that the secondary modern's scope for doing this is quite ted, but there is a sense in which it has the effect of instigating delinquency. There were eight offences for which there were ...gnificant differences by school type but for which there were no differences by class. So that far it can be said that the secondary modern stimulates new forms of delinquency, these mostly in the petty theft field. However the weight of evidence from this survey is that the modern school acts to increase the same offences for which working-class children have already shown some affinity – rather than inducing new forms of delinquency.

Delinquency and the Streaming System

So far the discussion on the influence of the educational system has been based exclusively on the type of school attended – whether grammar or modern. There is one other system to be considered, one based on the same purposes and premises as the system of separating children into different types of secondary schools; this is the streaming system. It has been summarily described by one writer as an education system in miniature.[66]

Like the system of developing different schools for children of different levels of ability the streaming system is based on the belief that children are better educated if taught with other children of the same ability. Ability, usually as measured by an I.Q. test, provides the means of ranking pupils for assignment into different schools and into different streams within the schools. As measured ability is the criterion for determining the child's place in both systems we should expect streaming to produce the same results *vis-à-vis* delinquency admissions that school type produced.

From the literature on education it is known that which stream a child is in has much to do with whether or not he goes on to university. In the junior schools the stream a child is in is a good predictor of whether or not he will go on to a grammar school or a secondary modern.

The spread of comprehensive schools will alter the effect of the streaming system. Streaming may be used less in the junior school as there will be no eleven-plus examination on which to focus. But it will probably maintain its influence in the secondary system as a substitute for the tripartite system. For example there could be grammar, technical and nonacademic streams as rigidly

[66] Brian Jackson. *Streaming*. London: Routledge & Kegan Paul, 1964.

separated as the present grammar, technical and secondary modern schools. In fact, when this subject is taken up again in the last chapter, it will be seen that much of the rigidity of the tripartite system has been transposed into the comprehensive.

So, at the present time, and in the foreseeable future, the stream plays a crucial role in the child's academic career. The implications of streaming include aspects of life well beyond the child's formal schooling. The child's stream is a matter of concern from an early age in the more ambitious families. It is used as a measure of worth within peer friendship groups as well. In some secondary modern schools demotion to a lower stream is used as a punishment for bad behaviour.[67]

In a couple of the secondary modern schools in this sample complete streaming had been abolished. Instead the children were in sets for the academic subjects and were not streamed at all for the other classes. However, this change had taken place only in the last year. Children were therefore, rated on the streams they had been in in the third form. Needless to say, though, the children were no longer visibly separated by ability or achievement, they had been for so long that they were well aware of where they stood.

In some schools the titles 'A stream', 'B stream', and so forth were no longer in use. The master's initial was usually substituted for identification. However the children knew that the groups were ranked and knew what the order was. Thus stream was, for all the children in the sample, a known and important element of life.

Social Class Distribution by Stream

It is by now well known that the distribution of the social classes amongst the streams is not a random one. Middle-class children disproportionately often wend their way into the A streams. The lower social classes more often find their way into the C and D streams. This distribution was clearly found for the secondary modern schools in this sample. However in the grammar schools the middle-class children were only slightly over-represented in the high streams and under-represented in the low, not to a degree

[67] David H. Hargreaves. *Social Relations in a Secondary School.* London: Routledge & Kegan Paul, 1967.

that was statistically significant. Therefore in the analysis of the grammar school data it was not necessary to control for social class. Of course in the analysis of the modern school data it was necessary to control for social class in all tables. These distributions are shown in Appendix D.

Stream and Delinquency Admissions in Grammar Schools

There was a very consistent association between the stream a child was placed in and his admissions to delinquent acts. The association was significant for half of the tests made, 23 tests out of 47. All were in the expected direction of higher rates of admission for boys in the lower streams. The trend was in the same direction for all but two of the other items as well. The significant items appeared in about equal proportions in all five types of offence.

The items for which significant associations by stream appeared tended to be the items for which a significant association with social class and type of school had already been demonstrated. There were only seven items for which there was a significant association by stream but not by social class. Of these, three were associated with school type.

Table 4.6 illustrates the effects of all the three variables analysed so far.

TABLE 4.6

Theft Admissions by Social Class, Stream and School Type

	high stream			low stream		
	grammar	modern		grammar	modern	
		MC	WC		MC	WC
shoplifting (per cent)	1	7	7	12	14	19
larceny	3	4	9	8	16	24

Stream and Delinquency Admissions in Secondary Moderns

The association between stream and delinquency admissions was not nearly so great for secondary modern children as for grammar school. For middle-class children only six out of the 45 chisquare tests made were significant. For working-class children 15 out of the 48 tests produced significant differences.

The six items for which significant differences appeared in the tests on middle-class subjects were distributed evenly between the offence groups. Admissions to all but six items were also known to be significantly associated with social class and admissions to five were known to be significantly associated with school type as well.

The fact that only six of the compared rates of admission proved to be significant under-estimates the association between the two factors. The N for this table is low, only 151, consequently a much greater difference is required for it to be statistically significant at the five per cent level. The trend is in the expected direction for the vast majority of the other items.

The findings for working-class boys at modern schools were quite different from those of middle-class boys at modern schools and all boys at grammar schools. The items for which there were significant differences by stream were concentrated in the serious theft group of offences. Eight out of nine tests in this group produced significant results. There was at least one other significant result in each of the other offence groups.

Again, those items that showed significant differences by stream tended to also have shown significant differences by social class and type of school attended. The exceptions to this were the serious theft offences.

From this pattern of associations it is suggested that the stream dimension is an extension of the social class one. Earlier in the chapter this account was given for a similar finding in the pattern of school-type findings. The same sort of evidence and reasoning is offered here in support. When the data on the influence of the area are reported it will be seen that a pattern of this type did not appear. Half of the items for which significant differences by area were produced were not significantly associated with the social class dimension.

Streaming is a system of stratification, as is the class system of society as a whole. In the streaming system children are stratified on academic criteria, which is of course not the case in society as a whole. However the streaming system has incorporated more of the features of general social stratification than is supposed. Selection within the streaming system is affected by broader social values, for example those held by the teachers and heads who make the initial selection and later transfers. Once the system is in operation it then affects a range of behaviour, including much outside the educational sphere.

This point is well-documented for primary school children in Douglas's study.[68] A good illustration at the secondary modern level is provided by Hargreaves.[69] As that study is relevant to the delinquency question as well its results bear repetition here. Hargreaves found that boys in the high streams conformed more to their teachers' middle-class expectations in dress, manners, and standards of conduct than boys in the lower streams. The boys with high status amongst their peers in the higher streams particularly conformed in this respect, thus setting an example for their high-stream fellow pupils. The reverse was true in the lower streams. There the boys who were looked up to most were the least conforming to the school's standards.

The matter of conformity in dress and manners seemed to be the most important issue in the school at the time Hargreaves was doing his research. The school had a policy of no long hair or blue jeans, which it attempted to enforce at all cost – with frequent requests, pronouncements, reminders, ridicule, and various punishments from caning to ignoring offending students. So the issue of acquisition to middle-class standards for these boys was a very salient one, and therefore a useful one for illustration here.

Hargreaves compared rates of delinquency by stream, with similar conclusions to those made in this study. There were differences between the streams both for official delinquency and for admissions made to him by the boys in informal conversation. Thus in the high streams the leaders were law abiding and generally conformed to the school's expectations, while in the low streams the leaders were strongly and visibly nonconforming and actually delinquent.

Conclusions

The stream variable was as powerful a variable for differentiating delinquents from nondelinquents as the school-type variable was. It was not, however, as strong or nearly as consistent a variable as the social class of the child's family of origin. The basic social class

[68] J. W. B. Douglas. *The Home and the School*. London: MacGibbon & Kee, 1964.

[69] David H. Hargreaves. *Social Relations in a Secondary School*. London: Routledge & Kegan Paul, 1967.

variable was significantly associated with rates of admission for over half of the items. For both the stream and the school type variables nearly a third of the items showed significant associations at the five per cent level or better.

The source of the power of the school system to influence delinquency cannot be precisely determined or even estimated in this study. There are two obvious possible explanations but the data collected does not contain any information that can be used to determine which if either of the explanations is correct.

The first explanation to be advanced is a psychological one. It is that intelligence exerts some causative effect on delinquency and/or delinquency admissions. Children in the lower streams and children in secondary modern schools are lower in intelligence than children in higher streams and in grammar schools, and they admit to a much larger number of delinquencies. However, while this association has been clearly demonstrated it is not necessary to conclude that low intelligence is the cause of higher rates of delinquency.

There is an alternative explanation which accounts for the intelligence variable, but does not make it the causative factor. It is that the lower intelligence children become delinquent as a result of certain social implications to their being separated from higher-stream and grammar-school children. Actually there are several sociological theories that could account for the associations found.

One could apply, for example, Cohen's theory of delinquent gangs to this material.[70] Cohen says that lower-class boys, as a result of being unsuccessful in the middle-class institution of the school, go through a process of reaction formation. With the support of other boys in a gang they develop delinquent norms and increasingly engage in delinquent activities.

This explanation would have to be modified somewhat to adequately explain the data collected in this survey. Note that the less successful children of middle-class families as well as working-class were more delinquent than the more able. But the principle is the same.

Toby and Toby[71] as well as advancing a similar explanation

---

[70] A. K. Cohen. *Delinquent Boys*. New York: Free Press, 1955.
[71] E. Jackson Toby and Marcia L. Toby. *Low School Status as a Predisposing Factor in Subcultural Delinquency*. United States Office of Education and Rutgers University, 1957.

report data in support of the theory. They found a progression over time from disliking school to seeking of alternative satisfaction outside school in delinquent activities. The children who disliked school tended to come from the lower status homes. Any explanation along these lines would be consistent with the findings of this survey.

Research on the effect of streaming on achievement, independent of that of intelligence, has yielded findings which are relevant to this problem.[72] In this study it was found that the children in the higher streams and the children in unstreamed schools improved their reading scores over the school year. The children in the lower streams failed to improve although they would not have been of lower intelligence than the average children in the unstreamed school. This can be illustrated by the diagram below.

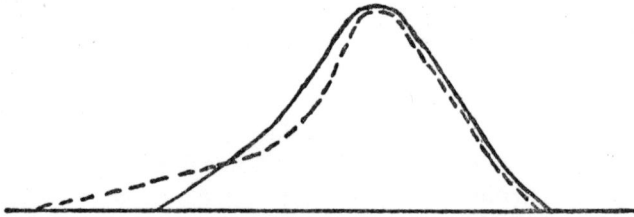

solid line: unstreamed school   broken line: streamed school

Reading Improvement

Intelligence is distributed normally. Reading improvement scores in an unstreamed school similarly fall approximately on the normal curve, in line with intelligence. In a streamed school the more able do not do any better than the more able in an unstreamed school. But in the streamed school there is a large number who do very badly – what Jackson refers to as the long C stream tail, visible in the diagram above.

Streaming clearly has an effect independent of measured intelligence. Extrapolation from this to delinquency admissions would not be warranted and is not suggested, but the finding can be construed as an indication of the powerful effect of the streaming system.

[72] Brian Jackson. *Streaming.* London: Routledge & Kegan Paul, 1964.

The important point about the explanations offered above is that the causal factor in the process is not intelligence but status frustration of some kind. It is not that lower-stream children are less able intellectually (although they are), but that they experience more humiliation and gain less satisfaction than more successful children. They certainly receive less stimulation and fewer rewards than higher-stream and grammar-school children. It is not that they are less able, but that everybody else knows they are and deals differently, even punitively,[73] with them.

Both the sociological and the psychological explanations are readily testable. If intelligence alone is the factor then children of lower intelligence would admit to higher rates of delinquency than more able children even in situations in which they were not separated from the more able children and subjected to more humiliation.

For example, children of lower ability in unstreamed schools would show the same higher admission rates that children in the lower streams of streamed schools show. Children of lower ability in comprehensive schools would admit to the same high rates of delinquency that children in secondary moderns admit to.

No data was collected on delinquency admissions by children in comprehensive schools. And all the schools in the sample were streamed. So no evidence from this study can be brought to bear on the problem. However, there has been a considerable amount of research showing no correlation between intelligence and criminality.[74] This clearly discredits the intelligence explanation. But it does not serve to confirm any of the others.

It is perhaps appropriate at this point to consider what changes to the current pattern of delinquency admissions should be expected with the coming changes in the education system. The government is committed to the comprehensive principle and while the changes will take years to be accomplished they are going ahead.

This writer would suggest that if these schools are really

[73] One teacher of a C stream class apologized (to the reasearcher, but loud enough for all in the classroom to hear) for not preparing a lesson that day: 'C stream here, can't do a thing with them anyway.' The researcher heard many such remarks in visits to schools prior to the giving of the questionnaire.

[74] See page 34.

comprehensive then there should be substantial changes in the pattern of delinquency. However, this proviso that the comprehensive principle be fully implemented is one that must be taken seriously. What is involved should be spelled out rather carefully.

Some comprehensive schools have been formed by joining a grammar school with one or more secondary moderns. These may be miles apart with the children of different ability levels segregated from each other to the same extent as before. Probably we should not expect any changes in the delinquency admission pattern in this sort of situation. The vital point is that children judge by how they are treated. An egalitarian sign on the door will not make up for a rigid hierarchy and sense of failure inside.

The essential point about the comprehensive system for our purposes is its reluctance to brand children as failures and treat them as such. Thus the possibility exists that secondary education can be interesting, useful and rewarding, and can be so perceived by even the pupils of low ability.

Frequent transfers of the children from class to class within the system must make it more difficult to operate both on a day-to-day basis and for purposes of planning. But without such flexibility the comprehensive system cannot work properly. The usual practice is to place children in sets for the academic subjects only. The sets are based on achievement in the particular subject. For art, music, games, religious instruction and any other nonacademic subjects the children are not grouped by ability. It is of course still possible that some children will be in all the highest or all the lowest sets. And of course it is possible that children in the lowest sets would be made to feel that they were really an impossible burden. However a good comprehensive school should prevent this from happening, or at least should certainly keep it to a lower degree than secondary moderns.

Along with the different organization in the school a different mentality is required. Perhaps it is not too much to say that teachers must be prepared to adopt a different philosophy of education, certainly a different attitude to the pupil and a different concept of the teacher's role in the learning process. Too often the researcher felt teachers did not consider that they had any responsibility to the pupil. The pupil had the duty of obeying orders and not causing trouble. But if the pupil could be seen to be dim or unmanageable the teacher could no longer justly be expected to teach him anything. The child could be written off as impossible to educate. The teacher's responsibility was then reduced to that of merely keeping the child off the streets until his school-leaving age.

It is well known that teachers receive prestige according to the calibre and level of the pupils they teach. Some like the challenge of dealing with the less able and the more unruly and accept the consequences. But not many. Few teachers subscribe to the view that the best teacher is the one who teaches his pupils more than other teachers manage to teach theirs. This may be in bringing an average class to perform well above average or it may mean seeing that an outstanding class becomes even more outstanding. And of course it could mean a teacher bringing a class that is two years behind in achievement to a level only one year behind.

Now, however, let us assume that there are some schools with the full comprehensive vision and with teachers eager to put it into practice. How would such schools manage to change the distribution of delinquency and what would the new distribution look like? We should see delinquents distributed more evenly throughout the school and quite possibly there would be a reduction in numbers. With a generally increasing crime rate perhaps it is too much to expect a real reduction, but certainly there should be a lessening of the increase.

The principle relied on is that the end of segregation for the brighter pupils will not harm them academically or socially. They will progress just as well as they did in grammar schools. They will face even more competition in the academic subjects than they would have faced in grammar schools, and this should be all to the good. In the past able children who did not manage to obtain places in grammar schools tended to give up the fight. Now they will not and some will successfully challenge the early starters.

In the long run comprehensive schools should alter in a profound way relationships between the social classes. However we shall have to wait for many years of comprehensive school graduates to make their way in adult life before we should expect to see such results. And if the social classes are effectively segregated from each other by area of residence, then of course even comprehensive schools will not help to break down these barriers. This is what happens in the larger American and Canadian cities. However, this subject will be gone into in the next chapter, so will be left without further comment here.

It is time for a note of caution in this speculation. There are many factors which will continue to operate against the full implementation of the comprehensive system, and so against the changes suggested above. First of all the comprehensives will not include those children educated in the private sector. We can assume that there will always be people who will want to and can afford to educate their children at public schools. The better the state schools become the fewer these families will be, but there will be some. It is so extremely unlikely that a government would abolish them that we should dismiss the idea. (It is a ludicrous one anyway; if a man is allowed to spend his fortune on all sorts of luxuries and vices why should he be prohibited from spending it on his children's education?)

The egalitarian principles of comprehensive education are more easily proclaimed than lived by. Children may not take advantage of the opportunities peculiar to the comprehensive system, especially of making friends with children of differing social backgrounds. The more able middle-class children may dominate the school societies making the less able unwelcome. It is certainly known that cliques on social-class lines develop in American high schools and a similar pattern may develop here.

Administrators may not keep the system flexible and therefore open to the less able to advance when they show talent. The tripartite system of grammar, modern and technical schools was supposed to be an open one, with transfers between all three types of school when appropriate. But in practice only a very small percentage of pupils were ever transferred.

Yet with all these provisos and warnings the fundamental point must not be lost sight of. The comprehensive system provides a structure much more amenable to the developments discussed above than the rigid tripartite system ever did. It is therefore that much more worthy of optimistic speculation than the system it is intended to replace.

Some of the findings on this part of the study have rather clear implications for policy-making in the field, as well as implications of a more academic nature. It was thought that the policy implications especially should be dealt with at some length. So, while the question of education is now to be left for a discussion of the last section of survey results, it will be returned to later. In the last chapter these issues, especially the question of streaming, will be further elaborated, with particular emphasis on expected developments and policy.

5

DELINQUENCY AND THE NEIGHBOURHOOD

The influence of the neighbourhood or area on delinquency admissions is the last element in the class constellation to be discussed. It is also the last variable of the survey data to be considered. After that the discussion will turn to the testing of the hypotheses on social class and school type with the data on official delinquency.

The survey's foremost purpose was to ascertain the degree of association between the social class (of the family) and delinquency admission rates. And so it was with this task in mind that the sample was selected. The problems next in priority were the association of admission rates with school type and area. Had the immediate question, of the association of area and delinquency, been the only one to be investigated much better data could have been obtained. Should that have been the case the sample would have contained a larger number of areas, with a small number of boys in each, and probably only secondary modern schools.

However the sample that was in fact used contained only four areas. Still, with only the four a satisfactory range in terms of class composition was covered. The areas were distinct social entities, each different from the others.

This can be illustrated objectively through reference to the published census material. As so many of the census indices clearly depict the contrasts between the areas a few of them have been included here. However before drawing on the census material a note of caution about its use must be made. The census areas concerned, which were boroughs, did not correspond exactly to the areas used in the survey. The school catchment areas, which formed the areas for this study, formed only a part of the boroughs, from about a sixth to a half. So the population covered by the census was much larger. From the figures shown, though, it can be seen that the schools sampled were not too unrepresentative.

In the selection of schools for the Suburb and North London areas the attempt was made to obtain schools with as high a concentration of middle-class pupils as possible. In East London, schools in the section reputed to be the most heavily working class were selected. Obviously it was desirable to have a strong contrast between the middle-class and working-class areas in the sample. In the small city no attempt was made to obtain schools either disproportionately middle class or working class. It is in this area then that the census distribution and sample distribution are closest.

TABLE 5.1

Social Class Distribution by Area— The Sample Compared with Census Data*

		I†	II	III	IV	V	N
Suburb (per cent)	census	7·1	22·4	56·0	7·5	7·0	76,069
	sample‡	9·1	35·4	49·5	4·5	1·5	
West Country	census	3·9	16·0	56·6	11·2	12·3	25,698
	sample	2·4	14·6	66·3	12·7	3·9	
North London	census	1·9	12·7	61·5	10·6	13·3	37,475
	sample	1·2	12·9	67·5	12·9	5·5	
East London	census	0·9	7·8	49·5	14·9	26·9	60,224
	sample	0·7	4·8	43·8	25·3	25·3	

* From the 1951 Census, County Report.
† The Registrar-General's classification is used here so that the data from this survey can be compared with the census. Throughout the rest of the chapter the four-fold classification, which has been used up to now, will again be used.
‡ The sample had a disproportionately large number of grammar-school children in it, thus over-representing the middle-class population. To remove this source of bias the figures were weighted so that grammar-school children would form the same ratio in the sample as they did in the population.

That the areas differ strongly in social class composition is readily apparent. It will become equally obvious that these social class differentials are reflected in a host of other characteristics. Housing facilities are one major example. A look at a few of the basic indicators of housing amenities will suffice to make this point.

TABLE 5.2

Housing Facilities by Area

	per cent class I & II	rooms per house- hold	per cent sharing a dwelling	per cent households with H/C water, bath & Wc.	per cent owner- occupier
Suburb	29·5	4·60	15·7	90·3	66·2
West Country	19·9	4·53	15·8	76·9	47·1
North London	14·6	4·23	24·9	68·8	54·1
East London	8·7	3·71	47·0	34·8	21·8

First three columns from the 1951 census, County Report; last two columns from the 1961 census, County Report.

The ranking of the areas in proportions of classes I and II is almost perfectly matched by the ranks for space and facilities in the homes.

Another good index of the difference between the four areas is the proportion of young persons staying on at school or at other educational institutions. This is shown in table 5.3.

TABLE 5.3

Boys in Full-time Education by Area

	per cent class I or II	per cent in full-time educ.
Suburb	29·5	28·9
West Country	19·9	22·4
North London	14·6	18·5
East London	8·7	11·0

From the 1951 census, County Report; the age group is 15–19.

For the four areas there is a perfect rank order correlation between the proportions staying in the educational system and the proportions in the higher social classes. Nearly three times as many boys in the suburb are in full-time education at ages 15–19 as in the East End. These figures cogently summarize a large number of words. At a glance they convey the salient points about the educational values, facilities and traditions of the respective areas.

Despite the fact that all these descriptions of the state of the four areas bring in the concept of social class it is not the social class of the family itself that is the subject of study here. Rather it is the impact of the prevailing class, the numerically dominant class of the area, that is under scrutiny. It is not the fact that a boy lives in a home where the father is a manual worker that is relevant here. It is that he lives in an area where most people are manual workers, and participates in a social life concomitant with that.

In the American surveys the concept of the prevailing class of the area was found to be extremely important with regard to delinquency admissions. In one study, by Reiss and Rhodes,[75] it was found to be a more important factor than social class itself. However, as that study was of official delinquency rates other factors, such as bias in policy processing, and different numbers of police in the different areas could have affected the result.

In another study, by Clark and Wenninger,[76] the prevailing social class was found to be the only class factor that was important; social class of the family itself was not a significant factor.

On the other hand research conducted by Reckless and others[78] in America demonstrates the ability of the good family in a high delinquency area to insulate its children from bad companions, attitudes and behaviour. While this does not necessarily mean that the area has no influence it does mean that the area influence can be counteracted. Presumably in families that do

[75] Albert J. Reiss, Jr. and A. Lewis Rhodes. 'Delinquency and Social Class Structure.' *American Sociological Review*, v. 26, 1961, p. 720.

[76] John Clark and Eugene Wenninger. 'Socio-Economic Class and Area as Correlates of Illegal Behavior Among Juveniles.' *American Sociological Review*, v. 27, 1962, p. 826.

—. 'Goal Orientations and Illegal Behavior Among Juveniles.' *Social Forces*, v. 42, 1963, p. 49.

[78] Walter C. Reckless and others. 'Self Concept as an Insulator Against Delinquency.' *American Sociological Review*, v. 21, 1956, p. 744.

not insulate their children the negative area influence might be strong. Reckless gives no information as to the prevalence of either the strong or the weak families in this respect; and in an area study the comparative proportions might be the crucial variable.

Survey Findings

As in the analysis of education data in the previous chapter the factor of social class was held constant by constructing separate tables for middle-class and working-class children. And as in all the discussions of survey findings the data will first be discussed by type of offence.

The pattern of admissions to appear most often was that of highest rates of admission by boys in East London or North London and lowest by boys in the West Country or the Suburb. This was the most frequent pattern amongst the items for which differences were not significant as well as amongst those which were. There were only ten items out of 98 tests which did not show at least one of these trends. That is, either East or North London boys had the highest rates, or the Suburban or West Country boys had the lowest.

Of the 29 significant differences found 20 were of the pattern with either the East or the North London boys most delinquent and with either Suburban or West Country boys in the least delinquent place. There were seven items which conformed in only one respect and two did not follow the pattern at all. Those two have not been counted as significant differences.

The number of significant differences therefore should not be taken as the number of items showing a clear and consistent pattern. In this part of the analysis the pattern is simply not as consistent as it was in the previous two chapters.

Serious Theft

It was shown in the last two chapters that there is some association between high theft admission, low social class and secondary modern schooling. However the serious theft rates did not show nearly as great an association with the social factors as the rates of other types of crime did.

The serious theft data, when related to the area factor, depart from this pattern. The association of theft admission and area was very strong. Amongst middle-class boys there were significant differences by area for three items: larceny, theft of a motorcycle and vehicle theft. Amongst working-class boys there were significant differences for many more items – six out of the seven specific offences, and the vehicle theft category.

For larceny there were strong differences by social class and area so the range of admissions by both factors can be shown.

TABLE 5.4

Larceny Admissions by Social Class and Area

	MC	WC
Suburb (per cent)	5	11
West Country	5	9
North London	12	17
East London	17	20

The number of boys in the whole sample who admitted to larceny was very few. However, when the sample is dissected by the two variables as it was in the above table the data take on a new appearance. Of the working-class boys who live in heavily working-class areas a large proportion, actually a fifth, admitted to larceny. But of the middle-class boys in the middle-class suburb or small city only a few out of every hundred did.

In the group of serious theft offences there were a large number of significant differences by area. There were almost as many as by stream, and more than by any other social factor. But the area factor did not appear to be very important with regard to the other crime categories. It was less important than social class in all the other categories. And it was less important than school type for all the other crime categories as well.

Damage

The area variable showed very little association with damage admissions. There were no significant differences by area amongst middle-class children. Amongst the working-class boys there was one significant difference, for general damage. Thus out of the sixteen chisquare tests made only one proved to be significant. This is close to what would be expected to occur by chance.

Violence

The factor of area was not much more important for the violence offences than it was for damage. Area was significantly associated with admission rates for only three offences, two amongst middle-class boys only and one amongst working-class boys only. However, the two offences for middle-class boys were fairly important ones – assault and gang fights.

Neither the rates of violence nor damage admissions showed anything but a minimal association with the factor of area. These two crime categories have shown similar patterns of association with the other social variables as well. Both were strongly associated with social class. Both had some, but comparatively weak, associations with school type.

Working-class boys who live in the industrialized dock area did not admit to any great amount more of damage or violence. Yet this is the area where the opportunities are greatest. Mays found a large amount of delinquency in his study of a dock area in Liverpool.[79] But in London it seems that virtually the same amounts of destructive delinquency are committed by working-class boys in other parts.

If any groups of offences can be said to characterize juvenile gang delinquency the violence and damage groups must be them. In fact this is one of the few points on which criminologists from the various schools do agree. There is in the literature widespread agreement with Cohen's summary description of the juvenile gang's delinquency: nonutilitarian, negativistic and malicious.[80]

While this description does not exclude theft offences it is the damage and violence offences that best fit it. Now if these offences are characteristic of organized gangs we would expect admissions of them to vary by area. But the admission rates for the damage and violence offences are those which are the least associated with area.

[79] J. B. Mays. *Growing up in the City*. Liverpool University Press, 1954.
[80] A. K. Cohen. *Delinquent Boys*. New York: Free Press, 1955.

On the other hand if damage and violence are the offences of mere ordinary friendship groups, which exist in all areas, they would show very little or no variation by area – which is the case. At the same time as this interpretation is made it must be made clear that the evidence for it is very limited. It is based on only four areas. And the sample contained only the 14-year-old age group. It is possible that had an older group been used more damage and violence offences would have been discovered in East London. This could have reversed the result.

From the evidence produced in this survey it appears that the causative factors for property damage and personal violence do not lie in the opportunities available. The example of other adults, the existence, perhaps, of older gangs in the area, and the actual abundance of damageable material a dock area or industrial area presents do not seem important.

Rather it seems that the variables associated with social class that are not particularly influenced by the neighbourhood are the important ones. These include the child-rearing practices of the parents, control and discipline of the children, and the example of the parents. This is intrafamilial behaviour and it is relatively uninfluenced by the neighbourhood.

Areas that have reputations for damage and violence offences may not really be that much different from other, urban, areas. The cause of these high crime rates may simply be the concentration of working-class persons in the area. When the damage and violence crimes are seen as a proportion of the working-class population they might not be greater than those of other areas.

Information on the relationship of area and delinquency is of more than academic interest. This kind of information can be turned to for guidance on housing policy amongst other things. The results of this study can be used for example to comment on one aspect of current housing policy: that of allowing or even encouraging families with delinquency problems, usually the lower working-class families, to rent homes only in certain parts of a housing estate. A concentration of families with delinquent children is known to produce a large number of delinquency problems (as well as other problems). It is not suggested that there is any geometric increase in problems with increased numbers of lower working-class families. It seems that an uncomplicated additive process is in operation. And should that be the case the problem is more manageable. If the housing estates increased the proportion of higher status families delinquency problems should show a corresponding decrease. Similarly if the families with delinquency problems were scattered throughout the estate (which apparently neither the delinquent families nor the respectable ones nor the administrative bodies want) the problems should decrease. Actually it is not true that the total problem would decrease. Rather on each estate or section of estate they would; the problems themselves would be dispersed to a wider range of areas.

The upper working or lower middle-class residents would not reform or inhibit the delinquent residents. But neither would the old delinquent families have an appreciable influence for bad on the new. Both would maintain their earlier patterns with respect to the damage and violence offences. Lower working-class families who moved out would take their problems to their new homes and areas. Instead of there being a small number of virtually permanent problems to deal with there would be a larger number of smaller, more tenable, problems.

However, if one were seriously concerned with applying the results of this study to the prevention of delinquency one would be less concerned with the influence of the neighbourhood and more concerned with making fundamental changes in the school system.

Petty Theft

There were not many associations between petty theft admissions and area although there were more than in the damage and violence categories.

There were significant differences for three offences amongst middle-class boys – petty shoplifting, receiving and not using money in automatic machines. Amongst working-class boys there were significant differences for petty shoplifting, making bad loans, family theft and holiday theft.

As has been the case with the admission rates by area for the other crime categories, no intelligible trend in the data is apparent. No reason can be suggested as to why there were significant associations for some offences but not for the others in the petty theft category. The number of significant associations was greater than would occur by chance. However there were not nearly so many associations as there were by social class, school type or stream.

Misconduct

The category of misconduct offences, a very heterogeneous group, is the one for which the data up to now have been most mixed and inconclusive. The data on misconduct admissions by the area factor do not make the situation any clearer.

The effect of area on the misconduct rates was not unsubstantial. Amongst working-class children there were significant differences for six offences. Amongst middle-class children there were only two significant differences. The school misconduct item showed significant differences for both social classes and so can be used to illustrate the range of admissions found.

TABLE 5.5
School Misconduct Admissions by Social Class and Area

	middle class	working class
Suburb (per cent)	60	70
West Country	51	63
North London	70	69
East London	76	79

The effect of area on this group of offences was not as great as the effect of social class. Social class was a significant factor in about half the cases. The area effect was significant for half the working-class chisquare tests, but only for a sixth of the middle-class tests. The measured effect of the school system on misconduct admissions was clearly less strong than either area or social class. There were only four out of the total 24 chisquare tests for which significant differences were found.

Summary of Findings on the Area Influence

It was a simple matter to sum up the effect of area on all the crime categories. It was a highly significant factor for only one group of offences, serious theft, and that mostly for working-class boys. For the petty theft, damage and violence groups there were some significant associations, but only for a small proportion of the offences. The significant associations in all cases occurred more frequently than could be expected by chance. Altogether area was not nearly so powerful a factor as social class, school type or stream.

In Clark and Wenninger's study,[81] it was found that working-class boys were more influenced by the type of area they lived in than middle-class boys. That is, certain values adhered to by working-class boys varied by area, whereas the values of middle-class boys did not. (For delinquency admission rates both classes varied by area to about the same degree.)

Clark and Wenninger then concluded that middle-class socialization must be more successful because the values inculcated were less mutable than those acquired by the child experiencing working-class socialization. The working-class child in a middle-class area acquires some of the majority values subscribed to there more readily than does the middle-class child acquire working-class values in a working-class area. The working-class child proves to be the more impressionable in this respect.

A similar tendency, with regard to delinquency admission rates, appeared in this study. For middle-class boys there were differences by area in admission rates for ten of the 44 items. For working-class boys there were 17 significant differences by area.

Comparison of Findings with American Surveys

Now that the survey results have all been reported an overall comparison with the results from the American surveys can be made. There are two sorts of finding that can be compared: the level of delinquency admission for the whole sample and the conclusion as to the influence of social class on rates of admission.

It is questionable that a comparison of levels of admission between the two societies has any use. Any interpretation of the comparison is open to a lot of criticism, and there is no simple way of finding out which interpretation is the best one. However,

[81] John P. Clark and Eugene P. Wenninger. 'Socio-Economic Class and Area as Correlates of Illegal Behavior Among Juveniles.' *American Sociological Review*, v. 27, 1962, p. 826.

the comparison here did seem to be worth reporting as it is somewhat contrary to the conventional wisdom on the subject. So the data will be outlined, but with little comment.

There were three American studies sufficiently similar for comparison with this study. The first one, by Erickson and Empey,[82] had a total list of 22 delinquency items, of which only ten were worded closely enough for comparison.

TABLE 5.6

Comparison of Study Findings with Erickson-Empey Findings*

	Erickson-Empey	McDonald
larceny or shoplifting	22%	14%
b and e	32	23
taking car	2	6
any damage offence	66	74
any petty theft offence	92	86
truancy	66	37
betting	90	63
run away	22	9
liquor	52	58
driving car	72	18
N	50	912

* Maynard L. Erickson and Lamar T. Empey. 'Court Records, Undetected Delinquency and Decision-Making.' *Journal of Criminology, Criminal Law and Police Science*, v. 54, 1963, p. 456.

The first observation that can be made about the relative proportions admitting to the delinquencies is that they were fairly similar. The damage and petty theft proportions were nearly the same; the findings for this study were higher for damage but lower for petty theft. There were some fairly substantial differences in the serious theft and the misconduct brackets. But some of the misconduct differences are probably the result of age differences, and in any event are not too important. For example, boys in the 15 to 17 age range are much more likely to have done

[82] Maynard L. Erickson and Lamar T. Empey. 'Court Records, Undetected Delinquency and Decision-Making.' *Journal of Criminology, Criminal Law and Police Science*, v. 54, 1963, p. 456.

some illegal driving than boys aged 14. And of course boys in America have more access to cars than British boys.

Two of the three serious theft items, shoplifting-larceny and breaking and entering showed higher rates on the part of the American boys. One item, however, car theft, actually showed a higher proportion of British boys admitting. Other minor items as well showed slightly higher proportions of British boys admitting than American. There was no consistent tendency for a higher proportion of American high-school boys to admit to delinquencies than British boys.

This is a most unusual finding as there were many factors present which could be expected to produce the opposite result. And, in view of the fact that conditions militated against the finding that was made, the finding becomes that much more credible. The boys in the Erickson-Empey study were asked if they had ever committed the offence in question while the boys in the British study were asked if they had in the last year. As well the American boys were from one to three years older. So the American boys had had many more years in which to accumulate delinquencies, at a stage of life marked by high delinquency.

The method used to acquire delinquency admissions in the Erickson-Empey study is often thought to be more effective than the questionnaire method in terms of sheer quantity of admissions induced. Interviews are thought to produce larger numbers of admissions, and in one important sense, frequency of delinquency, this is true. Erickson and Empey kept their sample small and used lengthy interviews with their subjects so that they could obtain detailed information about the delinquencies committed, and gain a better estimate as to their frequency. If the subject said he had not committed an offence but gave some expression of guilt, uncertainty or nervousness he was questioned further.

However, even with these special conditions the proportion of boys who admitted to delinquencies was not substantially different from that of boys who admitted delinquencies through a written questionnaire. The extensive interviewing was undoubtedly successful in tracing the precise kind of delinquency committed and the number of times it was. It had boys admitting to enormous quantities of all kinds of delinquencies and even to many instances of serious offences. This was essential in the Erickson-Empey study as the authors were investigating the relationships between undetected delinquency, detected delinquency, and court appearances. So frequency of admission of undetected delinquency was a crucial variable. However, when the focus of the inquiry is on the subjects and some aspects of their lives (for example social origins) rather than the offences and some aspects of their history, it would seem that the written questionnaire method is at least as effective.

Comparison of proportions of admissions of subjects in the British study and subjects in the Clark-Wenninger study produced a slightly different result. While the proportions were roughly similar for most offences the British boys actually had slightly higher rates of admission on average.

The tables produced for this comparison were rather long, so have been confined to an appendix. The comparison had to be made in two stages. One of the publications from the study, by Clark and Haurek, lists rates of admission by age, but does not control for social class or area. These rates were compared with the rates of admission for the whole sample of this study. (Appendix E.) In the other comparison the tabulations were by area, but a wide age range (12–18) was included. These were compared on an area by area basis with the findings of this study. (Appendix F.) Similar results were produced in the two comparisons.

For the two serious theft items and the petty shoplifting item, and for a few other scattered items, the rates for the American boys were higher. For most of the petty theft, damage, violence and misconduct items the rates for the American boys were lower.

The most interesting point about these findings is that they do not show the American boys admitting to vastly higher amounts of delinquency than the British boys. Note that the finding of higher rates of admission for British boys holds even for a comparison of a stable working-class section of East London with a Negro ghetto of Chicago.

Comparison of the findings of Akers's study with those of this study produced a slightly different picture again from the two comparisons just made. In most instances the proportions admitting to the delinquencies were higher in the Akers study than in this one. In no instance did the Akers subjects admit to a lower amount although the proportions were about the same for a number of items. The differences in rates of admission in any event were not great.

The Akers study and this one can be compared in some detail as similar procedures were followed in the most important aspects of method. Akers's questions came from the Nye-Short study, as did many in this study. The socio-economic groups in the Akers sample were based solely on occupation, as they were in this study. However, the occupational divisions were not made at the same places. As is the practice in American surveys, craftsmen and foremen were in the same group as white collar workers, small proprietors and lower professionals. The merits of this classificatory scheme will not be debated here. But it is necessary to point out that there is a serious deficiency in the scheme when it is used with Akers's sample. The lowest group, of unskilled workers, contained only 13 members, or two per cent of the sample. It is to be suggested that the results of Akers's survey were grossly distorted by such an unbalanced classification system.

Akers's results, as has been discussed in chapter one, were that there were no differences by social class in rates of admission to delinquencies. As these are absolutely contrary to the findings of this survey, and other American surveys, the task of demonstrating that his interpretations and conclusions are not warranted is a legitimate one for the writer to attempt. Of course the studies were effected in different societies and this alone could account for the differences in results. However, the studies were carried out with similar methods, similar, often identical, questions, and fairly similar age groups. The Akers subjects were from an area of the United States about as similar as any American community could be to the areas used in the English sample. The American area used was a city of Ohio – northern, urban and industrial. So there is reason to expect similar results.

Table 5·7 gives the percentages of the two samples who admitted to the delinquencies which the questionnaires had in common.

The defect of the Akers findings should be noticeable at this point. There were no statistically significant differences by social class in his admission rates. Yet for some of the offences the range in response was as great or greater than it was in this study, for which there were significant differences at the 0·05 level. For several offences it is particularly noticeable that the lowest class group has admission rates markedly above the others. Yet this is such a small group – two per cent of the sample – that even if it

TABLE 5.7

Comparison of Study Findings with Akers's Finding

	Akers*						McDonald					
	4†	3	2	1	X²	P	UM	LM	UW	LW	X²	P
larceny	15	11	18	23	3·90	> 0·50	6	9	13	17	13·50	< 0·005
taking car	10	15	14	38	6·51	> 0·05	4	6	7	5	1·41	> 0·70
theft under $2.00	72	63	61	77	3·67	> 0·20	52	61	58	63	4·97	> 0·10
damage	43	47	44	69	3·12	> 0·30	28	38	35	42	8·87	> 0·05
truancy	30	31	41	54	6·41	> 0·10	32	29	38	49	16·26	< 0·005
driving car	45	43	56	62	7·60	> 0·05	21	15	20	12	8·88	> 0·05
run away	12	17	44	69	6·86	> 0·10	6	8	10	13		
	df=3; N=429						df=4; N=912					

* Ronald L. Akers. 'Socio-Economic Status and Delinquent Behavior: A Retest. *Journal of Research in Criminology and Delinquency*, v. 1, no. 1, January 1964. p. 44. Akers has both boys and girls in his sample; only the data on boys are referred to here.

† The highest social class.

were compared with all the others as a group the differences would not be significant.

If this lower-class group were larger the differences between the classes, which by inspection appear to be large, might be statistically significant. This lower group is more numerous in the populations of most industrial cities. So it seemed reasonable to recompute the chisquare values using the same proportions of admissions for admissions for the lower-class group, but making the N larger. The number 100 was chosen arbitrarily for the size of this hypothetical lower-class group. This would make it larger than the highest social class but smaller than the lower middle- and upper working-class groups. The results from these new computations are shown in table 5.8.

TABLE 5.8

Comparison of Akers's Chisquare Values with Values Computed from an Adjusted Sample

| | Akers* | | hypothetical | |
	X^2	P	X^2	P
larceny	3·90 >	0·20	6·82 >	0·05
taking car	3·12 >	0·30	31·72 <	0·001
theft u$2.00	3·67 >	0·20	9·49 <	0·025
damage	3·12 >	0·30	18·59 <	0·001
driving car	7·60 >	0·05	11·90 <	0·01
run away	6·86 >	0·10	16·56 <	0·001
truancy	6·41 >	0·10	16·84 <	0·001
	N=429; df=3		n=516; df=3	

* Ronald L. Akers. 'Socio-Economic Status and Delinquent Behavior: A Retest.' *Journal of Research in Criminology and Delinquency*, v. 1, no. 1, January 1964, p. 44.

With the adjusted sample there are now six offences for which the differences between the social classes are statistically significant at the five per cent level. Only for larceny are the results still not significant.

However it must immediately be stated that the hypothetical results, as they are given above, are misleading. The overall chisquare values are significant for six out of seven of the offences. But this is due mostly to the high rate of admission in the lowest group, rather than to differences occurring throughout all four gradations.

This is demonstrated when the degrees of freedom are partitioned and separate values of chisquare are computed for the component parts. In table 5.9 the values of the two components

TABLE 5.9

Partitioned Values of Chisquare from the Adjusted Sample

taking car	X^2	df	P
components of X^2 due to			
differences between classes 4, 3, 2	1·03	2	> 0·50
differences between class 1 and 4, 3, 2 as a group	30·69	1	< 0·001
total	31·72	3	< 0·001
theft under $2.00			
differences between classes 4, 3, 2	2·20	2	> 0·30
differences between class 1 and 4, 3, 2 as a group	6·99	1	< 0·01
total	9·19	3	0·05
damage			
differences between classes 4, 3, 2	0·19	2	> 0·90
differences between class 1 and 4, 3, 2 as a group	18·40	1	< 0·001
total	18·59	3	< 0·001
run away			
differences between classes 4, 3, 2	1·43	2	> 0·30
differences between class 1 and 4, 3, 2 as a group	15·13	1	< 0·001
total	16·56	3	< 0·001
truancy			
differences between classes 4, 3, 2	4·37	2	> 0·10
differences between class 1 and 4, 3, 2 as a group	12·47	1	< 0·001
total	16·84	3	< 0·001

For one offence, driving a car, the differences within both parts of the table are significant.

driving car	X^2	df	P
differences between classes 4, 3 and 2	6·33	2	< 0·05
differences between 1 and 4, 3 and 2 as a group	5·57	1	< 0·02
total	11·90	3	< 0·02

For the larceny offence partitioning shows that the difference between the unskilled group and the three others is significant at the 0·05 level even though the overall chisquare value is not significant. The differences between the three higher groups are clearly not significant.

larceny	X^2	df	P
differences between classes 4, 3 and 2	2·86	2	> 0·20
differences between class 1 and 4, 3 and 2 as a group	3·96	1	< 0·05
total	6·82	3	> 0·05

of the chisquare value are given. The first is for the differences between the three highest social groups. The second is for the differences between the lowest group and the three highest as a group.

It may be thought that significant differences (real as well as hypothetical) between the lower working class and the higher groups should not be considered important. They were not specifically sought when the research was designed, so should be treated as incidental if and when they turn up.

Against this view it is suggested that in research on social class any significant differences, even if along unsought lines of classification, should be carefully considered. There is nothing sacred or immutable about a four-fold classification or a two-fold one split near the middle.

Miller and Mishler[83] recomputed data on social class and

[83] Frank Riessman and others, ed. *Mental Health of the Poor*. New York: Free Press of Glencoe, 1964.

mental illness from the well-known Hollingshed-Redlich study.[84] By leaving out the lower working class from the calculations, Miller and Mishler found that the differences in incidence of new neuroses, old neuroses, and psychoses – between the four higher social groups – were not significant. When the original calculations were done, on all five groups, the total chisquare values were significant for two of the three mental illness categories. Accordingly the writers concluded that the incidence of those two groups of mental illness increased level by level down to the lowest group. In fact the significant class differences in the original tables were due almost entirely to the enormity of the differences between the lowest group and the other four. These findings lead the writers of the Reissman book to further theoretical formulation and research on the problem of lower working-class mental illness.

The method used to recompute the Akers material was not the same as that used by Miller and Mishler. But the idea of recomputing it and the defence for doing it came from them.

It should not be thought that the findings of this survey in any way necessarily corroborate or disconfirm those of the American surveys. Obviously any comments made must be understood in the light of the fact that two different nations are being considered. However, it is useful to put these findings into the perspective of the whole literature on the subject, which in this field means relating them to American work.

First of all the findings in this survey differ in some important respects from all the previous studies. Obviously these conclusions are exactly contradictory to those of Nye and Short and Dentler and Monroe (and Akers). The Nye-Short and Dentler-Monroe studies were the first surveys done on this subject. Later work by Clark and Wenninger (discussed in Chapter I) suggests that those two studies' conclusions probably apply only to small communities – rural areas and small towns.

This researcher's work does not directly help to solve this problem of discrepant findings. This survey was carried out in larger communities and of course differences by social class in admission rates, were found in all areas. So it indirectly supports Clark and Wenninger's interpretation.

However, the conclusions to the present study are not the same

[84] August B. Hollingshed and Frederick C. Redlich. *Social Class and Mental Illness*. New York: Wiley, 1958.

as Clark and Wenninger's. Those authors found important differences in admission rates by status area, but not by social class. In this study, of course, there were significant differences by area, but these were much less important than those of class.

The findings to this study more closely approximate those of Reiss and Rhodes than any other study. The two studies are similar in that they found strong social-class differences along with significant but less pronounced differences by status area. However, the Reiss-Rhodes study was of official delinquency only, which constitutes a different level of delinquency and involves a different (though overlapping) group of delinquents. However, this subject of official delinquency is the subject of the next chapter, so need not be pursued further here.

6

OFFICIAL DELINQUENCY

The study has up to now been concerned solely with delinquency as it has been admitted to by boys. Delinquency, for this chapter only, is to be considered at the level at which it has been detected and dealt with in some way by the law enforcement agencies. The boys termed delinquent in this part of the study accordingly form a smaller proportion of the sample than the delinquent groups did in the admitted delinquency part of the study. But the official delinquents should not necessarily be thought of as more seriously implicated in delinquency. This would probably be the case in most instances, but it is not the basis of differentiation. What distinguishes the official delinquents from the unofficial is that they have all been detected for some delinquency and have appeared in court to answer for it.

The index used to measure delinquency for this part of the study was court appearances. As this is a sample of juveniles, appearance in court with rare exception meant conviction. However, it was thought that court appearances would be a slightly better measure for the study than actual convictions. The level of court appearances is the one least liable to the effect of bias in police and court processing. Failure to convict a child is probably more indicative of lack of evidence than of lack of guilt. And lack of evidence can be affected by the social background of the child, through the intervening factor of whether or not the child has legal counsel. Children from homes with more money and greater knowledge as to how to deal with legal problems, in other words children from middle-class homes, obtain legal counsel more frequently than children from working-class homes.

In the survey of admitted delinquency it was shown that there is a consistent association between certain social variables and the rates of admitted delinquency. More working-class boys admitted to delinquency than middle-class boys, and working-class boys admitted to more delinquency than middle-class boys. These findings can now be put into better perspective. They can now be related to the social-class distribution of delinquency that is officially dealt with.

This does not mean that one part of the study can verify the other. It is possible for working-class status to be associated with high rates of delinquency at one level, but not at the other. The two different concepts of delinquency result in two different groups of boys being defined as delinquent. Boys assessed as delinquent by the criterion of having appeared in court are only a small minority of the boys at risk in their areas. Boys assessed as delinquent in the admitted delinquency study, at least for the less serious offences, are actually a majority of the sample.

If no differences by social class had been found in the study of admitted delinquency it would have been rather important to ascertain whether or not there were such differences in official delinquency. If it had been found that there were no differences by class in the admitted sphere of delinquency, but that there were significant differences in the official sphere, the possibility of bias in police and court processing would have to be considered. However, social-class differences in the admitted sphere were amply demonstrated, so it did not prove necessary to consider the possibility of social-class bias in police processing. This does not of course mean there was none.

The association between social class and delinquency in the admitted sphere gives rise to the prediction of a similar association in the sphere of official delinquency. Yet there was cause, from the literature, to suggest that this might not be the case, that there might not be important social-class differences in the official delinquency sphere.

The only available data on the social-class distribution of delinquency in Britain (at the time this study was planned) showed that social-class differences in rates of court appearances had radically diminished over recent years.[85] The Little-Ntsekhe

[85] W. R. Little and V. R. Ntsekhe. 'Social Class Background of Young Offenders from London.' *British Journal of Delinquency*, v. 10, 1959, p. 130.

study was based in large part on material gathered in the same area as this study, London, and its data were on juveniles as well. So its findings must be considered as particularly instructive for the problem at hand. If the process described by the authors, of diminishing social-class differences in rates of court appearances, has in fact been occurring one would have to predict either very small differences by class in rates of court appearances in this study, or none whatsoever. With such contradictory evidence, and more fundamentally, in view of the scarcity of evidence generally, no firm prediction in this regard could be seriously made.

The data collected for this part of the study were deficient in one respect, but appear to be fairly satisfactory in all others. It was not possible to determine rates of delinquency for the various social classes within the schools or areas, as was done for the data on admitted delinquency. Rates of delinquency could only be assessed on a school-by-school basis. The data on court appearances came from the records of the Children's Department in each of the boroughs of the admitted delinquency survey. These records did not contain any information on fathers' occupations, nor was this information available in the schools for a sufficient number of cases for it to be worth using.

Despite this the Children's Department records were the best source of information on the subject. They are considerably more complete than the records kept by the police, courts or schools. Police and court records contain information only on court appearances or contacts made within their jurisdiction. The Children's Department keeps information on all court appearances of children who live in their area, whether they appeared in local courts or in courts in any other part of Britain. This includes appearances at the magistrates' and higher courts as well as at the juvenile courts. Of course most of the children's appearances were in the local juvenile courts. The following data was collected on each school:

    number of children of all classes
    number of working-class children
    number of lower working-class children
    number of court appearances of all children

The data on court appearances were further divided so that the theft group and the group of serious offences could be looked at apart from the total group. The theft group included the following matters:

    larceny
    shoplifting
    housebreaking
    shopbreaking
    attempted breaking and entering
    housebreaking implements
    loitering with intent
    taking and driving
    attempted taking and driving
    fraud
    receiving

Every kind of theft except rail fraud (which is treated separately from theft in the courts) was subsumed into this category. Most of the thefts were of simple larceny, shoplifting, breaking and entering, and taking and driving.

The group of offences referred to as serious offences was comprised of the theft group plus the damage and violence offences. Any kind of property damage, including fireworks offences, was included in the damage group. As well violations involving an airgun and trespassing on the railway were included in this group. It was thought that these offences would result in property damage more than anything else – theft in the case of railway trespassing or violence in the case of the air-gun. The violence group contained all assaults, including a few indecent assaults, wounding, robbery and possession of an offensive weapon.

The last or total group contained all court appearances for any offence. As well as all the serious offences it had traffic violations, truancy, rail fraud and a number of minor items such as insulting behaviour.

All court appearances during the two-year period were counted. If a boy appeared for a number of offences all were counted. Appearances for which the accused was not convicted were also counted: however, there were very few of these.

The figures for the number of children in each social class in each school were taken from the survey data. As the boys in the survey constituted almost the whole of their forms, at an age before legal school-leaving, these figures may be considered representative of the whole school populations.

Analysis of Data

The data analysis consisted of several multiple regressions in which the independent variables were added to the regression one at a time, and in a specified order. There were three separate regressions, one each for the three dependent variables: total court appearances, serious offences and theft offences. In the regressions the independent variables were introduced one at a time and kept in the analysis. Thus the amount that each new variable added to the total correlation coefficient could be determined for each type of delinquency.

The values of all variables, their means and standard deviations are given in Appendix G. The proportion of explained variation, values of t, degrees of freedom and probability of occurring by chance are all reported in the text.

The most general and most familiar dependent variable, total court appearances, will be considered first. The analysis was begun by regressing it on to the variable of sample size. This made it possible for the most obvious question to be answered immediately. If the number of delinquencies committed by boys in the schools was highly correlated with the number of boys in those schools we would have to conclude that official delinquency was not related to the social-class variables, but rather occurred randomly. It would simply mean that the more boys there were in any school area the more court appearances there would be in that area. Further regressions using the social-class variables would confirm this conclusion by showing nonsignificant correlations.

However the clear result of the first regression was that court appearances were not related to sample size. The coefficient of determination was the very low 0·05 (t = 0·73; df = 10; P > 0·40). Sample size was not correlated either with the other measures of court appearances. The amounts of explained variation for the regressions on sample size were as follows:

serious offences and sample size: $r^2 = 0·03$
    t = 0·52; df = 10; P > 0·60
theft offences and sample size: $r^2 = 0·07$
    t = 0·85; df = 10; P > 0·40

At the next stage, when the social-class variables are considered, it can definitely be said that any correlation they might show could not be the result of sample size. Any increment to the value of r^2 found would be almost entirely due to the effect of the particular social variable introduced.

The next independent variable, and the first of the social-class variables, to be introduced, was the number of working-class children in each school. Size of the working-class population at risk proved to be highly correlated with rates of delinquency, for all three delinquency variables. For the total offences category the addition of the social-class variable increased the explained variation from the clearly nonsignificant level of 0·05 to 0·87, which indicates a very high degree of correlation. The value 0·87 is significant at the 0·001 level ($t = 7·54$; $df = 9$). The increases for the other two delinquency variables were also substantial.

serious offences and number working class:
from $r^2 = 0·03$ to 0·66 $t = 4·10$; $df = 9$; $P < 0·005$
theft offences and number working class:
from $r^2 = 0·07$ to 0·72 $t = 4·62$; $df = 9$; $P < 0·001$

The results in this part of the study could hardly be more clear. The factor of sample size has been eliminated as an active variable. And the factor of social class has been shown to be extremely powerful. It explains a large portion of the variation in delinquency rates, for all three measures of official delinquency.

Although the proportions of explained variation increased markedly when the data of working-class numbers were introduced it was thought that one further test of the social-class association with delinquency rates should be made. It could be that the strength of the association was due more to the delinquent activity of lower working-class children than to that of the entire working-class. Studies of social class and mental health[86] have shown that what appeared to be a high and significant correlation between certain kinds of mental illness and working-class status was really a correlation of lower working-class status and mental illness. Differences between upper working-class and middle-class groups were not significant.

In the admitted delinquency part of the study it was shown that delinquency rates increased progressively as the social levels were descended; the differences between the classes were not just due to high delinquency rates on the part of the lowest social group. So it was important to find out which pattern appeared in

[86] Frank Riessman and others, ed. *Mental Health of the Poor*. New York: Free Press of Glencoe, 1964.

the case of official delinquency. This question could be easily investigated. A separate series of regressions of the numbers of lower working-class children in the areas and the various delinquency rates was run. The result of this series was as follows:

Total offences and number lower working class:

from $r^2 = 0.05$ to $r^2 = 0.68$

$t = 4.16$; $df = 9$; $P < 0.005$

serious offences and number lower working class:

from $r^2 = 0.03$ to $r^2 = 0.68$

$t = 2.53$; $df = 9$; $P < 0.05$

theft offences and number lower working class:

from $r^2 = 0.07$ to $r^2 = 0.42$

$t = 2.36$; $df = 9$; $P < 0.05$

Use of the data on lower working-class children did not improve the explanation of the various delinquency rates. On the contrary lower working-class status explained less variation of all three rates of delinquency than simple working-class status. Still the association was fairly strong, and was significant at the five per cent level or better.

School Type

Type of school was the last variable to be introduced into the regression. It will be seen that this variable did not add significantly to the explained variation. However this statement should not be taken at face value. The school-type variable did prove to have the power to explain variation in delinquency rates, but not when the variable of social class was already active in the regression. When the social-class factor is introduced into the regression it accounts for most of the variation. So when the school-type variable is added later there is very little left to explain. But the school-type variable could have independently explained some of the variation observed in relation to social class.

These points will be demonstrated one at a time. The figures below show the negligible effect which appeared when the school-type variable was added after social class.

total offences: without the school-type variable $r^2 = 0.87$;

with the school-type variable r^2 was increased only to 0.88;

$t = 0.90$; $df = 8$; $P > 0.30$

serious offences: without the school-type variable $r^2 = 0.66$;

with the school-type variable r^2 was increased to only 0·69;
$t = 0·91$; $df = 8$; $P > 0·30$
theft offences: without the school-type variable $r^2 = 0·72$;
with the school-type variable r^2 was increased to only 0·75;
$t = 0·90$; $df = 8$; $P > 0·30$

However, when a simple regression of the various delinquency rates on the school-type variable was made the strong effect of the school-type variable was clearly demonstrated.

total offences and school type: $r^2 = 0·61$
$t = 3·91$; $df = 10$; $P < 0·005$
serious offences and school type: $r^2 = 0·62$
$t = 4·02$; $df = 10$; $P < 0·005$
theft offences and school type: $r^2 = 0·62$;
$t = 4·01$; $df = 10$; $P < 0·005$

The association between school type and official delinquency was still not as strong as the association between social class and delinquency. But the association was an important one, and a statistically significant one.

In the analysis of the admitted delinquency data it was seen that the variable of school type tended to be associated with the same items that social class was. This occurred as well when social class was controlled. In interpretation it was suggested that the variable of school type was not really a new or separate dimension, but was rather an extension of the social-class complex. The type of school attended results in a heightening of either middle-class or working-class associations and experiences. Grammar schools, which have a predominantly middle-class population, are middle class in many aspects of belief and behaviour. Secondary modern schools, which have pupil populations even more disproportionately working class, immerse their children progressively into a way of life that minimizes middle-class associations, activities, ways of dealing with problems, and opportunities. In short these children become more working class.

The conclusions in this part of the study are not of use except as they are treated in relation to the conclusions of the survey part of the study. Ecological correlation taken by itself can produce highly misleading results. Just because there is a correlation between social class and delinquency at the level of the areas being studied it does not necessarily follow that this correlation will hold when individuals are studied. In fact, there are examples of situations in which two variables are positively correlated when individuals are the units of study, but negatively correlated when the areas are.[87] Ecological correlation is not an adequate substitute for the study of the behaviour of the individuals in the areas.

The other problem with ecological correlation is that it exaggerates the extent of correlation. If it had been possible to collect information on individuals who appeared in court and their social-class background, rather than the overall levels of court appearances and the levels of the various social classes in the areas, probably the correlations would be much lower. Whoever first said that 'correlation is not causation' most likely had ecological correlation in mind, or if not, he should have.

The value of ecological correlation is that, when used properly, it can extend the scope of the study. In this study specifically it means that two different concepts of quantity of delinquency can be compared, as well as two different levels, admissions and official involvement. The amount of crime in an area can be conceived of either as the number of criminals in the area convicted or arrested or defined as criminal in some way, or as the number of crimes that are reported to the police.

These concepts are more important for a longitudinal study and their usefulness is most easily demonstrated in reference to changes over time. For example it is quite possible for the number of crimes reported to the police to decrease in a certain area, but the number of criminals dealt with to stay the same or increase. That would mean that more people were committing crimes, but fewer per person. Conversely the number of criminals could decrease but there could be an increase in the number of crimes committed and/or reported to the police. That is, fewer people would be committing crimes, but more each.

So it is possible that the number of court appearances might be highly associated with the social-class variable, while the number of criminals were not. This would mean equal proportions of all classes appeared in court, but working-class persons appeared for many more offences each than middle-class persons.

This study, of course, deals with both concepts, the number of delinquencies and the number of delinquents. The data on court appearances were of delinquencies only: a person who appeared

[87] W. S. Robinson. 'Ecological correlations and the behavior of individuals.' *American Sociological Review*, v. 15, 1950, p. 351.

for five offences was counted as if he were five offenders. The data on admitted delinquency were of numbers of delinquents primarily, most frequently used as proportions of social-class groupings. However, a measure of frequency of admissions was also employed, although only in the social-class section of the analysis. Both the number of boys admitting to delinquencies, and the number of delinquencies admitted, were associated with the social-class factors. And the number of delinquencies per area dealt with as court appearances was associated with social class.

Seriousness of Delinquency

Throughout the discussion of both official and unofficial delinquency the only measure of delinquency was the frequency of the event, either of admissions or court appearances, or the number of persons admitting. There has been no attempt to measure the seriousness of the offences in terms either of the physical injury to the victim or the value of property involved. Before any such measure could be made a considerable amount of work to develop a system of quantifying such variables as injury and property loss and relating them to each other would have to be done, for a study of this kind as well as many others. A good example of such a scale is that developed by Sellin and Wolfgang.[88] However, Sellin and Wolfgang developed their scale in Philadelphia, taking their offences from police files there and using police officers and students in that area for rating the seriousness of the offences. Such a scale could not be applied directly to another society. There probably would be substantial differences in opinion between raters in Britain and the United States as to what weights should be given the various crimes. For example attitudes about violence would certainly be very different in the two countries.

To overcome the problem of measuring only frequency of delinquency, yet being without the means of assigning weights for relating the seriousness of delinquencies to their frequency, a rather laborious approach to the handling of the data had to be taken. Offences were considered individually first, and then in groups before any summary statement about the influence of the social factor on delinquency generally was made. By analysing

[88] T. Sellin and M. E. Wolfgang. *The Measurement of Delinquency.* New York: John Wiley, 1964.

the theft, damage, violence and misconduct items in separate groups it was not necessary to determine weights that could convert them into a single dimension.

Assertions about characteristics of a delinquent group could much more easily be made if frequency and seriousness were both measured on one scale. However, it should be noted that a scale that did not do this properly would seriously distort the findings.

For example it was found that the theft group of offences (which would be relatively serious) were less strongly associated with social class than were other offences. So the more the weight given to the theft items in the scale the weaker would be the finding of association between social class and delinquency. A scale which gave relatively more weight to the misconduct group of offences would produce findings of a higher degree of association of social class and delinquency. Similarly a scale which gave more weight to frequency than seriousness (indirectly giving more weight to the misconduct items) would over-estimate the degree of association between social class and delinquency.

Attention to the factor of seriousness was paid of course, though not by means of a scale. Car theft and breaking and entering are more serious offences than truancy or petty shoplifting. (And raters in studies published so far agree on this.) Accordingly these more serious offences were given more attention in the discussions of results.

Analysis by Type of Offence

Analysis of the offences in groups (theft, petty theft, violence, damage and misconduct) made it possible to consider whether or not any one of the groups was particularly associated with the social variable in question. So far as the section on social class was concerned the results were very clear. The damage and violence items were consistently associated with social class. The petty theft and misconduct items were less associated and the serious theft category had the fewest significant associations.

A similar pattern emerged with respect to the findings on official delinquency. The theft offences group was the one least correlated with social class. Comparison between the official and unofficial spheres could not be made precisely on this point as no distinction between serious and petty theft was practicable for the data on court appearances. (Values involved in the crimes were frequently not specified.) The serious theft offences were the least associated with social class in the sphere of admitted delinquency, and while petty theft had a somewhat higher association, it was still in the intermediate bracket. So it can be said that theft offences as a group are generally less influenced by social class than are all delinquencies as a group. This occurs at both the level of official delinquency and at the level of anonymous and confidential admissions by a sample of boys in the ordinary community.

The damage and violence offences were the ones most associated with social class in the admitted sphere. However the same did not prove to be true in the case of official delinquency. The group of serious offences, which was comprised of thefts for the most part, but also the damage and violence items, acted in the same way as the group composed solely of theft offences. In other words court appearances for serious offences as a group were less associated with the social-class variable than were all offences as a group. The figures below demonstrate the comparative strengths of the associations.

total offences and number working class: increment of
r^2 from sample size was 0·82
serious offences and number working class: increment of
r^2 from sample size was 0·63
theft offences and number working class: increment of
r^2 from sample size was 0·65

The finding was the same when the data on lower working-class associations were referred to instead. Of course all the associations were weaker.

total offences and number lower working: increment of
r^2 from sample size was 0·63
serious and number lower working: increment of
r^2 from sample size was 0·41
theft offences and number lower working: increment of
r^2 from sample size was 0·35

The only study with which the results of this study could be compared was that of Little and Ntsekhe. The findings of this study are not necessarily in disagreement with those of Little and Ntsekhe, but there is disagreement as to their interpretation. Little and Ntsekhe stated that their study showed greatly diminished class differences in rates of official delinquency, compared with a period ten years earlier. Yet there still were·differences between the classes, even at the time the authors made their inquiry. Application of the chisquare test to them, by this researcher, shows that the differences are statistically significant.[89] Little and Ntsekhe emphasize the reduction, over time in class differences in official delinquency rates. They could have pointed out that the remaining differences were substantial enough to be significant, but this is a matter of emphasis.

Using the material of the present study it can be said that there has been no appreciable reduction in class differences in official delinquency rates in the five years since the Little-Ntsekhe study. However, it could not be said either that there has been any increase. The two studies could not easily be related as their analyses were done in different ways. (The present study is a regression analysis, the Little-Ntsekhe study a tabulation of delinquents by social class.) So the above statement must be made with the qualification that it is a very rough and approximate interpretation of trend. The results of the present study consistently and unequivocably indicate that class differences in rates of official delinquency are still very strong.

Conclusions to the Study of Court Appearances

The variable most strongly associated with rates of official delinquency was that of social class. The factor of school type was second in importance and it showed quite a strong association. However, once the social-class factor had been used to explain variation the variable of school type had nothing more to add. The factor of school type explained only the same variation that social class was able to explain, and then did not explain quite as much.

This finding is directly parallel to the findings on admitted

[89] For the total sample of delinquents $(N = 381)$ $X^2 = 28 \cdot 08$;
$$df = 5; P < 0 \cdot 001$$
For the London juvenile court cases $(N = 209)$ $X^2 = 24 \cdot 47$;
$$df = 5; P < 0 \cdot 001$$
For the remand home cases $(N = 100)$ $X^2 = 18 \cdot 01$;
$$df = 5; P < 0 \cdot 005$$
But for the approved school cases $(N = 72)$ the social-class differences were not statistically significant: $X^2 = 8 \cdot 24$; $df = 5$; $P > 0 \cdot 10$

delinquency. The main conclusion of the three chapters on admitted delinquency was that the variable most strongly associated with delinquency rates was the social class of the home. The variable next in importance was the type of school attended. The school-type variable had a considerable association with the rates of admitted delinquency, but this was substantially reduced when the social-class factor was controlled. (In the case of official delinquency no significant effect remained when the social-class factor was allowed to operate.)

The Juvenile Liaison Scheme in East London

In one of the areas of the survey, East London, it was possible to look at the delinquency question with further perspective. Delinquency is dealt with there by police at a level of seriousness between the two used so far in this study. The police in the borough concerned operate a juvenile liaison scheme. Officers investigate cases of delinquency brought to their attention and in appropriate instances give supervision to the juveniles involved. This is done without any court appearance and in fact supervision can only be carried on with juveniles who have never appeared in court. So the scheme embraces a group of juveniles who have admitted to delinquencies, but who also (and this distinguishes them from the boys who merely admitted to delinquencies on the questionnaire) have been reported to the police for their crimes or misdemeanours.

Often the children have been found to have committed minor delinquencies, such as shoplifting of very small amounts, by persons or firms who do not wish to prosecute. A few retail stores in the area make it their policy not to lay charges. Children caught shoplifting in them are almost automatically referred to the juvenile liaison police for investigation.

For the child to be placed under supervision he must admit to the delinquency in question. Also his parents must agree to his being supervised. (In only one instance so far has this been refused.) The parents are included in the supervisory process to a considerable extent so their co-operation is important. The child is visited at home for the initial investigation and is visited there regularly afterwards if supervision is thought advisable. Usually the parents are seen at the same time as the visit to the child is made. So close contact is established immediately with the parents and this is maintained.

Almost all of the boys covered by the juvenile liaison scheme have admitted to delinquencies that could have been dealt with by a court, and which frequently would have been had the scheme not been in operation. The exceptions consisted of a very few boys who admitted to arson but who were too young to be charged. In the case of girls there were some under supervision for moral danger. But the boys fell clearly into a legal definition of delinquency, a broader one than that of court appearances, but a more narrow and more serious one than that used in the admitted delinquency survey.

A study of juvenile liaison cases in Greenock showed that the scheme was in fact dealing with the children it was intended to – the less serious offenders.[90] Introduction of the juvenile liaison scheme in that city had the effect of keeping these minor offenders out of the juvenile court. The cases that the courts continued to receive were the more serious ones and this was reflected in the sentences imposed. There were fewer discharges but more probation orders and committals to approved schools, after the juvenile liaison scheme began to operate.

The data on the juvenile liaison scheme in East London were collected so that a further estimate of the social-class distribution of delinquency could be made. The two other sources of data on delinquency have yielded consistent and statistically significant trends in the direction of higher working-class delinquency. As the concept of delinquency contained in the juvenile liaison scheme falls between the two concepts already used it provides an appropriate third check. The juvenile liaison scheme data differ from those collected for the other two parts of the study in that they apply to only one area, and that a very homogeneous working-class area. Thus it is testing social-class differences that can be considered exclusively the influence of the family. The influence of the area is the same for all the children in the sample, so area is not a variable.

The social-class distribution of the juvenile liaison cases was determined and this was compared with the social-class distribution of the borough, which was taken from the census. The sample

[90] J. A. Mack. 'Police Juvenile Liaison.' *British Journal of Criminology,* v. 3, 1962.

of juvenile liaison cases consisted of all the cases of boys for whom supervision was begun during a nine-month period in 1962, and for whom social class information was available.[91]

It can be seen in table 6.1 that the juvenile liaison cases are clearly representative, in terms of social class, of the population of the borough.

TABLE 6.1

Juvenile Liaison Cases by Social Class

	cases	per cent	population*	per cent
Class I	0	0	512	0·9
Class II	8	6·3	4,689	7·8
Class III	69	54·8	29,860	49·5
Class IV	22	17·5	8,946	14·9
Class V	27	21·4	16,217	26·9
total	126	100·0	60,224	100·0

$$X^2 = 3·35; \ df = 4; \ P > 0·50$$

* 1951 Census, County Report.

For the first time in the study working-class children were not over-represented in the group of delinquents. Middle-class children produced their full quota of delinquencies. This is not delinquency at as serious a level as that of court appearances, but it is probably more serious than the delinquency involved in the admitted delinquency survey. More importantly, it has been detected and openly admitted. Some official action has been taken.

These findings are clear enough at face value, but it is not clear how they should be interpreted beyond that, except that no attempt should be made to consider them applicable to other areas or situations. As the findings were not consistent with those of the admitted delinquency survey and the study of court appearances some detailed attention to the handling of the data is necessary.

The Registrar-General's classification was used as the measure of social class. This was necessary so that a comparison with the census data could be made. However, the Registrar-General's groupings are such that important differences could be hidden.

[91] Thirteen cases had to be omitted as there was insufficient information in the files for a classification to be made.

The class III group does not distinguish between skilled manual workers and lower middle-class persons, mainly clerks and sales workers. And so while the class III group is fairly accurately represented in the delinquent sample, the delinquents could have come disproportionately from the working-class sector of that group. There is no way of finding out whether or not this occurred. However the proportions of the borough population and the juvenile liaison cases at the other levels of the class structure were so similar that it is reasonable to suggest that there was no distortion at the centre of the distribution. The two highest classes were very slightly under-represented in the delinquent group. But the lowest, unskilled worker class was also very slightly under-represented in the delinquency group, which cancels the trend. While the Registrar-General's classification is certainly not the best classification for use in this analysis, there does not seem to be sufficient grounds for discrediting it.

Another point to be considered is that there is probably less to distinguish middle- from working-class people in an area such as East London than in most places. What middle-class people there are there are mostly lower middle class. Persons who in the census are rated Class II, by virtue of their owning small businesses are probably quite unrepresentative of those classes. Their businesses are small shops and they are operated often with the help of family members only. The daily work involved would be very routine. An area such as this is a poor one for testing social-class differences. There are middle-class people in the borough but they are more similar to the working-class people of the borough than middle-class persons of other areas would be. At least the differences in work routine and income would not be so great as they would be on average in the whole country.

This is not meant as a further criticism of the Registrar-General's classification. Many classificatory schemes do not make any distinction between very small shopowners of this kind, and larger business and managerial persons. And these distinctions could not be expected except in a classification with many divisions. In a sample that has a larger middle-class group or is not confined to a rather homogeneous working-class area this difficulty does not arise in any event. The effect of these border-line lower middle-class cases would be mitigated by the larger number of upper middle-class persons in the sample.

159

This inadequate distinction between the social levels in this part of the study is a factor which operates quite separately from that of the influence of the area itself. A fairly homogeneous area has a tendency to level differences between the classes of the area. And this distinctive working-class East London dock area is one in which the levelling process must be considerable. So, differences with respect to the individual characteristics of occupation and income are initially less strong than indicated by the formal ratings of the Registrar-General's classification. These differences are then further muted by the levelling influence of the area. The area influence, according to the findings of the admitted delinquency survey, was not as strong as that of the social class of the family, nor even as strong as that of the school. But its effect was significant.

Another factor which could possibly account for the findings would be bias on the part of police in selection of cases for juvenile liaison supervision. It could happen that the working-class children were less frequently considered suitable for police supervision and accordingly more frequently charged formally and sent to court. The middle-class children, who would form a smaller proportion of the cases investigated by police, would be less frequently charged formally and more frequently placed under supervision by the police. So, though the proportion of middle-class children reported to the police would be smaller than the proportion of working-class children, the proportion placed under supervision could turn out to be exactly the same.

There is no doubt that police have considerable discretion, certainly as to who is arrested, also as to who is charged and who is not proceeded with.[92] It is not known what factors are taken into account in making these decisions and the police themselves are not given specific criteria to use in judging. However, social class is probably a very important variable here as it is associated with the appropriate deference, articulated remorse, the appearance of stability, good home background and so forth.

Yet despite the possibility of bias in selection of cases there was no indication – either from the stated criteria for judging suitability for juvenile liaison supervision, or from discussions with the head of the juvenile liaison operation in the borough – that such bias exists. Apparently there is no practice of excluding cases

[92] Wayne R. LaFave. *Arrest*. Boston: Little, Brown, 1965.

on the basis of the problem being too difficult to handle. If there were such a policy perhaps more working-class children would be excluded. The result of that would similarly be an over-representation of middle-class children in juvenile liaison caseloads.

One last possible source of bias would be differential acceptance of supervision on the part of parents. However, as only one family has refused to co-operate since the inception of the scheme, this could not be a factor.

Conclusions to the Juvenile Liaison Scheme Discussion

The findings of this part of the study appear to contradict those of the major part of the study, and those of the other subsidiary section. However, a case for not relying too much on the discrepant findings has been made. At the very least it is insisted that the findings not be considered applicable beyond the borough limits within which the data were collected.

Although the value of the data has been seriously doubted it was thought essential that it be reported. The data were collected as a further test of the hypothesis that working-class status and delinquency are associated. Its findings are negative. While it is certainly not thought that they undermine the major findings of the study they do point out a useful qualification. Social class of the home is still the most important factor associated with rates of delinquency, at both the admitted level and at the level of court appearances. But it now appears that there are circumstances, or to be precise that there is one situation in which the effect of the social class of the home may be mitigated. This occurs with respect to the distinctive homogeneous working-class area.

The findings suggest that the influence of the area might be an important factor even at the level of official delinquency. This is not something that could be dealt with within the scope of the present study. Also, considering the intervening factor of differential police administration in the various areas it is questionable whether a proper test of this could be made at all at the present time.

It is also possible that there are other sorts of areas, perhaps heavily middle-class areas, or rural areas, that would demonstrate similar low or nonexistent class differences within the area in delinquency rates. This again is something that would require a separate study. But it is a subject that could be researched much more easily than the immediately preceding suggestion.

So the major finding of this chapter stands with this additional and suggestive information. Rates of official delinquency are strongly correlated with social class. The rates of court appearances for theft offences and serious offences are associated to a somewhat lower degree than those of all offences. However even they are strongly associated.

Evidence from the survey is that more working-class boys admitted to delinquencies of all kinds than middle-class boys, and working-class boys admitted to having committed delinquencies more frequently than middle-class boys. Evidence from the official data is that more working-class boys appeared in court for all kinds of offences than middle-class boys. Delinquency at both the level of official action and unofficial anonymous admission is consistently associated with social-class position.

7

CONCLUSIONS AND SOME
IMPLICATIONS FOR POLICY-MAKING

In this chapter the findings from the various parts of the study are to be brought together for final discussion and evaluation. The summary will of course be a repetition of the main findings and can be skipped by anyone who has read the findings themselves thoroughly, or the conclusions to chapters three to five. After this general summary certain of the implications of the research for policy-making will be discussed.

Summary Discussion of Findings

Four hypotheses were posed at the beginning of the study. The first hypothesis, stated in the null form, was that there is no association between social class and rates of admitted delinquency. This must be rejected. The evidence from the admitted delinquency survey consistently showed higher rates of delinquency on the part of working-class boys than middle-class boys. This occurred for all categories of offences, though particularly for the damage and violence groups. The typical pattern was of increasing proportions of admission as the social levels were descended. The differences between the four social-class groups were not due to the unusual behaviour of only one of the groups.

As well as the differences in proportions of the social classes admitting to the items there were differences in frequency of admission. Of boys who admitted at all to the offences working-class boys tended to admit to having committed the offences more frequently than middle-class boys.

CONCLUSIONS AND SOME IMPLICATIONS

The second hypothesis investigated was that there is no difference between children from grammar and children from secondary modern schools, holding class constant, in rates of admitted delinquency. This hypothesis had to be rejected as well. The evidence was convincing although it did not form as solid and consistent a whole as the evidence on social class did. Amongst middle-class children those attending grammar schools admitted to less delinquency than those attending modern schools. And the same occurred with respect to working-class children.

Along with the testing of the hypotheses on school type was a test on the level of achievement at school, as judged by stream. It was hypothesized that children of lower streams would have higher rates of delinquency than children of higher streams, holding class and school type constant. This was found to be the case.

As the stream variable produced a pattern of results similar to that of social class and type of school it was thought that the effect of stream lay in its social implications rather than in an independent mechanism of intelligence. The separation of children on grounds of intelligence results in the creation of distinct social groups with clear concepts as to where they stand in the stratification system within the school.

The fourth hypothesis stated that there are no differences in rates of admission to delinquency between children from certain socially different and distinctive areas, irrespective of the social-class differences between their families. This hypothesis had to be rejected as well. Again, the evidence for rejecting the null hypothesis was not as imposing as that collected for the test of the hypothesis on the social class of the family itself.

The total number of significant differences by area was the same as the number of significant differences by type of school. The differences by type of school, however, were equally divided between the classes while the area differences held more for the working class (24 compared with 16). Also a few of the differences by area were not in the expected direction while all but one of the differences by type of school were. So the area influence is considered to be less strong than that of school, as well as of the social class of the home.

The area factor could not really be adequately studied within the framework of this survey, and probably cannot be in Britain at the present time, given any research design and any amount of funds. Authorities with access to subjects are still prone to refuse permission for the relevant questions to be asked. So the researcher must use what areas admit him, rather than choose his areas randomly or by any other method.

The range of areas obtained for this study, in terms of social-class composition, was extremely good. However, in view of the small number of areas and lack of choice in obtaining them, much caution must be exercised in formulating conclusions. Significant differences by area were found for the four areas included in this study. But this information could not be used to estimate how widespread differences by area are, or within what range they should be in other regions or cities.

The second part of the study involved a testing of two of the hypotheses, on social class and school type, with data on official delinquency. The findings were broadly the same as for the tests on admitted delinquency. However, there were points at which specific findings differed and these will be dealt with later.

The correlation of numbers of working-class boys per school and numbers of court appearances per school was extremely high; it explained 87 per cent of the variation. As in the admitted delinquency survey the simple social-class variable, father's occupation, was the variable most associated with rates of delinquency. And, as in the study of admitted delinquency, the data consistently pointed to this conclusion. The social-class variable stood above the others in the strength and consistency of its association with the delinquency variable.

The findings on admitted and official delinquency were found to be discrepant on minor points, for example when the specific types of delinquency were considered. In the admitted sphere the damage and violence categories were more strongly associated with the social-class variable than any other type of delinquency. Yet in the sphere of official delinquency the damage and violence items were associated to only the same degree as the theft items. However, for both official and admitted delinquency the association between class and delinquency was lower when only theft was considered than when total offences were.

There is one further point on which the findings at the two levels of delinquency differ. At the level of admitted delinquency the differences in rates of delinquency by school type were marked and significant when the social-class variable was controlled. This was not so for official delinquency. When the social-class variable was introduced into the regression, before the school-type variable, the proportion of explained variation was 0·87 (for total offences). When the school-type variable was introduced the proportion increased to only 0·88.

However, a simple regression of the rates of court appearances on to the school-type variable produced a very high and significant correlation. (For total court appearances $r^2 = 0·61$.) So it is correct to say that type of school is associated with rates of delinquency even in the official sphere. But it is not so important a variable as social class itself. It cannot add to the explanation of variation and in fact the social-class variable itself can explain any variation that type of school can, and more as well.

This interpretation has broader implications. It is suggested that type of school should be considered a part of the social-class variable rather than as an independent dimension. The reasons for this with respect to the sphere of official delinquency have been stated. It is slightly more difficult to make an effective case for this in the sphere of admitted delinquency.[93] The items for which significant differences by type of school were found tended to be the same ones for which differences by social class had already been found. And the items for which type of school was not a significant factor tended to not be associated with social class either.

The type of school attended serves to intensify the experiences and attitudes that are already affected by social class – deferred gratification and use of leisure time for example. The grammar school makes all its pupils more middle class in these respects and the secondary modern makes all its pupils more working class.

These processes will, it only follows, serve to mute differences between groups under cross-pressure. That is, middle-class boys at secondary modern schools will become more like working-class boys at grammar schools. So a large group of boys under these cross-pressures could accumulate in the centre of the distribution. But at the same time the boys at the extremes of the distribution would be pushed further out. The middle-class boy at grammar school would become more the subject-minded individualist thinking of higher education and a career, while the working-

[93] A more detailed discussion of this can be found in Chapter IV, page 109.

class boy at a modern school would become more the impulsive carefree delinquent that the literature depicts him. In short, boys of the different schools would become further differentiated from each other, but – and this is the key point – on lines on which the social classes have already been shown to be different.

The Survey Findings and Etiological Theory

Comparison of the strength of the three main social variables produced results which can be used to comment on certain etiological theories. The research was not designed to explicitly test any of these theories. More preliminary work on the distribution of delinquency and the relationship between different kinds and levels of delinquency was needed first. However, the information obtained can be used to reflect on the plausibility of the theories. While it cannot be used to assert, for example, that theory A is hereby verified and all others disconfirmed, it can be used to say that the findings are consistent with theories A, B, and C, but not with D, E or F. For example, if the area and school influence were very important but the social class of the family were not it would appear that the important delinquency causative factors lay in the peer group or in opportunities for committing delinquency. One would conclude that family interaction, parental norms and models were unimportant. The crucial period for delinquency causation would be later childhood and early adolescence, when the child is more exposed to the influence of the neighbourhood and the parents' influence is consequently mitigated by these other pressures.

However, the findings were that the social class of the family is the most important variable, more important than the type of school attended, stream or area. Precisely which aspects – whether parental example, the methods of inculcating morals in the child, the parents' norms themselves, or something else – cannot be determined at this stage. But the results do give clear indications of the more and less fruitful avenues for future investigation.

The data can be used as well to comment on what kind of social-class model is the most appropriate one. The rates of admission increased as the social-class level decreased. It is not just that the lowest class behaved differently from the rest of the society but that each level could be distinguished from the other in respect of delinquency admissions. Perhaps in the future differences between the three higher classes will disappear, leaving the boundary between these three and the bottom one the only important distinction. There is some indication that this is happening with respect to the attainment of grammar school places. Upper working-class children obtain the number of places proportionate to their numbers in the population. Middle-class children obtain more than their share and lower working-class children considerably fewer. But the main difference now is between the lowest group and the rest of the population.

Such a trend is nowhere in evidence in respect of delinquency admissions and court appearances. The differences between all four classes are equally strong. It is not that some kind of slum culture is present, or that the unskilled and insecure section of the population is distinguishable from the rest. Rather the model of society that seems most appropriate is a more traditional one, with four distinct strata. There may be important changes in the class system in the next decade, and certainly should be in the next generation. If the comprehensive system accomplishes even part of what it is intended to there will be, but probably not until a number of children have gone through the system and themselves have become adults.

The findings of no association between certain variables and delinquency rates can also be used to comment on the etiological theories based on those variables. (A finding of no association is of course always an equivocal finding. One can criticize it on the grounds that the variable was measured badly or that the wrong indicator was chosen.)

The study obtained information on a number of variables used in a range of etiological theories and hypotheses. These factors, listed below, failed to show any significant association with delinquency admission rates:

> broken home
> mother working
> number of brothers and sisters
> birth order
> part-time job
> youth club membership
> religion
> church attendance

CONCLUSIONS AND SOME IMPLICATIONS

These negative findings disconfirm several of the older, and now less popular, hypotheses about delinquency causation: the working mother and the broken home. Similarly disconfirmed is an even less sophisticated, old explanation, that the lack of con-constructive pursuits (such as a job or organized activities) forces adolescents into delinquency. Hypotheses based on religious influences, either the kind of religion or the extent of commitment as measured by attendance, also are disconfirmed. Religious commitment may well affect delinquency, but the indicator used to measure it in this survey did not reveal it.

While social class was the most consistently active variable it cannot be relied upon exclusively in any theory. On the evidence presented here both type of school attended and stream must be made part of the explanation. It has been suggested throughout that the operation of these variables is probably similar to that of social class. That is, it is not intelligence or any academic aspect of education that is so important but the social consequences of being defined a failure. The everyday fact of being low status in the sphere of education works in the same way that it does in society at large.

The anomie school of explanation clearly can account for this set of findings. The fact of social class and the school variables all being important (and the area factor being somewhat less important) is consistent with this theory. However, the main competitor with the anomie school, the working-class culture explanation, is also consistent with these findings. The cultural explanation actually requires some modification, but the modification respects the fundamentals of the idea. That is, the explanation must emphasize the culture of the school and classroom as agents in disseminating delinquent ideas and techniques rather than the neighbourhood. Instead of a neighbourhood gang being the focus the school or class group would play this role.

The findings did not help to solve this main theoretical dispute in the field. They demonstrated that several of the simple, single cause hypotheses which are still discussed in the literature are not supported. The study has shown what variables are associated with delinquency and in what direction these should be further explored.

CONCLUSIONS AND SOME IMPLICATIONS

Implications for Policy-making

The material collected in this piece of research is relevant to a number of practical problems. The research was not undertaken as an 'applied' project, but numerous of its findings have very obvious implications for practice. The more obvious of these have been discussed in the course of presenting findings. Now they are to be treated explicitly in reference to policy-making.

Education has been selected for emphasis here for various reasons. Its sheer importance as a variable influencing delinquency is one. The second reason for the focus on it is that the policy issues involved are particularly crucial at this period of time. The government is now engaged in the process of making profound changes in the system. These changes are based on a knowledge of the social-class structure and a desire to change it. The intention is to alter the class structure of the nation at large by changing the structure of the school system.

Of course there are economic reasons for the changes in the education system as well as those based on social philosophy. The need for upgrading the skills of the labour force at all levels is recognized. Certain of the contemplated changes can be attributed to this motive rather than, or in addition to, the motive of social change.

Yet despite the importance of these issues the changes being made have not been adequately thought out or researched. Insufficient attention has been paid to the possible adverse results of change. Very likely some of the changes being made will subsequently be found to not be improvements at all, and some will be found to be detrimental.

Good intentions and the approach of the reasonable man are insufficient at this time. What appears to be reasonable on paper may not prove to be that in practice. For example, what appears on paper as a comprehensive school may be administered more rigidly, and be more inhibiting to the average and below average pupil, than the secondary modern it replaced.

The problem with the approach of the reasonable man, the wise administrator or the Royal Commission is that it can easily be wrong. There was a time when the most learned people believe that the world was flat. Such learned people were mistaken. Most learned people are mistaken about some matters and the field of education is no exception.

Beliefs about the streaming system provide one example of very widely and firmly held opinions being quite out of touch with the real world. Empirical evidence on the effects of streaming is equivocal. Some studies show it helps, some show it harms the worse pupils and fails to help the brighter, some show it makes no difference at all.[94] Yet the vast majority of teachers and administrators believe it produces benefits for all levels of ability.[95] Many believe it would be impossible to run a school without a streaming system.

The connection between social class and education is clearly acknowledged by the bodies involved in educational change. Yet how the school system can be utilized as a means of change is not at all well understood. It is possible to discover this although the difficulties to be overcome are substantial. This can only be done through a process of experimentation, evaluation, revision of plans and further experiment.

The question as to the method of introducing change is perhaps as important for discussion here as the nature of the changes recommended. If decision-makers employ the wrong methods for reaching decisions, barring a ceaseless flow of good luck, they will usually arrive at the wrong decision, or at least fail to reach the best ones.

Attention to research findings, particularly evaluative studies, should play a much larger part in the decisions top policy-makers make. It is inconceivable that all the guesswork can be taken out of decision-making. And given the present stage of research in the field of education there is still a lot unknown on most questions. But there is no need to repeat the obvious mistakes of previous attempts.

Two kinds of decisions have to be made: the ends to be reached and the means to be employed. The empirical investigator as such has nothing to say on what the ends should be. But he can say

[94] Alfred Yates, ed. *Grouping in Education*. New York: John Wiley, 1966. Isobel Pfeiffer. 'Teaching Ability Grouped Classes.' *Education*, v. 87, 1966, p. 88.

[95] J. C. Daniels. 'The effects of streaming in the primary school. 1: What teachers believe.' *British Journal of Educational Psychology*, v. 31, 1961, p. 69.

much concerning how well any particular method is doing in reaching those goals. He can comment on the feasibility of any projected methods and evaluate the efficacy of current methods. Given agreement on the ends to be reached, choices, made after reference to empirical investigation, could be narrowed down and the worst mistakes avoided.

This presupposes that people familiar with empirical inquiry will be making the important decisions, or at least will be relied on extensively for advice. Unless that is the case there can be no hope for effective lasting changes throughout the system. What is required is not the rapid implementation of changes, even if substantial, but an ongoing approach of implementing change when shown to be desirable on the basis of empirical evidence.

What is needed is an empirical mentality on the part of administrators. It is now becoming widely admitted that the day of the gifted amateur has passed. Yet there is no consensus as to what type of professional ought to replace him. (And in many places of course the gifted amateur remains as powerful as ever.) To the writer it does not matter what kind of academic background or experience the decision-maker has, so much as to what extent he works within an empirical frame of reference. That is, a social scientist of any field would be preferred to a clinical psychologist or teacher no matter how skilled, successful or experienced with schools and children the latter might be.

This empirical approach assumes that there is substantial agreement on the goals to be reached. Such an assumption may not be valid at the present time in Britain. If so it is quite a distinct problem, and will not be dealt with at length here. For example, criticism of certain methods used in comprehensive schools may be motivated more by disapproval of the goal of comprehensive education (a more egalitarian society) than by disapproval of the method itself. Some middle-class parents are opposed to comprehensive schools because they do not want to see their children mix with the secondary modern type children at the same school. Certain teachers are opposed because they do not consider it possible to give as good an education 'to those who deserve it' at a comprehensive as at a grammar school. Some are opposed to them on the grounds that they are too competitive for the poorer students, and actually do them more harm than the modern school did. Some are opposed because they are more costly than the sparsely equipped secondary modern. Thus there are objections on many, conflicting, grounds: economic self-interest, social self-interest, pedagogical principles and humanitarianism.

The issues are confused ones, but can be sorted out. The writer would like to see a more egalitarian society, one which makes a concerted effort to provide opportunity to the disadvantaged, and which avoids distributing the reward of moral worthiness on the basis of status. The recommendations related below are directed to that end. While there may be no firm consensus on that in British society such is the official policy and it is therefore appropriate to work within that frame of reference.

Recommended Changes

Teaching the teachers

Changes in teacher training are given highest priority here. Changes in the structure of the system (the introduction of comprehensives for example) are also extremely important – and to some would be considered even more important than teacher training. However it was thought that structural changes would never be successfully implemented without prior and extensive changes in the knowledge and attitudes of the teachers and administrators who would work within any new system.

Teacher-training institutions should attempt to inculcate into teachers certain values and attitudes different from those presently espoused. It is the writer's opinion that potential teachers who are in extreme disagreement with these ideas should not be allowed into the profession, this screening to take place at the training stage.

Screening on grounds of values and attitudes is done in all professions to some degree. It is done in the teaching profession as well; the change recommended here concerns the content of such values. Certain attitudes now widely held are extremely detrimental to the effective teaching of a good range of children who are average or below average in IQ and social status. Material should be introduced showing that such children can learn, given certain conditions, which include the set of teachers' attitudes and concepts.

Social work students who believe that people cannot change are normally screened out of the social work profession. Similarly people who hate children are generally not accepted into the teaching profession. People who believe that schools and teachers are ineffective agents of education are normally kept out of it also. (Occasionally teachers acquire that belief after joining the profession – which is more difficult to deal with.)

The screening principle should be extended.[96] Potential teachers who believe that lower working-class children are ineducable should not be allowed to teach lower working-class children. We concede that there is evidence that lower working-class children are less educable than middle-class or upper working-class children *with the present methods of teaching.* Yet such evidence does not justify abandoning the lower working-class child. It might even be thought to point to experimentation to develop better ways of teaching him.

Teachers at all levels should be taught some sociology of education as well as the psychology, philosophy and history of education. Teachers must become aware of the range of variables other than IQ that affect scholastic performance. Here there is a glaring gap between the state of knowledge in the field and the knowledge that is communicated to the teachers.

Teachers are gradually becoming cognizant of the role of low social class in impeding learning in the school setting. But for the most part they are not aware of the possibilities of overcoming class obstacles. Rather they use the disadvantage of low social class as a rationalization for the child's poor performance at school. Thus they can slough off any responsibility for that child's failure. It was not that the school failed to teach him, but that his social class background made it impossible for him to learn, and concomitantly, for the school to teach him.

Experiments which have been successful in teaching lower working-class children indicate that radically different methods arc required. One very good example is Holbrook's experiment in teaching creative writing to a secondary modern third year C stream.[97] He took a highly permissive, encouraging approach to

[96] Some will call this recommendation unrealistic as there is a teacher shortage at present. However, the numbers that would be lost by more thorough screening would be replaced by others (attracted by the other changes in the profession recommended further below) who would not otherwise have considered becoming teachers.

[97] David Holbrook. *English for the Rejected.* Cambridge University Press, 1964.

his pupils. Every composition they did was marked 'good', or 'excellent!' and remarks of praise were liberally strewed throughout. There were no corrections for spelling, grammar or style. Holbrook encouraged the children to ask how to spell a word they did not know before they wrote it, so that he could prevent their making a mistake. Frequently he would edit their compositions, type them with correct spellings and a few other improvements and run them off on a mimeograph machine. Then the children could see their own work, in its most presentable form, and actually be proud of it.

Very few of his pupils failed to show some ability. Some wrote good dialogue, some wrote good description, some were able to convey the deepest emotions on paper and some produced elegant fantasies. Most of these pupils previously would not have been able to write a simple letter in response to an advertisement. This amount of change took place within one school year. With three or more years of such experience probably most of the children would be able to write fluently and correctly without editing.

Note that the principles involved in this approach are diametrically opposed to those employed by most teachers at the secondary level. Holbrook considered that the ban on giving negative criticism to the children was essential. The children had received so much negative criticism for so long that they gave up very easily. Yet many teachers would consider it a neglect of duty to fail to inform a pupil of his errors. Some teachers would consider it dishonest to tell a pupil a poor composition was good. (This can be rationalized in that the composition is good under the circumstances.)

It would require special training for teachers to learn new approaches such as the one outlined above. And it would certainly require a fundamental change of attitude to the pupil for the method to be successful. Concepts of the role of the pupil and the teacher in the education process both must change. The teacher must be motivated to achieve learning on the part of the child, by any means legal and decent. The teacher must become the initiator and at least temporarily the more active partner. As a result of this nourishment the pupil would eventually learn to play a more dynamic part in the process of his own education.

This approach already has a derogatory name: spoonfeeding. However the unpopularity of this approach is based on a distortion of certain moral principles, of dubious value in any event, and not on empirical evidence. The protestant ethic demands that one work and succeed. The pupil who does not work does not succeed and the pupil who has not succeeded probably is lazy. The pupil who does not work does not deserve the teacher's efforts (after all, the teacher works hard). So it follows that the pupil who does not succeed does not deserve the teacher's efforts.

But perhaps the original process is incorrect. Perhaps instead it is that the pupil who does not succeed does not work. Perhaps by making very early and very hasty decisions about the child's success or failure at school, the school, for those who fail, lowers motivation for work. Perhaps some enlightened form of spoonfeeding on the part of teachers instead of destroying the child's initiative would, with other measures, begin to restore it.

Motivation is influenced by various factors, including competition and previous success. A factor which would enhance motivation for a child with certain characteristics would decrease it for others. Increased competition for a child with a strong fear of failure would lessen his motivation to achieve; for a child without a strong fear of failure it would increase it.[98]

Whether or not spoonfeeding is desirable is an empirical question. If children learn more with such an approach it should be widely used. If they do not then it is all right to denigrate the idea, but on empirical evidence, not principle. Possibly the less intelligent children would learn more rapidly with such an approach while the brighter would learn less rapidly or at just the same rate as with the present methods.

Research can be done to find out what sort of child is best taught at what sort of school with what sort of methods and what sort of teacher. The research techniques involved are not complex or difficult in any way. There is no lack of knowledge as to how to conduct this kind of research, but a mentality prevails which is reluctant to set up the research and apply the results.[99]

Teaching involves a set of relationships: teacher-pupil and inter-pupil. Personality as well as ability levels affect these relationships. There is probably no one correct type of personality

[98] J. W. Atkinson, and N. T. Feather, eds. *A Theory of Achievement Motivation.* New York: John Wiley, 1966.

[99] For a good discussion of evaluative research on subjects of this kind see L. T. Wilkins. *Social Deviance.* London: Tavistock, 1964.

or one correct style for effective teaching. Certain children will learn faster with certain kinds of teachers and approaches and other children will do better with different teachers and styles. Research in the United States on this has shown that the various combinations of personality, style and ability level do produce different results and undoubtedly the same principle applies here.[100] The point is that research should be done here to find out specifically what combinations of ability level, personality and interests are most effective. This information should then be used to bring together those combinations.

The principle of using different methods with different children has been developed for use with children in the primary years who have particularly great problems. Known as 'prescriptive teaching' this involves the diagnosis of the child's difficulty by a clinician, usually a psychologist who is also knowledgeable about teaching or a group, for example, composed of the principal, clinician and a social worker. The clinician or group recommends a certain approach to the child's classroom teacher. The work with the child is done in the regular classroom with the regular teacher.

Employment of such techniques as prescriptive teaching requires further training of the appropriate teachers and clinicians. These techniques should be taught at the training colleges and institutes of education so that the next generation of teachers has an adequate repertoire of methods to use, and should be taught to present teachers who wish to try the new methods. These more varied work opportunities in the teaching profession would in time affect the pattern of recruitment. For example persons with a social science background and an interest in the particularly social aspects of teaching, who would not now be attracted to teaching, would with such increased scope.

The language and concepts of teaching

The greater emphasis on experimentation and the broadening of the sphere of education to include more of the social aspects should result in a rethinking of some of the fundamental concepts in the field. One cannot expect breakthroughs in the practice of teaching without breakthroughs in concepts. New concepts of

[100] Alfred Yates, ed. *Grouping in Education.* New York: John Wiley, 1966.

course must be tested in the classroom and evaluated. And so a process of interchange between practice and theory develops.

Concepts are useful because they subsume a number of observations and interpretations into one economical work. The price that is paid for this economy is that the assumptions involved become accepted as they are. They become 'the truth' and therefore need no longer be questioned. 'Ability level' is a useful concept, but has been badly over-used and flagrantly abused. It implies correctly and precisely measured levels of ability which require different kinds and levels of teaching. Use of the term blinds the user to the amount of error incumbent in measuring this host of attributes. As well it obscures the disagreement as to what constitutes ability anyway.

Concepts in the field of mental health are presently going through a stage of vigorous challenge by social scientists. This includes the most basic ideas, such as the nature of schizophrenia, the neuroses and even the 'illness' model of mental 'illness' itself. It is far too early yet to know how treatment results will be affected, but certainly one cannot expect substantial improvements without new approaches.

Changes of the same depth and scope are needed in the field of education. Bernstein's theory of language codes is the only example in the field of education known to the writer of the kind of rethinking that is advocated.[101] As well it applies to a significant proportion of the children who are problems at school. It is a highly imaginative challenge to the conventional wisdom.

There are numerous other aspects of education that should be subjected to the same fundamental re-examination. Several hypotheses are offered below. These ideas have not been thoroughly worked out (certainly not researched) and are intended to serve, in their present form, only as examples.

The role of the failure

Under achievement (meaning achievement at a level below that expected for the IQ) is a role a child plays in interaction with other people: his parents, siblings, teachers and peers. It is not that some kind of emotional block prevents him from learning but

[101] Basil Bernstein. 'A Public Language; Some Sociological Implications of a Linguistic Form.' *British Journal of Sociology*, v. 10, 1959, p. 311.

that he has learned to live in the role of a failure. It is functional for him. It protects him from the recurrence of what he perceives as more distressing events than nonfailure situations. When he plays the failure role the behaviour of the other people with whom he interacts is predictable. He knows how to respond; he can cope with life in that role. To assume another role would be very difficult, and would certainly disappoint all those who are counting on him to fail again.

To change this situation, that is to make a success out of such a child, one would first have to examine all aspects of this ongoing interaction, including the parts played by the parents and the teacher, and then deal with one or more of these relationships. Of course it would be far simpler to diagnose some neurotic difficulty which required individual therapy (preferably in a clinic removed from both home and school) than begin to involve parents and teachers in therapy.

This analysis applies to only a minority of children, and mainly to middle-class children. Working-class children from families which place a high value on education would also be included. For both classes of course the hypothesis refers only to those achieving at a level below that expected for the IQ. Bernstein's theory, as it applies to the whole normal population of lower working class or working-class people is relevant to a much larger group.

The ineducable majority

It is very curious and disturbing to the writer that the British population should define failure as the normal course of events for the majority of the population. (The British are not the only people to do this, but they stand in sharp contradiction to North America in this respect.) Most children are not in A streams or grammar schools. The median child in the state sector of secondary education is in the B stream of a secondary modern. Yet curiously the secondary modern school is defined by most of the population as a place for failures, for the 'dim', for the ineducable. The majority of the secondary school age group attend such schools. According to most people's views then the average child is dim and ineducable.

Why do teachers have to define most of their pupils as failures? What benefit do they get from such a definition? One could postulate (not without difficulties that will immediately become apparent) that teachers as a group have a vested interest in producing failures – fewer people with whom to compete for middle-class status and the respect of society for educated, cultured people. On the other hand there are some teachers who have a vested interest in the opposite, those whose income, prestige or promotions depend on a certain measured level of success. However far more are in the former position.

Doctors in most countries have a vested interest in keeping people sick. (The National Health list system reverses this in Britain.) Yet even where it is against their financial interests they work very hard to heal. Some would argue that the same is true for teachers. However here it is going to be suggested that the situations are not at all comparable. Children cannot choose their teacher as patients can their doctor. Teachers are not normally judged on their success in developing their pupils' abilities. In fact it has only been very recently that there have been any ways of evaluating teachers' performance – and these only roughly. Doctors on the other hand are evaluated extensively, throughout a long period of training, and less extensively throughout their practice. Doctors' worst mistakes result in deaths, not as easily concealed as school failures.

Most teachers realize that a well-educated population is desirable as such. In addition it produces benefits for them in greater productivity, and more support for some of their interests – the fine arts for example and general standards of law, order and respectability which they value. The point is that for most teachers there is a conflicting pressure – to produce failures. This is certainly not consciously discussed although there are manifestations of the attitude from time to time. Teachers are frank in conceding that certain of their pupils are considerably brighter or more gifted in some way than they are. Such discussion is usually marked by nervous laughter and comments about what their reaction would be should said child be running their city, country or school.

The idea that teachers are driven by such fear of competition to produce an inordinate number of failures at school is of course highly speculative. Yet until a better reason is advanced it deserves attention. It cannot be denied that there are an inordinate number of failures in the system, and that teachers accept that state of affairs as normal. Indeed at every attempt to provide more high level education to the mass of the population there have been many teachers who declared that the system was already scraping the bottom of the barrel. Should a lower intelligence range of the population be admitted to academic studies teachers would be faced with an impossible task and all academic standards would drop.

The role set of the C stream teacher merits particular study along the lines discussed above. It becomes obvious immediately that the role relationships of the C stream teacher pressure him to produce failures in the classroom. The sheer preponderance of relationships in which the other person would expect the teacher to have failing pupils lends weight to this hypothesis. The teacher's college professors, headmaster, advisers or inspectors, friends, family and colleagues would all help him to fulfil the prophecy that C stream children fail.

Other conditions add to these personal influences: the teacher's paucity of training for teaching children of low social class, the less adequate facilities he is given and generally worse conditions under which he works with such children, and the lower rewards he receives for doing a good job, in comparison with those the teacher of a high stream receives.

Some teachers begin their professional training with high ideals; they will teach the more difficult secondary-modern children, and with sufficient effort, will be at least moderately successful. Most of such teachers eventually assimilate the majority point of view, that the great mass of such children are not educable. Or their concept of what constitutes success changes radically – to order in the classroom, decent social behaviour, and the exceptional pupil who shows enough promise to be promoted to academic work.

The process of losing ideals and accepting a cynical 'reality' deserves study. Presumably with an understanding of the process it would be possible to break into it at some point. The premise after all – that most children must be educational failures – is untrue and unnecessary.

There is a lot of material written in the United States on the problem of the difficult-to-educate child that is germane to the problem in Britain. A lot more experimentation in methods of teaching and types of school organization has been done in America than Britain. While the same faults of inadequate evaluation apply there is still a residue of properly researched projects for some conclusions to be made.

Comparison of the literature from the two societies yields several interesting observations. The descriptions of the children involved in the two societies sound like the same children. Whether they are called slum children, culturally deprived or disadvantaged, lower working-class, inner-city children, public language speakers, insecure working class, poor kids or ghetto children the same characteristics keep reappearing. What makes this important is the next observation – that the proportions of the population referred to are not at all similar. The American literature is primarily referring to the unskilled recently urbanized Negro minority, next to an unstable, multi-problem white population. Some reference is made to working-class persons more generally but far more often the problem is assumed to apply only to these two groups. In England of course even the average child is considered virtually ineducable.

The American literature expresses considerable optimism about solving this problem. It is seen as a highly undesirable and unnecessary result of certain conditions of American life. All that is required is more know-how, funds and effort. Such an attitude is not at all evident in Britain. Poor academic achievement is not considered a difficult problem to solve but a fact of life to be accepted. Rather than face the problem and develop ways of teaching these children it was decided that such children should have their school days filled with noneducational activities – and not be allowed to interfere with the education of the capable few. Thus citizenship training, games, arts and crafts and any subject with a practical bent became the natural curriculum for the average child.

About the only encouragement that can be derived from this comparison is that many of the research findings, ideas and information about the problem are probably exchangeable. Neither society need make all of its educational mistakes independently. Each can profit from the other's experience.

The reversal of cause and effect

One of the most dangerous tendencies in the field of education is the reversal of cause and effect, which itself is a special case of a more general dangerous tendency, the erroneous assessment of cause. The danger involved is that if the cause of a problem is incorrectly assessed probably the means employed to improve the situation will be wrong too.

Numerous problems might be thought to be the cause of low achievement on the part of the pupil:

old and over-crowded facilities

inadequately-trained teachers

poor curriculum

psychological problems of pupils

poor health of pupils

demoralizing effect of mixing with brighter pupils

demoralizing effect of being isolated from brighter pupils

Depending on what is thought to be the cause, the action taken might be to:

build new buildings

build more training colleges and expand university departments

hire experts on curriculum

hire doctors and expand the school meals service

separate children of different ability levels as much as possible

avoid such separation

Clearly the solutions possible differ enormously from each other and if the wrong ones are chosen the problem will remain, and possibly become worse.

In some cases the action taken may actually engender more of the problems it was intended to solve. It is suggested that that is one way of looking at the tripartite system. The official point of view would explain that certain children (in fact the majority) did not have sufficient ability or interest for an academic education. Therefore, they were separated from those who did so that they could be taught at their own speed and with methods especially devised to suit them. It is now becoming more and more apparent that the cause has been confused with the effect. Children become incapable of academic education as a result of being denied it. They lose interest in it as a result of being told they cannot have it and being separated from those who do. This is of course an oversimplification; other factors such as family aspirations are important too, but the element of the self-fulfilling prophecy is very strong.

CONCLUSIONS AND SOME IMPLICATIONS

The irrelevance of research

Educational research now has sufficient prestige for it to be accorded polite references. Like the plea for more facilities for handicapped children and more tolerance between the races respectable people agree that educational research is good and there should be more of it. But it is often not relevant to their system, their school, or their methods. The paucity of grants for educational research in relation to the need, and even more so the failure to implement research findings when they are available, demonstrate that educational research is not yet taken seriously. Also research that is offered to the education system free of charge is often declined. Graduate students, for example, with outside grants in support of their projects, are frequently refused permission to do research in the schools. Research at that level is of course not an adequate substitute for well-funded extensive studies. However, the plea for more research money would sound more genuine if the available research were fully made use of.

Research needs will not be discussed here as a separate subject because, as previous discussion should have made clear, research is not here conceived of as a separate entity. If the educational system is to become and then continue to be as effective as possible research must be built into the system. Research findings must be consulted at every level of decision-making – changes in teacher training, administration and school structure.

The inevitability of rigid stratification

A very widespread belief amongst teachers is that a school cannot be run without streaming. The only exception would be a school with a pupil population too small for division of any kind. Unfortunately this belief is widely held by teachers in comprehensive schools as well as grammar and secondary moderns. Opinions about this are typically asserted in no uncertain terms, often with no documentation at all; streaming is natural and self-evident so no justification for it need be offered.

The following illustration, which comes from a report written by teachers in comprehensive schools, is representative of official policy as well as informal opinion.

'On the first morning of the new school-year a comprehensive has to deal with its new pupils and divide them into teaching units. . . . If selection has not already been made on previous tests, selection

184

must begin now. . . . When the results of the eleven-plus examination are available for guidance, schools are grateful. In fact, more than one school is of the opinion that if they were not available, the staff would have to devise one of their own for the same purpose. Certainly, eleven-plus selection is unavoidable. . . . Everywhere the need for careful selection is realised and great care is taken so that each child can start in the right group.'[102]

When reasons for streaming are supplied at all by defenders of the system they usually consist of 'personal experience' and anecdotes. Proof by personal experience is of course highly suspect because the self-fulfilling prophecy operates here. It is inevitable that the top streams, when given the most and best in pupil intelligence, teaching ability and experience, facilities, stimulation, prestige and rewards, will do substantially better than the low streams.

Streaming in comprehensives seems progressive because the total effect is more flexible than the previous system. There are more transfers between the ability levels in comprehensive schools than in the other system. There is more opportunity for the late developer to show his ability in even a thoroughly streamed comprehensive than when pupils are divided into physically separate buildings and different administrative units. However, that does not necessarily mean that the streaming system as it presently operates is good, or that it is as good as it could be. It may merely indicate that the previous system was abysmally bad.[103]

Research findings on the effect of streaming are equivocal, except that they do point to the self-fulfilling tendency of the system.[104] There is no consistent evidence that streaming either promotes or hinders the progress of the pupils of any ability level. This has been found in other societies that use variants of the

[102] Incorporated Association of Assistant Masters in Secondary Schools. *Teaching in Comprehensive Schools, a second report*. Cambridge University Press, 1960, pp. 14 and 15.

[103] Much of the praise for the tripartite system can be treated analogously. The 1944 Education Act did mark the end of selection on the basis of parental income. However, almost any new system, no matter how mistaken its assumptions, would seem good in comparison.

[104] Alfred Yates, ed. *Grouping in Education*. New York: John Wiley, 1966. J. W. B. Douglas *et al*. 'Delinquency and Social Class.' *British Journal of Criminology*, v. 6, 1966, p. 294.

streaming system as well as in Britain. Certainly there has been no substantiation for the claim often made by teachers in defence of the system that it helps and protects the lower ability groups. However much it does help them by separating them from the stiffer competition it also deprives them of the stimulation and contribution of the brighter group. At the present time the research evidence runs somewhat against streaming, as harmful especially to the low ability groups, and not particularly helpful to the brighter groups.[105] An extensive study of this in Britain is currently being made by the National Foundation for Education Research. Its findings may serve to resolve some of the contradictions which now dominate any discussion of the topic.

Some of the research findings already available indicate that some of the bases on which grouping decisions are made may be mistaken. For example one American study of streaming at the junior school level found that teachers were more effective teaching one or two subjects to pupils of varied ability, than teaching several different subjects to even a narrow ability range or stream.[106] This may not be true of teachers in Britain, but as it has such important implications for practice one should not simply assume that it does not apply. The finding is markedly contrary to the convictions of most teachers. The rationale for streaming, setting and dividing pupils into different schools and classrooms is of course that more effective teaching can be gained.

The Crowther Report's discussion of the tripartite system provides another example of the inevitability of stratification mentality. It mentions – as a deficiency in the systems – that there was found to be considerable overlap in ability levels, and therefore educational requirements, between the children in grammar and modern schools. There was far more than anticipated when the system was inaugurated. In fact there was so much more that the solution of transferring individual children from the modern to the grammar or the contrary was not practicable. Consequently Crowther recommended that there be courses in the modern schools for those more able. Thus instead of transferring individuals there would be in a sense a transfer of courses.

[105] Alfred Yates, ed. *Grouping in Education*. New York: John Wiley, 1966.
[106] M. L. Goldberg *et al*. *The Effects of Ability Grouping*. New York: Teachers College Press, 1966.

CONCLUSIONS AND SOME IMPLICATIONS

This state of affairs is mentioned in the Report with little apparent awareness of the enormity of the revelation. The founders of the tripartite system really believed that there were three types of child – with three different abilities, aspirations, interests, and schooling requirements. The system subsequently exerted every effort it could to produce these three distinct varieties, but there are limits even to the self-fulfilling prophecy. And in 1959 it did not yet appear extraordinary that the three distinct types did not materialize, that there were many pupils who did not fit the system. The possibility that the whole system was based on mistaken notions was not entertained.

However the tripartite system is on the way out and new problems have arrived. The comprehensive school is gradually taking its place, with local authorities having the power to decide what brand of comprehensive they want.

To this writer there is no doubt but that many of the new structures will not be better than the old, and perhaps worse in some respects. One of the worst possible repercussions of the comprehensives, which was discussed in Chapter IV, is the fulfilment of the conditions for anomie.

School systems in other countries, Canada and even more so the United States for example, afford numerous examples of what not to do, as well as some good examples which are applicable to Britain. Yet many of the British comprehensives are adopting the worst features of the American high school. In the introduction of any new system some mistakes will be made, but these should be new, progressive mistakes that will eventually lead to further improvements. Remaking the mistakes of 20 years ago only brings one to the situation of 19 years ago.

The point is that it is possible to test the new structures on a small scale, before committing large sectors of the country to it. There are already a large variety of comprehensive schools in operation. Research could be done to find out which of them are most successful academically: in producing a high proportion of A levels for example. It is also important to find out which are successful with the average and below average pupils. The type of school that is most successful in producing A levels amongst the top minority might not be commensurately successful with the less able pupils, in increasing their reading or mathematics performance for example. And the converse may also be true. Should that be the case then a difficult policy decision has to be made. Whose interests should be sacrificed – the bright minority or the average majority. Perhaps it is more painful to have to make such a decision openly, but it is surely more fair. Honesty yields one other advantage for its pains. With the knowledge of the relative success patterns of the different types of comprehensive experimentation could begin to improve the schools in the areas in which they are found to be deficient.

Another very important question of structure concerns the method of streaming within schools. The comprehensive system will place a wider range of children both socially and academically within the same building. However, this affords no assurance that there will be significant interaction across the social class or achievement lines within the school or any opportunity for this. Neither is there any assurance that a climate more encouraging for learning will exist. The same spirit that produced the tripartite system and a rigid streaming system in the first place could produce the same effective separation and rejection within the comprehensive school.

The results of this survey showed that there were many significant differences between the streams in rates of admission to delinquency. And this occurred particularly in the grammar schools. Clearly the problem of dealing with the various ability levels is a complex and difficult one. No assumptions about the desirable structure for doing this should be made, rather considerable experimentation and evaluation of present methods should be accomplished first.

Research should also be made into the social aspects of life in the present comprehensives. A study of the delinquency rates in the various types of comprehensives would be one obvious test of the success of the comprehensive in reaching their espoused social goals. Studies of aspiration, political and social views, friendships across the social-class lines would all provide information as to the effect of the different kinds of comprehensives.

No specific recommendations as to what kind of comprehensive, what kind of courses to be offered, or what kind of classroom organization is most desirable will be offered here. The writer does not possess the knowledge or expertise necessary to make recommendations on such subjects. There are doubtless several equally effective ways of organizing secondary schools to meet the needs of the various ability levels and interests. There is no call here for uniformity throughout the country in methods or organization although there is a strong recommendation for uniformity of standards: high.

There are many advantages of decentralized authority. However, the present system takes little advantage of them, while it capitalizes on most of the disadvantages. There is a tradition of experimentation in all aspects of education in Britain, which is facilitated by the decentralization of authority. However, the results of the experiments are rarely properly evaluated. Usually they are reported somewhere in the educational press, with a description of the new approach being tried and a partisan account of its success. With adequate facilities for research and the dissemination of research results the whole country could benefit from the enterprise of any one area.

The science of learning

Virtually everyone in the education field would agree that teaching is an art, but not many would be equally aware that learning is a science. The success or failure of the art of teaching is measured by the extent of learning on the part of the pupil. At least no one would seriously suggest that a teacher whose pupils learned little was good, or that a teacher whose pupils did well was poor. A teacher's success in working his art depends on his knowing something of the science of learning. For the most effective practice of the art one must constantly adapt one's methods to make the most use of the science. And the science itself grows as research findings in the field accumulate.

More often than not this obvious relationship is ignored. The art is shrouded in mystery. Such intangibles as experience, the gift of teaching, a good teaching personality, and an intuitive grasp of teaching are made to be even more intangible. The outsider, the person who has never taught, cannot reasonably aspire to understand.

During the formal training period some emphasis is put on the scientific foundations of education. Yet the fact that very few teachers keep up with the science demonstrates that the connection between the art and the science is not regarded as important. It would be relatively easy to organize the dissemination of new findings and suggested application of them through refresher courses and publications.[107] That this is rarely attempted shows that there is little demand for such information. The publications in the field most widely read devote very little space to the subject.

It must be conceded here that psychology and sociology have not yet contributed very much that is directly applicable in the classroom. However, development in this field is taking place rapidly and it will not be long before much more specific recommendations for practice will come out of research. Unfortunately the means of substantially increasing this contribution will probably be strongly resisted, especially in the case of psychological research.

In order to measure learning it is necessary to break up the operations of teaching into very small steps. This requires, amongst other things, controlling for the teacher's personality and interaction with other pupils. Clearly at least some of this research will require machinery – which means teaching machines with elaborate feed-back equipment, a threatening prospect to the more traditionally oriented teachers. This whole area of relating the art and science will of course have to be re-examined from time to time as the science is better developed.

Implications for Treating Delinquency

Up to now discussion has centred on changes needed in the educational system. Now the discussion will be focused on the specific use of the education system in treating delinquency. If it were necessary to relate the previous discussion to delinquency it would have to be considered delinquency prevention; it is intended of course as much more than that. Now the discussion will turn to the treatment of children who have been detected as and adjudged delinquent. This involves only a minority of school children, although in some areas this would be a substantial minority. It is going to be suggested that the schools take on as one of their functions the treatment of delinquents. However, before explaining how this could be done some explanation as to why it should be done will be attempted.

---

[107] For a good discussion and recommendations as to how educational research could be organized from the national to the local level see Michael Young. *Innovation and Research in Education*. London: Routledge & Kegan Paul, 1965.

CONCLUSIONS AND SOME IMPLICATIONS

One of the most compelling reasons for utilizing the school system in the correction of delinquents is that the other methods presently in use are not very effective. The most commonly used treatment methods are social work in the form of probation, and institutional care. For juveniles the institutions are approved schools and borstals, both of which incorporate some social work principles and methods. Contrary to popular opinion there is no evidence that any of these three methods of treatment actually works. And this opinion is shared by most of the professional, experienced people in the field. Yet no studies have ever shown that applying any of these treatments results in less recidivism than applying no treatment at all to the offender. Neither have such methods of treatment been shown to have made any other significant improvements in the lives of the offenders.[108]

Most people are entirely unprepared for such findings. Yet this reaction itself is part of the tyranny of the helping professions. Good intentions are supposed to produce good results. If the personnel involved is well trained and experienced in addition to being well motivated, good results are taken for granted.

On deeper reflection it should be comprehensible why social work treatment methods are not very successful. Probation consists of counselling periods, of at best half an hour every fortnight, more in times of crisis, but less far more often. Yet the problem the social worker is dealing with stems from the offender's early childhood very often, and usually pervades his family and neighbourhood environments. Counselling of a juvenile offender cannot overcome the problems of an inadequate home, illiteracy, suspicion and hatred of authority. Counselling methods simply apply too little too late.

Institutional care is at least theoretically a more powerful tool for reform. The offender is under the influence of the method for all his waking hours for some months or years. However, the majority of the changes made are superficial. Cleanliness, order,

---

[108] L. T. Wilkins. 'A Comparative study of the result of probation.' *British Journal of Delinquency*, v. 8, 1958, p. 201. D. C. Gibbons. 'Comments on the Efficacy of Criminal Treatment.' *Canadian Journal of Corrections*, v. 2, 1960, p. 165. C. F. Jesness. *The Fricot Ranch Study.* California Department of Youth Authority Research Report no. 47, 1965. J. P. Seckel. *The Fremont Experiment.* California Department of Youth Authority Research Report no. 50, 1967.

and respect for the staff are stressed and achieved. Normally in approved schools and borstals the offender would not be released until he learned to comply with orders and say 'yes, sir' while doing it. Unfortunately, however, there does not seem to be any causal link between such superficial manifestations of obedience and law-abiding behaviour outside the institution.

Also while the institution has more opportunity to influence the offender to reform it has as well more impediments to reform embedded in its structure.[109] The offender is cut off from all the normal, law-abiding influences of his family and perhaps of friends. He is surrounded by other offenders; all his friends now are officially adjudicated delinquents, which delinquents do not choose when, as outside the institution, they have the choice.

It has been well documented over the last fifty years that certain attitudes and habits of the family are conducive to delinquency amongst the children. These are for the most part class-linked characteristics. Quite reasonably it has been thought that social work of some form with the family would be the best way to change these criminogenic factors. The methods of social work have changed over time but the principle has remained the same. And the principle does make sense. Yet it is the results which are important, not the principle. If a certain approach does not work one should begin to look for another no matter how reasonable it appears in theory.

In some areas an attempt has been made to prevent and control delinquency by changing neighbourhood influences, particularly the adolescent peer groups in the neighbourhood. This is a different approach from treating the individual or the family through counselling methods. Usually the focus is on the patterns of leisure-time use by the adolescent population. Recreational facilities are improved. Recreation personnel who have some social-work training and experience are brought in. Street workers are assigned directly to gangs which are not in any other contact with conforming society.

There have been some accounts of spectacular success with the use of detached workers, but also some equally spectacular stories of failure. Generally the projects have not been set up properly

[109] Erving Goffman. *Asylums*. Garden City, New York: Doubleday, 1961.

for evaluative research, even the very expensive and elaborate American projects. Thus no summary comment about their success or failure is possible.

Most of the other attempts to change neighbourhood influences through the peer group have been more manifestly unsuccessful.[110] Where such programmes have been researched it has been found that the delinquency rates were not affected at all. Neither was there any other kind of measurable improvement.

Upon eliminating the attempts to change the individual, the family and the neighbourhood through some form of social work we must turn to some new form. And here the school system poses itself again. The survey done by the writer showed admissions to delinquency and failure at school to be connected. This relationship will probably increase over time. Formerly a poor education meant very little to a working-class boy; he expected no better. Moreover he could obtain as good a job as his father without much education, which is no longer true.

The role of the school system in producing delinquency will probably then increase. Yet if this is correct it is likely that the potential role of the school in preventing and correcting delinquency will increase in proportion. It requires little imagination then to advocate using the school in treating delinquency. This idea is not at all new. It has been discussed for decades in the United States. There has even been some attempt to put it into practice.[111] Here it is suggested that attempts be made in Britain. They should follow the process of evaluation and revision (including abandonment of the idea) recommended above for the institution of any new idea.

The schools could be used for several purely educational programmes clearly needed by delinquent children. Remedial reading is the most obvious need, in terms of the number of people affected and the severity of the problem imposed by this handicap. The number of children in Britain – with normal intelligence – who cannot read must be staggering. The survey done for the

---

[110] W. E. Amos and C. F. Wellford. *Delinquency Prevention*. Englewood Cliffs, N.J.: Prentice-Hall, 1967.

[111] The Mobilization for Youth programme in New York City is a good example. It is comprised of many facets, including recreation, but is based primarily on increasing employment opportunities through education, which itself is broadly conceived of and includes many approaches.

Newsom Report found that for one quarter of the secondary moderns sampled the average reading level of their 15-year-olds was age 13 or lower.[112]

Another widespread need is that of programmes and space for assisting children with homework. These have been tried in many places in America, with success where well organized. The programmes require good volunteers and good supervision for them. With the tradition of voluntary service Britain has this would be one of the programmes most easily implemented. Those requiring vast increases in personnel at the professional level would be much more difficult to start.

These changes however could only be made in the context of an improved secondary-school environment. They presuppose some interest on the part of the children concerned, and some confidence that they will be rewarded for their efforts. Such an assumption could not properly be made at the present time in most high-delinquency areas.

As secondary schools are gradually better equipped they will become useful as community centres. Some already are used for sports, discussion groups, adult education, art and craft work and so forth. This facet of the school could then be used in correctional work, both for juveniles and adults. The connection between correctional work and community centres may not be an obvious one for many readers, but it will be in the future. Already more varied probation programmes are being developed, which employ 'constructive' outlets for leisure time. These are intended to fill the gap between the two extremes of institutionalization and probation supervision.

Such programmes satisfy society's demand 'that something be done with this child', yet they do not do too much. It is not yet known if these programmes do what they were intended to do – reduce recidivism. At worst they are safe programmes. It is highly unlikely that any of them would cause any harm to the children involved, as institutionalization can. It is unlikely that they would result in an increase in rates of recidivism, which institutionalization can do in certain instances. These programmes are attractive also in that they are much cheaper to run than institutional care

[112] Newsom Report. Ministry of Education, Central Advisory Council for Education (England). *Children and Their Primary Schools*. H.M.S.O., 1967, p. 119.

and probably not much more than probation. They clearly have potential and should be experimented with widely.

The school system is an appropriate place for society to intervene in respect of controlling delinquency. The school system itself is society's intervention in people's lives to make them the kind of citizens it wants. If this is acceptable then there can be no objection to the use of the school system in delinquency treatment. Using the schools to treat delinquents would require giving them no more power than they already have. (This is a lot of power and some would question the necessity for it; however, that is a separate question and will not be discussed here.)

The recommended use of schools in delinquency treatment is lower in priority than any of the other broad changes discussed above: teacher training, school structure, and incorporating research into policy-making of all kinds. Without change in the attitudes and concepts of teachers probably no effective programme for delinquents could be put into operation. And certain of the other recommended changes would increase the effectiveness of the delinquency programme, though they may not be essential to it.

Some Final Remarks and Prognosis

It is interesting that the changes recommended in the education system for social purposes (reducing delinquency and increasing opportunity) are also coming to be recognized as pedagogically worthwhile. The same changes that would have desirable effects in the social climate (at least to the writer) would also result in higher levels of academic performance.

The opposite could be the case. That is it might be necessary to sacrifice egalitarian goals in order to have a well-educated population, or to sacrifice educational standards to have a more egalitarian society. Such a situation would be difficult to work out. Unfortunately many people believe the conflict exists – that an egalitarian society and a well-educated one are mutually exclusive. And probably this belief impedes reform in the system.

There are now ways to overcome the problem of teaching the range of abilities without dividing and separating pupils and promoting misunderstanding across these divisions. Programmed instruction provides one answer, a far more elegant one than grouping by school or stream. It allows for the full range of ability levels to be served efficiently. No form of grouping can claim it caters to all ability levels as well as individualized instruction can. Schools and streams have attempted to form homogeneous groups (and over time do make their groups more homogeneous), but they still contain a wide range of ability within them.

Within the traditional frame of reference there are still other ways of coping with the range of ability. Grouping within the classroom is one which solves the problem apparently without producing others which are worse. This requires more skill on the part of the teacher, and, as always, a change in attitude. Training institutions are improving and the level of teacher training is rising. Thus it is not at all unreasonable to expect and require better teaching in the future.

The rigid structuring of ability levels between and within schools cannot be maintained on the grounds of the necessity of maintaining academic standards. There are other solutions available now and more will be developed as the need is recognized.

The problems presented in this chapter cannot be said to have been only recently discovered. Most have been known about for some time although many individual teachers and administrators would be unaware of various specific ones, and some would dispute the existence of others of them. Specific recommendations for policy have been made in other books. Young's *Innovation and Research in Education* makes the plea, eloquently and at great length, that it would be a good idea to innovate in education, but in relation to research knowledge.[113] Vaizey's *Education for Tomorrow* provides a good discussion of many of the basic issues and makes recommendations for reorganization.[114] The universities and institutes of education have personnel who do research and write about the problems involved, and who are competent to advise on reform. It is necessary then to ask why these most basic problems have not been acted upon.

It is always easier to leave a system as it is rather than change it, or make superficial changes rather than fundamental ones, but in

[113] Michael Young. *Innovation and Research in Education*. London: Routledge & Kegan Paul, 1965.

[114] John Vaizey. *Education for Tomorrow*. Harmondsworth: Penguin, 1967.

the case of education there are several other impediments to change as well. The status of teachers is related to the ability of the pupils and the level of sophistication of subject-matter they teach. A grammar-school teacher has more status than a secondary modern, a sixth form than a first form, and a high stream than a low stream. The comment is often made that 'there are C stream teachers as well as C stream children'. It is not intended as a compliment for the gift of teaching the less able children.

If a high status, 'A stream', teacher had his bright pupils taken away from him he would lose in status. Obviously he is not likely to favour changes in the system that would do this. Equally obviously the main recommendations made here involve threatening changes of that sort.

It might be thought that the teachers presently with lower status might favour the recommendations, as they have the chance of gaining in the shift. However, they have opportunities, as individuals, for gaining status within the system, by transferring upwards, which many of them do as soon as they can. For any individual it is easier to obtain a promotion within the existing structure than reform it. And of course once one has been promoted he has at least as much interest as the teacher who started off at the higher levels has in maintaining it.

Education in England has traditionally been more the preserve of the elite than it has been in other countries. Scotland, Wales, Canada and the United States would all contrast markedly with England in this respect. The composition of the educational elite has changed over time, from an aristocracy to what is succinctly described as a meritocracy. The criteria for joining the elite then has changed, but it is still necessary to belong to an elite in order to get an education even at the secondary level. The idea that large numbers of people can be well educated is entirely out of tune with the folklore on the subject at all levels of society.

With these difficulties in mind the writer is not optimistic that the very deep changes in mentality, empirical orientation and pragmatic continuous evaluation of programmes and structures will come into being. What then are the possibilities for change? Who are the best prospects for the role of instigators? Unfortunately no likely candidates immediately spring to mind, so the process of elimination will have to be relied upon to make any comment on this question.

CONCLUSIONS AND SOME IMPLICATIONS

The teaching profession at the present time cannot be expected to play any leading role here as it simply lacks commitment to the fundamental ideas recommended. Undoubtedly there are members who have the training and mentality to do the experimentation and evaluation necessary. Means could be devised to assure that such people were found, and then put into a position such that their talents could be used. With a more open and vigorous challenge to the conventional wisdom, to be advocated below, many of those presently unaware of the issues would become informed, and some would subscribe to the new mentality.

In the writer's opinion there is no lack of ability or dedication in the profession. With rare exception the teachers and heads met during the research appeared to be intelligent and concerned about the state of education. It did seem, however, that most were concerned about the wrong issues, for example with how selection should be made, not whether or not a selection and division system is advisable at all.

These teachers have learned what they have been formally taught, and what they have read in their field since. Indeed they could not have become teachers if they had not. Very few of them have been exposed to an orientation that would equip them to challenge the sacred wisdom of education.

The other obvious source to consider for leadership in innovation is the Department of Education. If there is not much hope that the profession will persuade the civil service that change is necessary, perhaps the civil service will inspire or commission the profession into action. The writer however holds little hope for this possibility. The Department has shown no initiative in relating innovation with research in the past, and has given no indication that it is about to adopt such a policy. It occasionally makes the appropriate utterances, but we are judging on performance. It was this department that must bear the responsibility for instituting the tripartite system: according to Vaizey it 'single-handedly imposed' it on the country.[115]

For any fundamental changes to be made in the system the civil service and the teaching profession must both be involved. The point is that it appears unlikely that either of these two

[115] John Vaizey. *The Economics of Education.* London: Faber & Faber, 1962, p. 105.

important, highly conservative, groups will actually take the initiative in working for change. Pressure for reform will then have to come from outside, from the political sphere possibly, and from the interested public, particularly parents. If the public refuses to be satisfied with assertions that all is well and requires proof the schools will have to provide such proof. They will be forced to turn to experimenters and researchers to provide them with the answers.

If a political party in office is firmly committed to improving the system it will make this known in some authoritative way to the professional civil service. Again the administrators involved will be forced to turn to the people who can demonstrate their effectiveness with more than anecdotes and the clichés of the conventional wisdom. When results are required that will be evaluated objectively it is no longer good enough to assert that the correct methods are being utilized by decent well-motivated administrators and teachers.

The discussion in this chapter has ranged far from that of the research carried out on the subject of delinquency. (For the reader who is interested only in the research findings the end to the discussion arrived half a chapter ago.) The education system was an obvious choice for emphasis. Its effect on delinquency has been clearly demonstrated in this study. Its relationship with the total social-class complex has been known for a long time. Many of the links between social class and delinquency clearly are made through the education system. And for purposes of applying corrective measures to delinquency the education system is of growing importance.

The tenor of the remarks in this last section has not been optimistic. The writer's expectations for substantial improvements in the education system are probably lower than those of most writers on the subject. They certainly are more pessimistic than the published remarks of the experts. Needless to say, the failure of the authorities to seriously deal with the more fundamental issues is regarded as a drastic mistake, with long-term repercussions.

The Plowden Report gives some cause for hope. In it most of the issues are discussed with at least some degree of empirical orientation. The recommendation of educational priority areas, as the most urgent concern, is commendable. The main criticism of this report that the writer would make is that it does not go far enough. It gives extensive documentation to the failings of the system, then calmly discusses relatively mild measures for reform. The reader might well ask how such measures could ever be expected to work, given that the system is as bad as the evidence presented has it. Highly incriminating facts are juxtaposed with other pieces of description, with little apparent awareness of their relative importance.

One short example will have to suffice. There is mention to the extent of one sentence that classrooms of C stream children more often are in annexes and other out of the way places than for higher stream children, and that these C stream classrooms significantly more often face north. Discrimination is so thorough that C stream children do not even get as much sunshine as A stream children.

To the writer it seems wrong and futile to seriously regard any advice from administrators and teachers who distribute children this way, and then affirm the benefits of streaming and point out that the case for unstreaming has not yet been substantiated. Moral indignation is conventionally toned down in reports of this kind, so was not expected in the Plowden Report. However, the writer would have been more optimistic had the deeper implications of certain of the findings been more carefully considered, and reflected in the recommendations.

The lack of optimism throughout the discussion in this chapter has not resulted in any modification of the criticism. The remarks could have been softened on the grounds that the more severe of them would not be considered anyway. Or they could have been overdrawn in the hope that with exaggeration they would shock the reader into paying attention. Rather the criticisms and recommendations have been made on the basis of the evidence it seemed proper and necessary to the writer to consult. The implications have been extended as far as deemed appropriate, which involved some restraint to the imagination. Necessarily some of the discussion has been highly speculative. The writer has attempted to note this where it occurs.

While the range of material introduced has been extensive, the framework for analysis has been extremely simple. The principle appealed to at all stages in this discussion of implications for policy-making has been that the basis for decision-making be experience, evaluated according to the best-known methods of the time, or, in other words, research. This will not guarantee success, but will keep the probability of it as high as possible at any time.

APPENDIX A

QUESTIONNAIRE

For your information this questionnaire is about what boys your age do in their leisure time, what they want to do in the future, and what they think about rules and discipline. From the answers the activities and ideas of British boys can be compared with those of boys in other countries, such as Canada and America. Many studies like this have already been done in Britain and America. In fact most of the questions have been asked in different places and schools, but the whole questionnaire has not been given together before. So it is very important that you answer *all* the questions. Your answers will be treated as strictly confidential. Your answers will not be given to your parents, teachers or anyone else. Do not put your name on the questionnaire.

1. Age .... years, ... months

2. Number of brothers: ....

3. Number of sisters: ....

4. Which are you in your family?
   an only child   ....
   the eldest-child   ....
   the youngest child   ....
   between the eldest and youngest child ....

5. With whom do you live?
   mother and father   ....
   mother only   ....
   father only   ....
   mother and stepfather ....

    father and stepmother ....
    foster parents   ....
    relatives   ....

6. Religion:
    Church of England ....
    Methodist   ....
    Presbyterian   ....
    Roman Catholic   ....
    Jewish   ....
    No Religion   ....
    Other (which one?) ....

7. How many times have you been to church or Sunday School
   in the last month?
    not at all   ....
    once   ....
    twice   ....
    three times   ....
    four times or more ....

8. Your form in school: .... Teacher's name: ....

9. At what age do you expect to leave full-time education?
    15   ....
    16   ....
    17   ....
    18   ....
    19   ....
    20 or over ....

10. In your last report were you in the top ten, bottom ten, or in
    between?
    top ten   ....
    bottom ten ....
    in between ....

11. Did your father leave school at age 14 or before, or at 15 or
    after?
    at 14 or before ....
    at 15 or after   ....

12. Did your father go to a university or college? yes ....
                                                       no ....

13. Did your mother leave school at age 14 or before, or at 15 or after?

 at 14 or before ....
 at 15 or after ....

14. Did your mother go to a university or college? yes ....
               no ....

15. If you were free to do as you liked, at what age would you leave full-time education?

 15   ....
 16   ....
 17   ....
 18   ....
 19   ....
 20 or over ....

16. How important do you think it is to get good marks at school, for getting on in the world later?

 the most important thing of all ....
 very important   ....
 fairly important   ....
 not very important   ....

17. Do you belong to a youth club or group? yes ....
               no ....

18. If you do belong to a club or group, how many times in the last two weeks have you been to a meeting or some activity. (If you belong to more than one, count *all* the meetings or activities you have been to in the last two weeks.)

 none   ....
 one   ....
 two   ....
 three   ....
 four or more ....

19. How many evenings last week did you spend at least an hour out of your home? (Do not count times you spent on a spare-time job if you have one.)

 one evening   .... five evenings   ....
 two evenings .... six evenings   ....
 three evenings .... seven evenings   ....
 four evenings .... home every evening ....

20. If you have a spare-time job, what is it?
....

21. If you have a spare-time job, how many hours a week do you usually spend on it?
.... hours per week

22. Father's occupation: ....

23. Describe his job: ....
....

24. Mother's occupation (if your mother works as well as taking care of your home):
....

25. If your mother does not now work, what was the job she last had? (Include job before marriage.)
....

26. Is your mother's job (if she now works outside your home) full-time ....
or part-time ....

27. In the last two weeks, how many days have you been absent from school?
½ day ....
1–1½ days ....
2–3½ days ....
4–5½ days ....
6 days or more ....
o days ....

28. Do you have to get permission from your mother or father to go out in the evening?
all the time ....
usually ....
sometimes ....
no ....

29. Tick the following items if anyone in your family, living at home, has them.
car ....
motorcycle ....
motorscooter ....

30. Do you ever get told that you will be punished if you do something and then you are not?
    usually   ....
    often   ....
    sometimes ....
    never   ....

31. Do you feel that the punishment you get at home is fair?
    never   ....
    sometimes ....
    usually   ....
    always   ....

Everyone breaks some rules and regulations during his lifetime. Some break them regularly, others less often. Below are some frequently broken by boys your age. Tick those that you have broken *in the last year*.

32. Driven a car, scooter or motorcycle on the road?
    very often   ....   which one?
    several times ....   car   ....
    once or twice ....   motorscooter ....
    not at all   ....   motorcycle   ....

33. Skipped school without a legitimate or proper excuse?
    no   ....
    once or twice ....
    several times ....
    very often   ....

34. Had a fist fight with one other person?
    very often   ....
    several times ....
    once or twice ....
    no   ....

35. Started a fist fight with one other person?
    no   ....
    once or twice ....
    several times ....
    very often   ....

36. Told a lie?
    very often   ....

several times ....
once or twice ....
no   ....

37. 'Run away' from home?
no   ....
once or twice   ....
3 or 4 times   ....
5 times or more ....

38. Taken little things (like sweets, cigarettes, comics or other things worth less than £1) from a shop or store?
very often   ....
several times ....
once or twice ....
not at all   ....

39. Taken things worth £1 or more from a shop or store?
no   ....
once or twice ....
several times ....
very often   ....

40. Taken things that you really didn't want that did not belong to you?
very often   ....
several times ....
once or twice ....
no   ....

41. Taken things worth £1 or more from a car, house, or any other place?
no   ....
once or twice ....
several times ....
very often   ....

42. Taken a car for a ride without the owner's knowledge?
no   ....
once or twice ....
several times ....
very often   ....

43. Been in a car for a ride with someone else who took it without the owner's knowledge?
    very often ....
    several times ....
    once or twice ....
    no   ....

44. Thrown stones or sticks or any other thing in order to break a window, streetlight or something like that?
    no   ....
    once or twice ....
    several times ....
    very often ....

45. Taken a motorcycle or motorscooter for a ride without the owner's knowledge?
    very often ....   which one?
    several times ....   motorcycle   ....
    once or twice ....   motorscooter ....
    no   ....   both   ....

46. 'Beat up' kids who hadn't done anything to you?
    no   ....
    once or twice ....
    several times ....
    very often ....

47. Bought or drank beer, wine or spirits? (Do not count if with your parents' permission.)
    very often ....
    several times ....
    once or twice ....
    no   ....

48. Taken little things like cigarettes or money less than £1 from your friends or family?
    no   ....
    once or twice ....
    several times ....
    very often ....

49. Taken things from someone else's desk or locker at school without permission?
    very often ....

several times ....
once or twice ....
no   ....

50. Caused damage to railway carriages, tracks or stations?
very often   ....
several times ....
once or twice ....
no   ....

Below are some ideas about which people have different opinions. Tick the idea that you agree with most. Note that there are no right or wrong answers. The 'right' answer is the one closest to your opinion.

51. Which would you rather be?
very good at school work and not so good at games ....
very good at games and not so good at school work ....

52. If you were free to choose, which of these would you rather do?
go to a university or college ....
get a job straight away   ....

53. When you have left school, which of these jobs would you rather have?
a job where you have to think things out for yourself   ....
a job where, once you learn it, you always know how to do it   ....

54. And which of these jobs would you rather have?
a job where it is very necessary for you to be nicely dressed   ....
a job where it doesn't matter how you are dressed ....

55. Suppose you are out playing ball with the boys and having lots of fun. Do you (a) leave the boys and go home to eat because you are expected home for meals at a certain time, or (b) go home to eat whenever you get hungry or through playing or whenever you feel like it?
(a) ....   (b) ....

56. Suppose you and some of your friends go to a cinema. One of the boys hasn't any money and you have some extra. So

you lend him the money. Now with the boys who are your friends what would you usually do? (a) Would you expect him to pay you back or (b) just do you a favour sometime?

(a) ....   (b) ....

57. Which is more true:
(a) Nowadays in Britain everybody with the same ability has the same chance to move up in life, or (b) Nowadays in Britain it still seems that some people have a better chance than others to move up in life.

(a) ....   (b) ....

58. Despite more opportunities for education, boys like me don't have really much more of a chance to move up in life than people when my parents were young.

agree ....   disagree ....

59. It doesn't matter to me what kind of job I get so long as the pay is good.

agree ....   disagree ....

60. Which is more true:
(a) If a person doesn't have a good education he hasn't much of a chance to move up in life, or (b) There's a chance for everybody who works hard to move up in life, even people who don't have a good education.

(a) ....   (b) ....

61. If you could go to any college, university or technical college, or take any training you needed for the job, what job would you most like to do?
....

Below is another list of rules and regulations some of which everyone breaks during his lifetime. Tick those that you have broken *in the last year*.

62. Done things your parents told you not to do?
no   ....
once or twice ....
several times ....
very often   ....

63. Used swear words or dirty words out loud in school or on the street or some place like that so that other people would hear you?

    very often   ....
    several times ....
    once or twice ....
    no   ....

64. Showed or gave someone a dirty picture, a dirty story or something like that?

    no   ....
    once or twice ....
    several times ....
    very often   ....

65. Been out at night just fooling around after you were supposed to be home?

    very often   ....
    several times ....
    once or twice ....
    no   ....

66. Hung around other people who you knew had broken the law lots of times or who were known as bad people?

    no   ....
    once or twice ....
    several times ....
    very often   ....

67. Thrown stones, cans, sticks or other things at a passing car, cycle, or person?

    very often   ....
    several times ....
    once or twice ....
    no   ....

68. Gone into another person's house, shed, or other building without their permission and with no good reason?

    no   ....
    once or twice ....
    several times ....
    very often   ....

QUESTIONNAIRE

69. Bet money or something else with people other than your
own family?
   very often   ....
   several times ....
   once or twice ....
   no   ....

70. Got some money or something from others by saying that
you would pay them back even though you were pretty sure
you wouldn't?
   no   ....
   once or twice ....
   several times ....
   very often   ....

71. Have been sent out of class or school for bad behaviour?
   very often   ....
   several times ....
   once or twice ....
   no   ....

72. Slipped into a cinema or other place without paying?
   very often   ....
   several times ....
   once or twice ....
   no   ....

73. Been on a bus or the underground without paying?
   no   ....
   once or twice ....
   several times ....
   very often   ....

74. Taken a bicycle for a ride without the owner's knowledge?
   very often   ....
   several times ....
   once or twice ....
   no   ....

75. Used something other than money to get things from an
automatic machine?
   no   ....
   once or twice ....

several times ....
very often ....

76. Taken little things (like sweets, cigarettes, comics or money less than £1) when you were on a holiday or outing?
very often ....
several times ....
once or twice ....
no ....

77. Kept or used something that you knew had been stolen by someone else?
no ....
once or twice ....
several times ....
very often ....

78. Messed up a public or school lavatory by writing on the wall or leaving the water running to run on to the floor?
very often ....
several times ....
once or twice ....
no ....

79. Broken down or helped break down a fence, gate or door on another person's place?
no ....
once or twice ....
several times ....
very often ....

80. Carried a razor, flick-knife or other weapon to be used against another person?
very often ....
several times ....
once or twice ....
no ....

81. Purposely damaged or destroyed public or private property that did not belong to you?
no ....
once or twice ....
several times ....
very often ....

82. Taken fruit, vegetables or other things from a fruit stall or lorry?
     very often   ....
     several times ....
     once or twice ....
     no   ....

83. Damaged or taken things from a building site?
     no   ....   which one?
     once or twice ....   damage   ....
     several times ....   taking things ....
     very often ....   both   ....

84. Taken part in gang fights?
     no   ....
     once or twice ....
     several times ....
     very often ....

85. How old were you when you first took something that did not belong to you (if you have)?
     before school age ....
     between 5 and 10 ....
     11–12   ....
     13–14   ....
     15   ....

86. How old were you when you first skipped school (if you have)?
     between 5 and 10 ....
     11–12   ....
     13–14   ....
     15   ....

Below is a list of ideas and attitudes that some people think are very important and some people think not very important. For each idea tick whether it is very important, of some importance, or of little or no importance to you. These are all opinions, so there is no right or wrong answer. Just tick for each question what best agrees with your ideas.

87. Being able to stay out of trouble and handle any that comes my way.
     very important   ....

some importance ·········
little or no importance ·········

88. Doing the things that are right for me to do.
very important ·········
some importance ·········
little or no importance ·········

89. Getting my share of fun and excitement.
very important ·········
some importance ·········
little or no importance ·········

90. Being a success at what I do.
very important ·········
some importance ·········
little or no importance ·········

91. Being able to handle myself, being tough.
little or no importance ·········
some importance ·········
very important ·········

92. Not wasting time in getting things done.
little or no importance ·········
some importance ·········
very important ·········

93. Being smart enough to stay one jump ahead of the others.
very important ·········
some importance ·········
little or no importance ·········

94. Planning what lies ahead for me as much as possible.
little or no importance ·········
some importance ·········
very important ·········

95. Taking advantage of luck to get the most out of it.
little or no importance ·········
some importance ·········
very important ·········

96. Having good manners and getting along well with others.
    very important   ....
    some importance   ....
    little or no importance ....

97. Being my own boss.
    little or no importance ....
    some importance   ....
    very important   ....

98. Being able to pass up things now, can have things later.
    little or no importance ....
    some importance   ....
    very important   ....

99. Not taking too much from anyone.
    very important   ....
    some importance   ....
    little or no importance ....

100. Working hard at trying to get ahead.
    little or no importance ....
    some importance   ....
    very important   ....

101. Learning how to do the things I will need to know when I
     grow up.
    very important   ....
    some importance   ....
    little or no importance ....

102. Write down the job you expect to do when you leave school.
     ....

APPENDIX B

Delinquency Involvement by Social Class

Offence	Middle Class Vo	Sev	1–2	Working Class Vo	Sev	1–2	X²	P
shoplifting*	10	13	77	17	22	61	2·45	> 0·25
larceny	4	18	78	13	21	66	2·02	> 0·30
b and e	8	10	82	7	16	77	1·34	> 0·50
taking car	6	11	83	11	20	69	1·27	> 0·50
car possession	24	16	60	26	14	60	0·05	> 0·95
taking cycle	22	39	39	22	24	54	1·79	> 0·50
taking scooter	10	33	57	20	15	65	4·22	> 0·10
throwing stones	4	26	70	12	26	62	8·15	< 0·02
railway	10	17	73	9	16	75	4·37	> 0·10
car	5	11	84	7	17	76	2·42	> 0·30
lavatory	10	15	75	7	22	71	1·66	> 0·50
fence	6	15	79	13	15	72	2·52	> 0·25
general	3	6	91	7	15	78	9·95	< 0·01
site damage	5	18	78	14	18	68	4·15	> 0·10
fist fight	7	21	72	13	24	63	7·52	< 0·025
fight start	7	11	82	6	10	84	0·25	> 0·80
assault	1	8	91	6	15	79	9·29	< 0·01
gang fights	9	15	76	16	16	68	4·80	> 0·05
weapons	12	20	68	25	23	52	5·19	> 0·05

* per cent of those admitting

Offence	Middle Class			Working Class			X^2	P
	Vo	Sev	1–2	Vo	Sev	1–2		
petty shoplifting	6	20	74	9	17	74	1·68	> 0·40
neurotic	3	11	86	6	10	84	0·77	> 0·50
family	2	14	84	2	7	91	3·32	> 0·10
school	5	10	85	3	12	85	0·90	> 0·50
bad loans	3	16	81	6	14	80	1·43	> 0·50
cinema	12	24	64	23	19	58	7·72	< 0·025
bus rides	12	34	54	18	30	52	4·50	> 0·10
machine	6	19	75	13	18	69	19·68	< 0·00
receiving	2	17	81	7	14	79	4·40	> 0·10
fruit	6	11	83	12	16	72	5·93	> 0·05
site	4	12	84	9	20	71	5·86	> 0·05
driving car	8	29	63	19	26	55	3·20	> 0·10
driving cycle	13	20	67	25	23	52	3·44	> 0·10
driving scooter	11	26	63	17	24	59	0·83	> 0·50
truancy	4	19	77	9	12	79	3·67	> 0·10
run away	4	20	76	15	12	73	2·69	> 0·30
swearing	18	31	51	20	28	52	1·52	> 0·40
pornography	11	25	64	17	28	55	7·05	< 0·05
late nights	11	25	64	21	26	53	9·73	< 0·01
bad company	12	17	71	15	26	59	4·86	> 0·05
betting	11	26	63	17	29	54	5·95	> 0·05
school misconduct	8	24	68	19	22	59	13·14	< 0·005
liquor	17	30	53	25	30	45	5·77	> 0·05

N for each item is the total number admitting.   df = 2

APPENDIX C

Delinquency Admissions by School Type

Offence	MC				WC			
	Gr	Mod	X²	P	Gr	Mod	X²	P
serious theft	31	35	0·52	> 0·40	31	36	0·91	> 0·30
shoplifting	7	10	0·50	> 0·40	5	13	4·29	< 0·05
larceny	6	9	1·12	> 0·25	4	17	10·93	< 0·001
b and e	21	23	0·11	> 0·25	23	23	0·01	> 0·99
taking car	5	5	0·04	> 0·80	6	6	0·00	—
car possession	5	9	1·09	> 0·25	5	12	3·38	> 0·05
taking cycle	3	7	3·04	> 0·05	4	10	2·69	> 0·10
taking scooter	5	7	0·33	> 0·50	5	8	0·70	> 0·30
vehicle theft	10	18	3·68	> 0·05	10	28	12·88	< 0·001
throwing stones	41	59	10·41	< 0·005	51	72	16·23	< 0·001
railway	24	19	1·18	> 0·25	21	25	0·97	> 0·30
car	24	31	3·74	> 0·05	42	41	0·01	> 0·99
lavatory	15	19	0·78	> 0·30	21	27	1·63	> 0·10
fence	20	24	0·35	> 0·50	24	36	4·69	< 0·05
general	31	34	0·23	> 0·50	38	37	0·03	> 0·99
site	15	20	1·43	> 0·20	20	25	1·21	> 0·25
violence	58	67	5·20	< 0·025	66	74	3·70	> 0·05
fist fight	69	78	3·28	> 0·05	77	81	1·33	> 0·20
fight start	41	45	0·41	> 0·50	46	53	1·79	> 0·10
assault	27	19	2·95	> 0·05	30	32	0·07	> 0·98
gang fights	27	47	14·52	< 0·001	37	52	7·65	< 0·01
weapons	15	22	2·65	> 0·10	23	23	0·00	—

APPENDIX C

Offence	MC				WC			
	Gr	Mod	X^2	P	Gr	Mod	X^2	P
petty shoplifting	46	68	16·80	< 0·001	44	64	13·55	< 0·001
neurotic	44	66	16·70	< 0·001	27	34	2·37	> 0·10
family	36	33	1·33	> 0·20	29	23	1·41	> 0·20
school	29	20	3·74	> 0·05	44	18	33·11	< 0·001
bad loans	24	29	1·05	> 0·30	37	35	0·18	> 0·50
cinema	38	53	9·24	< 0·005	54	57	0·35	> 0·50
bus rides	85	90	0·01	> 0·99	89	81	1·71	> 0·10
machine	35	51	9·19	< 0·005	42	48	1·96	> 0·10
holiday	25	35	4·31	< 0·05	23	34	5·09	< 0·025
receiving	33	47	6·87	< 0·01	47	45	0·14	> 0·70
fruit	23	37	7·67	< 0·01	24	47	17·77	< 0·001
site	20	30	5·27	< 0·025	21	32	4·71	< 0·05
driving car	16	20	0·90	> 0·75	17	17	0·01	> 0·90
driving cycle	7	18	10·88	< 0·001	10	16	2·16	> 0·10
driving scooter	9	13	1·72	> 0·10	11	13	0·25	> 0·50
truancy	32	30	0·08	> 0·75	36	43	1·96	> 0·10
run away	5	9	2·14	> 0·10	5	13	4·52	< 0·05
swearing	79	76	0·55	> 0·40	83	74	3·65	> 0·05
pornography	76	76	0·00	—	77	71	1·19	> 0·25
late nights	56	70	6·38	< 0·01	60	69	3·37	> 0·05
bad company	29	37	2·96	> 0·05	44	49	0·76	> 0·40
betting	56	61	8·44	< 0·005	67	64	0·32	> 0·50
school miscon.	53	70	10·03	< 0·005	59	73	7·83	< 0·01
liquor	52	65	5·61	< 0·02	58	60	0·04	< 0·80
N	205	161			115	421		

APPENDIX D

Social Class and Stream: a Comparison of the Expected and Observed Distributions

| | Grammar Schools | | | | |
| | Middle Class | | Working Class | | |
	Expected Frequency	Observed Frequency	Expected Frequency	Observed Frequency	Observed Total
Stream A	53	56	30	27	83
Stream B	47	47	26	26	73
Stream C	75	70	42	47	117
Stream D	39	30	16	15	45
Stream N/K	1	2	1	0	2
Total	205	205	115	115	320

$X^2 = 3 \cdot 23$
$df = 4; P > 0 \cdot 50$

	Secondary Modern Schools				
Stream A	59	76	151	134	210
Stream B	48	42	123	129	171
Stream C	43	33	110	120	153
Stream D	4	0	11	16	16
Stream N/K	9	10	23	22	32
Total	161	161	421	421	582

$X^2 = 23 \cdot 56$
$df = 4; P < 0 \cdot 005$

APPENDIX E

Comparison of British and American Delinquency Admission Rates

	Clark-Haurek Survey*	McDonald Survey
major theft	41	35
b and e	44	22
throwing stones	43	60
car damage	62	36
lavatory damage	20	22
fence damage	27	29
fight start	36	49
assault	17	29
gang fights	17	44
weapons	16	21
petty shoplifting	89	58
cinema	46	52
bad loans	40	32
machine	31	46
receiving	34	43
swearing	71	77
pornography	70	74
late nights	59	65
bad company	53	43
betting	54	63
liquor	36	58
school misconduct	47	66
truancy	24	37
runaway	12	9

* John P. Clark and Eugene W. Haurek. *Age and Sex Roles of Adolescents and their Involvement in Misconduct: a Reappraisal.* University of Illinois, 1965, mimeo, data for boys aged 14–15 only.

APPENDIX F

*Comparison of British and American Delinquency Admission Rates
by Area*

	1	2	3	4	5	6
major theft	72	16	83	19	84	7
b and e	40	27	20	24	38	19
throwing stones	43	66	50	71	35	49
car damage	64	41	57	36	52	32
lavatory damage	24	25	30	24	13	20
fence damage	31	31	26	34	13	29
fight start	44	54	36	52	25	46
assault	14	34	12	31	9	28
gang fights	21	38	25	53	13	24
weapons	13	22	25	28	6	18
petty shoplifting	85	69	83	62	83	56
cinema	52	48	54	58	46	45
bad loans	45	36	65	46	40	28
machine	39	49	54	56	25	36
receiving	55	51	42	50	20	37
swearing	77	74	60	80	64	80
late nights	62	64	63	71	59	63
bad company	61	49	56	55	36	34
betting	50	57	42	72	52	60
liquor	49	69	42	64	33	60
school misconduct	45	68	44	79	45	63
truancy	34	48	45	45	23	31
run away	11	13	12	11	10	7
N	280	172	265	190	335	242

Clark-Wenninger*
1. industrial city
3. lower urban
5. upper urban

McDonald
2. N. London
4. East London
6. Suburb

* John P. Clark and Eugene P. Wenninger. 'Socio-Economic Class and Area as Correlates of Illegal Behavior among Juveniles.' *American Sociological Review*, v. 27, 1962, p. 826.

APPENDIX G

Regressions of Court Appearances on Social Variables

		Sample Size	No. Working Class	No. Lower Working ing	Total Offences	Serious Offences	Theft Offences
East London	mod	91	83	46	176	70	63
West Country	mod	108	80	21	174	99	83
North London	mod	84	62	18	162	95	88
Suburb	mod	82	48	6	33	20	19
West Country	mod	68	46	10	95	76	67
East London	mod	54	45	29	91	54	40
West Country	gr	113	44	6	31	26	23
North London	mod	52	37	12	73	27	23
East London	gr	49	33	12	33	17	16
Suburb	gr	123	21	1	4	4	1
Suburb	mod	55	20	5	23	14	14
North London	gr	39	17	1	7	3	3
Mean		76·5	44·7	13·9	75·3	39·2	36·9
St. Dev.		27·9	21·7	13·1	64·6	37·3	30·5

BIBLIOGRAPHY

Ronald L. Akers. 'Socio-Economic Status and Delinquent Behavior: A Retest.' *Journal of Research in Criminology and Delinquency*, v. 1, no. 1, January 1964, p. 38.

W. E. Amos and C. F. Wellford. *Delinquency Prevention*. Englewood Cliffs, N.J.: Prentice-Hall, 1967.

Robert G. Andry. *Delinquency and Parental Pathology*. London: Methuen, 1960.

Roger Armfelt. *Our Changing Schools*. London: Her Majesty's Stationery Office, 1950.

J. W. Atkinson and N. T. Feather, eds. *A Theory of Achievement Motivation*. New York: John Wiley, 1966.

Olive Banks. *Parity and Prestige in English Secondary Education*. London: Routledge & Kegan Paul, 1955.

H. C. Barnard. *A History of English Education from 1760*. University of London Press, 1947.

Milton L. Barron. *The Juvenile in Delinquent Society*. New York: Knopf, 1954.

J. M. Beck and R. W. Saxe, eds. *Teaching the Culturally Disadvantaged Pupil*. Springfield, Ill., C. C. Thomas, 1965.

W. S. Bennet, Jr. and N. G. Gist. 'Class and Family Influences on Student Aspirations.' *Social Forces*, v. 43, 1964.

George Z. F. Bereday. 'The Problem of Social Equality in English Education.' *Harvard Educational Review*, v. 23, 1953, p. 228.

Abraham Bernstein. *The Education of Urban Populations*. New York: Random House, 1967.

Basil Bernstein. 'Language and Social Class.' *British Journal of Sociology*, v. 11, 1960, p. 271.

BIBLIOGRAPHY

Basil Bernstein. 'A Public Language; Some Sociological Implications of a Linguistic Form.' *British Journal of Sociology*, v 10, 1959, p. 311.

Herbert A. Bloch and Frank I. Flynn. *Delinquency: the Juvenile Offender in America Today*. New York: Random House, 1965.

B. Bricklin and P. M. Bricklin. *Bright Child – Poor Grades: the psychology of underachievement*. New York: Delacorte Press, 1967.

W. H. Burton. 'Education and Social Class in the United States.' *Harvard Educational Review*, v. 23, 1953, p. 243.

Flann Campbell. *Eleven-Plus and All That*. London: Watts, 1956.

M. P. Carter and P. Jephcott. *The Social Background of Delinquency*. University of Nottingham mimeo., 1954.

Richard Centers. *The Psychology of Social Classes*. Princeton University Press, 1949.

Dennis Chapman. *The Home and Social Status*. London: Routledge & Kegan Paul, 1955.

H. R. Chetwynd. *Comprehensive School*. London: Routledge & Kegan Paul, 1960.

K. O. Christiansen, ed. *Scandinavian Studies in Criminology*. London: Tavistock, 1965.

John P. Clark and Eugene W. Haurek. *Age and Sex Roles of Adolescents and Their Involvement in Misconduct: A Reappraisal*. University of Illinois, mimeo., 1965.

John P. Clark and Eugene P. Wenninger. 'Socio-Economic Class and Area as Correlates of Illegal Behavior Among Juveniles.' *American Sociological Review*, v. 27, 1962, p. 826.

——. 'Goal Orientations and Illegal Behavior Among Juveniles.' *Social Forces*, v. 42, 1963, p. 49.

Richard A. Cloward and Lloyd E. Ohlin. *Delinquency and Opportunity: A Theory of Delinquent Gangs*. Glencoe, Illinois: Free Press, 1960.

——. 'Illegitimate Means, Anomie, and Deviant Behavior.' *American Sociological Review*, v. 24, 1959, p. 164.

Albert K. Cohen, *Delinquent Boys*. New York: Free Press, 1955.

Albert K. Cohen and James F. Short, Jr. 'Research in Delinquent Subcultures.' *Journal of Social Issues*, v. 14, 1958, p. 20.

BIBLIOGRAPHY

G. D. H. Cole. *Studies in Class Structure.* London: Routledge & Kegan Paul, 1955.

James S. Coleman. 'The Adolescent Subculture and Academic Achievement.' *American Journal of Sociology*, v. 65, 1960, p. 337.

E. B. Collier. *The Social Purposes of Education.* London: Routledge & Kegan Paul, 1959.

J. B. Conant. *The Education of American Teachers.* New York: McGraw-Hill, 1963.

W. F. Connell. *The Educational Thought and Influence of Matthew Arnold.* London: Routledge & Kegan Paul, 1950.

R. R. Dale and S. Griffith. *Down Stream.* London: Routledge & Kegan Paul, 1965.

J. C. Daniels. 'The effects of streaming in the primary school. 1: What teachers believe.' *British Journal of Educational Psychology*, v. 31, 1961, p. 69.

Allison Davis. *Psychology of the Child in the Middle Class.* University of Pittsburgh, 1960.

——. *Social-Class Influences upon Learning.* Harvard University, 1948.

Harry Davis. *Culture and the Grammar School.* London: Routledge & Kegan Paul, 1965.

Norman Dennis and others. *Coal is Our Life.* London: Eyre and Spottiswoode, 1956.

H. C. Dent. *Secondary Modern Schools.* London: Routledge & Kegan Paul, 1949.

——. *The Educational System of England and Wales.* London: University of London Press, 1961.

——. *Secondary Education for All.* London: Routledge & Kegan Paul, 1944.

——. *The Education Act, 1944.* University of London Press, 1944.

Robert A. Dentler and Lawrence J. Monroe. 'Five Self-Report Scales of Early Adolescent Misconduct.' Paper read to the American Sociological Association, 1961.

——. 'Early Adolescent Theft.' *American Sociological Review*, v. 26, 1961, p. 733.

C. H. Dobinson. *Schooling 1963–1970.* London: MacGibbon & Kee, 1964.

W. B. Dockrell. 'Secondary Education, Social Class and the

BIBLIOGRAPHY

Development of Abilities.' *British Journal of Educational Psychology*, v. 36, 1966, p. 7.

J. W. B. Douglas. *The Home and the School*. London: MacGibbon & Kee, 1964.

J. W. B. Douglas and J. N. Blomfield. *Children Under Five*. London: Allen & Unwin, 1958.

J. W. B. Douglas *et al.* 'Delinquency and Social Class.' *British Journal of Criminology*, v. 6, 1966, p. 294.

David Downes. *Delinquent Subcultures in East London*. London University. Ph.D. thesis, 1964.

——. *The Delinquent Solution: a study in subcultural theory*. London: Routledge & Kegan Paul, 1966.

O. D. Duncan and R. W. Hodge. 'Education and Occupational Mobility.' *American Journal of Sociology*, v. 68, 1963, p. 269.

Martha C. Ericson. 'Child-Rearing and Social Status.' *American Journal of Sociology*, v. 52, 1946, p. 193.

Maynard L. Erickson and Lamar T. Empey. 'Class Position, Peers and Delinquency.' *Sociology and Social Research*, v. 49, 1965, p. 268.

——. 'Court Records, Undetected Delinquency and Decision-Making.' *Journal of Criminology, Criminal Law and Police Science*, v. 54, 1963, p. 456.

J. Floud, ed. *Social Class and Educational Opportunity*. London: Heinemann, 1957.

D. C. Gibbons. 'Comments on the Efficacy of Criminal Treatment.' *Canadian Journal of Corrections*, v. 2, 1960, p. 165.

Daniel Glaser. *The Effectiveness of a Prison and Parole System*. New York: Basic Books, 1964.

David Glass, ed. *Social Mobility in Britain*. London: Routledge & Kegan Paul, 1954.

Erving Goffman. *Asylums*. Garden City, New York: Doubleday, 1961.

M. L. Goldberg *et al. The Effects of Ability Grouping*. New York: Teachers College Press, 1966.

E. W. Gordon *et al. Compensatory Education for the Disadvantaged*. New York: College Entrance Examination Board, 1966.

R. E. Gross, ed. *British Secondary Education*. London: Oxford University Press, 1965.

BIBLIOGRAPHY

A. H. Halsey, Jean Floud and C. Arnold Anderson. *Education, Economy, and Society*. New York: Free Press of Glencoe, 1963.

A. H. Halsey and L. Gardner. 'Selection for Secondary Education and Achievement in Four Grammar Schools.' *British Journal of Sociology*, 1954, p. 60.

R. M. Hardt and G. E. Bodine. *Development of Self-Report Instruments in Delinquency Research*. Syracuse: Syracuse University Youth Development Center, 1965.

David H. Hargreaves. *Social Relations in a Secondary School*. London: Routledge & Kegan Paul, 1967.

Tom Harrisson. *Britain Revisited*. London: Gollancz, 1961.

Robert J. Havighurst and Bernice L. Neugarten. *Society and Education*. Boston: Allyn & Bacon, 1957.

R. E. Herriott. 'Some Social Determinants of Educational Aspiration.' *Harvard Educational Review*, v. 33, 1963, p. 157.

H. T. Himmelweit, A. H. Halsey and A. N. Oppenheim. 'The Views of Adolescents on Some Aspects of Social Class Structure.' *British Journal of Sociology*, v. 32, 1952, p. 148.

Richard Hoggart: *The Uses of Literacy*. London: Chatto & Windus, 1957.

David Holbrook, ed. *English for the Rejected*. Cambridge University Press, 1964.

August B. Hollingshed and Frederick C. Redlich. *Social Class and Mental Illness*. New York: Wiley, 1958.

Brian Holmes. *Problems in Education*. London: Routledge & Kegan Paul, 1965.

Incorporated Association of Assistant Masters. *Teaching in Comprehensive Schools, a second report*. Cambridge: Cambridge University Press, 1960.

Brian Jackson. *Streaming*. London: Routledge & Kegan Paul, 1964.

Brian Jackson and Dennis Marsden. *Education and the Working Class*. London: Routledge & Kegan Paul, 1962.

Pearl Jephcott. *Some Young People*. London: Allen & Unwin, 1954.

C. F. Jesness. *The Fricot Ranch Study*. California Department of Youth Authority Research Report no. 47, 1965.

National Society for the Study of Education. *Juvenile Delin-*

BIBLIOGRAPHY

quency and the Schools. 47th Year Book, pt. 1, University of Chicago Press, 1948.

N. Kent and D. R. Davies. 'Discipline in the Home and Intellectual Development.' *British Journal of Medical Psychology,* v. 30, 1957.

Madeline Kerr. *The People of Ship Street.* London: Routledge & Kegan Paul, 1958.

Edmund J. King. *Education and Social Change.* London: Pergamon, 1967.

John I. Kitsuse and David C. Dietrick. 'Delinquent Boys, a Critique.' *American Sociological Review,* v. 24, 1959, p. 208.

Josephine Klein. *Samples From English Cultures.* London: Routledge & Kegan Paul, 1965.

Melvin L. Kohn. 'Social Class and Parental Values.' *American Journal of Sociology,* v. 64, 1959, p. 337.

——. 'Social Class and Parent-Child Relationships: An Interpretation.' *American Journal of Sociology,* v. 68, 1963, p. 471.

——. 'Social Class and the Exercise of Parental Authority.' *American Sociological Review,* v. 24, 1959, p. 352.

J. D. Krumboltz, ed. *Learning and the Educational Process.* Chicago: Rand, McNally, 1964.

W. C. Kvaraceus and W. B. Miller. *Delinquent Behavior, Culture and the Individual.* National Educational Association of the United States, 1959.

Wm. C. Kvaraceus and Wm. E. Ulrich. *Delinquent Behavior.* National Educational Association of the United States, 1959.

Wayne R. LaFave. *Arrest.* Boston: Little, Brown, 1965.

D. E. Lavin. *The Prediction of Academic Performance.* New York: Russell Sage, 1965.

John Lello. *The Official View on Education.* London: Pergamon, 1964.

Roy Lewis and Angus Maude. *The English Middle Classes.* London: Phoenix, 1950.

S. M. Lipset and Reinhard Bendix. *Social Mobility in Industrial Society.* London: Heinemann, 1959.

W. R. Little and V. R. Ntsekhe. 'Social Class Background of Young Offenders from London.' *British Journal of Delinquency,* v. 10, 1959, p. 130.

David Lockwood. *The Blackcoated Worker.* London: Allen & Unwin, 1958.

BIBLIOGRAPHY

R. Lynn and E. E. Gordon. 'Maternal Attitudes to Child Socialization.' *British Journal of Social and Clinical Psychology*, v. 1, 1962.

E. E. Maccoby and others. 'Methods of Child-Rearing in Two Social Classes.' In Martin, *Readings in Child Development*, p. 380.

J. A. Mack. 'Police Juvenile Liaison.' *British Journal of Criminology*, v. 3, 1962.

John S. MacPherson. *Eleven-Year-Olds Grow Up*. University of London Press, 1958.

H. Mannheim, J. Spencer and G. Lynch. 'Magisterial Policy in the London Juvenile Courts.' *British Journal of Delinquency*, v. 8, 1957, pp. 13 and 119.

Fortuen V. Mannino. 'Family Factors Related to School Persistence.' *Journal of Educational Sociology*, v. 35, 1962, p. 193.

David Matza. *Delinquency and Drift*. New York: Wiley, 1964.

David Matza and Gresham M. Sykes. 'Juvenile Delinquency and Subterranean Values.' *American Sociological Review*, v. 26, 1961, p. 715.

Martin Mayer. *The Schools*. London: Bodley Head, 1961.

J. B. Mays. *Crime and the Social Structure*. London: Faber & Faber, 1963.

——. *Education and the Urban Child*. Liverpool University Press, 1962.

——. *On the Threshold of Delinquency*. Liverpool University Press, 1959.

——. *Growing Up in the City*. Liverpool University Press, 1954.

——. *The School in its Social Setting*. Longmans, Green, 1967.

——. 'Delinquency Areas – A Reassessment.' *British Journal of Criminology*, v. 3, 1963, p. 216.

Joan and Wm. McCord. 'The Effects of Parental Role Model on Criminality.' *Journal Social Issues*, v. 14, 1958.

——. *Origins of Crime*. New York: Columbia University Press, 1959.

D. McIntyre *et al.* 'Social and educational variables relating to teachers' assessments of primary school pupils.' *British Journal of Educational Psychology*, v. 36, 1966, p. 272.

D. C. McKinley. *Social Class and Family Life*. New York: Free Press of Glencoe, 1963.

231

BIBLIOGRAPHY

J. C. McLendon, ed. *Social Foundations of Education*. New York: Macmillan, 1966.

Robert K. Merton. *Social Theory and Social Structure*. Glencoe, Illinois: Free Press, 1957.

Walter B. Miller. 'Implications of Urban Lower Class Culture for Social Work.' *Social Service Review*, v. 33, 1959.

——. 'Lower Class Culture as a Generating Milieu of Gang Delinquency.' *Journal of Social Issues*, v. 14, 1958. p. 5.

S. M. Miller and Frank Riessman. 'The Working Class Subculture: A New View.' *Social Problems*, v. 9, 1961, p. 86.

Daniel R. Miller and Guy E. Swanson. *The Changing American Parent*. New York: Wiley, 1958.

E. H. Mizruchi. *Success and Opportunity*. New York: Free Press of Glencoe, 1964.

J. M. Mogey. *Family and Neighbourhood*. London: Oxford University Press, 1956.

Oliver Moles and others. *A Selective Review of Research and Theory on Delinquency*. University of Michigan, 1959.

Thomas P. Monahan. 'Family Status and the Delinquent Child: A Reappraisal and Some New Findings.' *Social Forces*, v. 35, 1957, p. 250.

J. B. Montague, Jr. *Class and Nationality*. London: Vision, 1963.

T. P. Morris. *The Criminal Area*. London: Routledge & Kegan Paul, 1957.

Fred J. Murphy and others. 'The Incidence of Hidden Delinquency.' *American Journal of Orthopsychiatry*, v. 41, 1946, p. 686.

J. H. Nicholson. *New Communities in Britain*. London: National Council of Social Service, 1961.

F. Ivan Nye. *Family Relationships and Delinquent Behavior*. New York: John Wiley, 1958.

F. Ivan Nye, James Short and Virgil J. Olson. 'Socioeconomic Status and Delinquent Behavior.' *American Journal of Sociology*, v. 63, 1958, p. 381.

A. N. Oppenheim. 'Social Class and Clique Formation Among Grammar School Boys.' *British Journal of Sociology*, v. 6, 1955, p. 228.

Marie Paneth. *Branch Street*. London: Allen & Unwin, 1944.

A. H. Passow *et al.*, eds. *Education of the Disadvantaged*. New York: Holt, Rinehart, 1967.

BIBLIOGRAPHY

T. H. Pear. *Psychological Aspects of English Social Stratification.* Manchester University Press, 1942.
——. *English Social Differences.* London: Allen & Unwin, 1955.
Robert Peers. *Fact and Possibility in English Education.* London: Routledge & Kegan Paul, 1963.
Isobel Pfeiffer. 'Teaching Ability Grouped Classes.' *Education,* v. 87, 1966, p. 88.
Austin L. Porterfield. *Youth in Trouble.* Fort Worth, Texas: Leo Potishman Foundation, 1946.
Walter C. Reckless and others. 'Self Concept as an Insulator Against Delinquency.' *American Sociological Review,* v. 21, 1956, p. 744.
A. T. Ravenette and J. H. Kahn. 'Intellectual Ability of Disturbed Children in a Working-Class Area.' *British Journal of Social and Clinical Psychology,* v. 1, pt. 3, 1962, p. 208.
Albert J. Reiss, Jr. and A. Lewis Rhodes. 'An Empirical Test of Differential Association Theory.' *Journal of Research in Crime and Delinquency,* v. 1, 1964, p. 5.
——. 'Delinquency and Social Class Structure.' *American Sociological Review,* v. 26, 1961, p. 720.
Frank Riessman and others, ed. *Mental Health of the Poor.* New York: Free Press of Glencoe, 1964.
Leonard Reissman. *Class in American Society.* New York: Free Press of Glencoe, 1959.
E. A. G. Robinson and J. E. Vaizey, eds. *The Economics of Education.* London: Macmillan, 1966.
Sophia Moses Robinson. *Can Delinquency be Measured?* New York: Columbia University Press, 1936.
W. S. Robinson. 'Ecological correlations and the behavior of individuals.' *American Sociological Review,* v. 15, 1950, p. 351.
Hyman Rodman. 'The Lower Class Value Stretch.' *Social Forces,* v. 42, 1963, p. 205.
John F. Scott. 'Two Dimensions of Delinquent Behavior.' *American Sociological Review,* v. 24, 1959, p. 240.
J. P. Seckel. *The Fremont Experiment.* California Department of Youth Authority Research Report no. 50, 1967.
T. Sellin and M. E. Wolfgang. *The Measurement of Delinquency.* New York: John Wiley, 1964.

W. L. Slocum and C. L. Stone. 'Family Culture Patterns and Delinquent-Type Behavior.' *Marriage and Family Living*, v. 25, 1963, p. 202.

Patricia C. Sexton. *Education and Income*. New York: Viking, 1961.

John Sharp. *Educating One Nation*. London: Parrish, 1959.

James Short. 'Differential Association as a Hypothesis in Problem of Empirical Testing.' *Social Problems*, v. 8, 1960.

James F. Short, Jr. and others. 'Behavior Dimensions of Gang Delinquency.' *American Sociological Review*, v. 28, 1963, p. 411.

T. S. Simey, ed. *Neighbourhood and Community*. University of Liverpool Press, 1954.

Brian Simon. *Intelligence Testing and the Comprehensive School*. London: Lawrence & Wishart, 1953.

Jon E. Simpson and others. 'Delinquency Potential of Pre-Adolescents in High-Delinquency Areas.' *British Journal of Delinquency*, v. 10, 1960, p. 211.

John Spencer. *Stress and Release in an Urban Estate*. London: Tavistock, 1964.

B. M. Spinley. *The Deprived and the Privileged*. London: Routledge & Kegan Paul, 1964.

Irving Spirgel. *Racketville Slumtown Haulburg*. University of Chicago Press, 1964.

Gresham M. Sykes and David Matza. 'Techniques of Neutralization.' *American Sociological Review*, v. 22, 1957, p. 664.

Richard M. Stephenson. 'Stratification, Education, and Occupational Orientation: A Parallel Study and Review.' *British Journal of Sociology*, v. 9, 1958, p. 42.

Frances Stevens. *The Living Tradition*. London: Hutchinson, 1960.

E. H. Sutherland. *The Sutherland Papers*. University of Indiana Press, 1956.

Wm. Taylor. *The Secondary Modern School*. London: Faber & Faber, 1963.

Frederic M. Thrasher. *The Gang*. University of Chicago Press, 1927.

Richard M. Titmuss. *Income Distribution and Social Change*. London: Allen & Unwin, 1962.

E. Jackson Toby and Marcia L. Toby. *Low School Status as a*

Predisposing Factor in Subcultural Delinquency. United States Office of Education and Rutgers University, 1957.

Asher Tropp. *The School Teachers.* London: Heinemann, 1957.

Ralph Turner. *The Social Context of Ambition.* San Francisco: Chandler, 1964.

United Kingdom

Hadow Report. *Education of the Adolescent.* H.M.S.O., 1926.

Spens Report. *Report of the Consultative Committee on Secondary Education.* H.M.S.O., 1938.

Norwood Report. Board of Education. *Curriculum and Examinations in Secondary Schools.* H.M.S.O., 1941.

Ministry of Education pamphlet No. 1. *The Nation's Schools: Their Plan and Purpose.* H.M.S.O., 1945.

Ministry of Education. *The New Secondary Education.* H.M.S.O., 1947.

Ministry of Education. *Examinations in Secondary Schools.* H.M.S.O., 1952.

Ministry of Education. *Early Leaving.* Central Advisory Council for Education (England). H.M.S.O., 1954.

Ministry of Health and others. *An Inquiry into Health Visiting.* H.M.S.O., 1956.

Crowther Report. *15–18.* Report of the Central Advisory Council for Education (England), v. 1, Ministry of Education, H.M.S.O., 1959.

Ministry of Education. Secondary Schools Examination Council. *The Certificate of Secondary Education.* H.M.S.O., 1961.

Newsom Report. Ministry of Education, Central Advisory Council for Education (England). *Half our Future.* H.M.S.O., 1964.

Plowden Report, Ministry of Education, Central Advisory Council for Education (England). *Children and their Primary Schools.* H.M.S.O., 1967.

John Vaizey. *Education for Tomorrow.* Harmondsworth: Penguin, 1967.

——. *The Economics of Education.* London: Faber & Faber, 1962.

Edmund W. Vaz, ed. *Middle-Class Juvenile Delinquency.* New York: Harper and Row, 1967.

BIBLIOGRAPHY

Thelma Veness. *School Leavers*. London: Methuen, 1962.

Harwin L. Voss. 'Ethnic Differentials in Delinquency in Honolulu.' *Journal of Criminal Law, Criminology and Police Science*, v. 54, 1963, p. 322.

James Walters *et al*. 'Interaction of Mothers and Children from Lower-Class Families.' *Child Development*, v. 35, 1964, p. 433.

W. Lloyd Warner, Robert J. Havighurst and Martin B. Loeb. *Who Shall be Educated?* London: Routledge & Kegan Paul, 1946.

John Webb. 'The Sociology of a School.' *British Journal of Sociology*, v. 13, 1962, p. 264.

L. T. Wilkins. 'A Comparative study of the result of probation.' *British Journal of Delinquency*, v. 8, 1958, p. 201.

Rupert Wilkinson. *The Prefects*. London: Oxford University, 1964.

Peter Willmott and Michael Young. *Family and Class in a London Suburb*. London: Routledge & Kegan Paul, 1960.

Harriett Wilson. *Delinquency and Child Neglect*. London: Allen & Unwin, 1962.

Percy Wilson. *Views and Prospects from Curzon Street*. Oxford: Basil Blackwell, 1961.

Roger Wilson. *Difficult Housing Estates*. London: Tavistock, 1963.

Stephen Wiseman. *Education and Environment*. Manchester University Press, 1964.

Alfred Yates, ed. *Grouping in Education*. New York: John Wiley, 1966.

Michael Young. *Innovation and Research in Education*. London: Routledge & Kegan Paul, 1965.

Michael Young and Peter Willmott. *Family and Kinship in East London*. London: Pelican, 1957.

SUBJECT INDEX

AUTHOR INDEX

Akers, Ronald L., 16–18, 135–138, 141

Amos, W. E., 193n

Andrey, Robert G., 69

Armfelt, Roger, 40n

Atkinson, J. W., 176n

Bernstein, Basil, 24–27, 35–38, 178–179

Clark, John P., 14, 16, 37, 47n, 50, 68n, 125, 132, 135, 141, 142

Cloward, Richard A., 49, 50

Cohen, Albert K., 15, 45–47, 50–51, 115, 128

Daniels, J. C., 39n, 171n

Davis, Allison, 22

Dentler, Robert A., 13, 14, 41

Douglas, J. W. B., 114n

Downes, David, 50

Erikson, Maynard L., 13, 14, 79n, 133, 134

Floud, J., 55n

Gibbons, D. C., 191n

Glass, David, 55n

Goffman, Erving, 192

Goldberg, M. L., 186n

Hargreaves, David H., 11n, 114

Havighurst, Robert J., 22, 54

Himmelweit, H. T., 53, 55

Hoggart, Richard, 108

Holbrook, David, 174, 175

Hollingshead, August B., 141

Jackson, Brian, 36, 106n, 108n, 116

Jephcott, Pearl, 22, 58

Jesness, C. F., 191n

Klein, Josephine, 43

Little, W. R., 18, 19, 84, 85, 144, 154, 155

Mack, J. A., 157

McKay, Henry D., 58

Mannheim, H., 18, 19

Martin, F., 55

Matza, David, 11n, 46, 47

Mays, J. B., 22, 57, 58, 128

Merton, Robert K., 48, 49, 52, 57

Miller, S. M., 140, 141

Miller, W. B., 23, 24, 46, 51, 52

Morris, T. P., 18, 19, 22, 23, 43, 58

Nicholson, J. H., 44n

Nye, F. Ivan, 11, 12, 14, 16, 58n, 136, 138, 141n

Oppenheim, A. N., 106n

Park, Robert, 45

Parsons, Talcott, 45

Pfeiffer, Isobel, 171n

239

AUTHOR INDEX